HBJ SOCIAL STUDIES

STATES AND REGIONS

Titles in this series:

Friends
Families
Neighborhoods
Communities
States and Regions
The United States: Its History and Neighbors
The World: Past and Present

SENIOR PROGRAM ADVISERS

JOHN BARBINI
Director of Program Services
School District 54
Schaumberg, Illinois

PAUL S. HANSON
Social Studies Supervisor
Dade County Public Schools
Miami, Florida

CHERYL BILES MOORE
Director, Staff Development,
Research and Evaluation
Orange County Department of Education
Costa Mesa, California

DR. WILLIAM D. TRAVIS
Curriculum Coordinator
Pittsfield Public Schools
Pittsfield, Massachusetts

DONALD P. VETTER
Supervisor of Social Studies
Carroll County Public Schools
Westminster, Maryland

THOMAS GREGORY WARD
Social Studies Specialist
Fairfax County Schools, Area II
Fairfax, Virginia

ALICE WELLS
Curriculum Consultant
Cartwright School District No. 83
Phoenix, Arizona

SENIOR CONTENT SPECIALISTS

DR. BILIANA CICIN-SAIN
Associate Professor of Political Science
University of California
Santa Barbara, California

DR. IRVING CUTLER
Chairman, Geography Department
Chicago State University
Chicago, Illinois

DR. STEPHANIE ABRAHAM HIRSH
Consultant, Staff Development and
Free Enterprise Education
Richardson Independent School District
Richardson, Texas

DR. DONALD O. SCHNEIDER
Associate Professor of Social
Science Education
University of Georgia
Athens, Georgia

DR. PETER J. STEIN
Professor of Sociology
William Paterson College
New York, New York

SKILLS DEVELOPMENT

DR. H. MICHAEL HARTOONIAN
Madison, Wisconsin

HBJ SOCIAL STUDIES
STATES AND REGIONS

HARCOURT BRACE JOVANOVICH, PUBLISHERS

Orlando   New York   Chicago   San Diego   Atlanta   Dallas

CLASSROOM CONSULTANTS

ANITA T. DAVIDSON
Wesconnett Elementary School
Jacksonville, Florida

GLORIA GEDROSE
Phil Lewis Elementary School
Tigard, Oregon

JOANNE G. GIBSON
College Park Elementary School
Wilmington, North Carolina

KATHYLEEN GUARNIER
Howe Elementary School
Schenectady, New York

JOHN P. HUGHES
Hayes-Leonard Elementary School
Valparaiso, Indiana

CELIA ANN JEFFERS
Wendell Phillips Elementary School
Kansas City, Missouri

DOROTHY KUEKER
Bamber Valley Elementary School
Rochester, Minnesota

SARAH LEE LITTLE
Our Lady of Lourdes School
Greenville, Mississippi

DOROTHY MARCOUX
Adams Elementary School
Boise, Idaho

GEORGIA E. MASSA
Calvary Christian Day School
Baltimore, Maryland

ELENA M. MIDOLO
W. A. Driscoll Elementary School
Centerville, Ohio

MARCIA D. MUSE
Fair Oaks Elementary School
Highland Springs, Virginia

JUDY PARKER
Ruus Elementary School
Hayward, California

DOROTHEA C. RAMSEY
Lincoln Elementary School
Schenectady, New York

NANCY D. RODNEY
Oliver Wendell Holmes
  Elementary School
Chicago, Illinois

TANIS ROELOFS
Victor Fields Elementary School
McAllen, Texas

JUDY SULLIVAN
Hamilton Park Elementary School
Dallas, Texas

RUTH SWANZY
Mark Twain Elementary School
Houston, Texas

DENNIS E. WAGESTER
Clarkston Community Schools
Bailey Lake Elementary School
Clarkston, Michigan

WENDELL GENE WARD
Bradley Elementary School
Columbia, South Carolina

READABILITY

DR. JEANNE BARRY
Jeanne Barry and Associates, Inc.
Oakland, California

The publisher would like to thank Roy Franz (for assistance with information on the Ouray, Colorado, fire department) and Thomas Pagenhart of the geography department at California State University in Hayward and Marcia Pagenhart (for advice on geographical terminology).

1986 Printing
Copyright © 1985 by Harcourt Brace Jovanovich, Inc.

PHOTOGRAPH ACKNOWLEDGMENTS

KEY: T, Top; B, Bottom; L, Left; R, Right; C, Center.

RESEARCH CREDITS: © Alec Duncan: 2. Contact, © David Burnett: 14. West Light, © Craig Aurness: 15B. Photo Researchers, Inc., © Porterfield-Chickering: 16TR. Bruce Coleman Inc., © D. P. Hershkowitz: 16BR. West Light, © Bill Ross: 17L. Stock, Boston, © Bohdan Hrynewych: 18. Photri, © B. Kulik: 19. Bruce Coleman Inc., © David Madison: 20. Folio, Inc., © David Marie: 21. Woodfin Camp and Associates, © Annie Griffiths: 33. © John Elk III: 34TL. Bruce Coleman Inc., © Nicholas Devore III: 35. Click, Chicago, © Jim Pickerell: 39TL. Woodfin Camp and Associates, © Al Stephenson: 39TR. © Tom Tracy: 39B. Woodfin Camp and Associates, © John Blaustein: 52. Freelance Photographers' Guild International, © Mary Wolf: 57TR. The Image Bank, © Jay Maisel: 57B. © R. Rowan: 60. Stock, Boston, © Stacy Pick: 64. Magnum Photos, Inc., © Alex Webb: 67. Photo Researchers, Inc., © Earl Roberge: 68. Photo Researchers, Inc., © Robert A. Isaacs: 72B. West Light, © Craig Aurness: 84TL. Taurus Photos, © Eric Kroll: 84BL. Bruce Coleman Inc., © Phil Degginger: 84R. Photo Researchers, Inc., © David R. Frazier: 86. Peter Arnold, Inc., © Clyde H. Smith: 87. West Light, © Ric Ergenbright: 95T. Photo Researchers, Inc., © Tom McHugh: 96R. Freelance Photographers' Guild International,

© Rick Stockton: 100. Photo Researchers, Inc., © George Gerster: 101. Photo Researchers, Inc., © Tom McHugh: 102. Stock, Boston, © Arthur Grace: 130. West Light, © Chuck O'Rear: 135. Woodfin Camp and Associates, © Sepp Seitz: 136. Bruce Coleman Inc., © A. Avis: 137BL. Contact, © Douglas Kirkland: 137TR. Magnum Photos, Inc., © Costa Manos: 147. Woodfin Camp and Associates, © Dan Budnik: 148BR. After-Image, © Cary Wolinsky: 149. After-Image, © Ron Sherman: 154L. Woodfin Camp and Associates, © William Strode: 154R. After-Image, © Paul Dix: 156. Contact, © Chuck Fishman: 157R. After-Image, © Jack Fields: 157L. Woodfin Camp and Associates, © Akhtar Hussein: 159. © Yale University Art Gallery, *The Declaration of Independence,* John Trumbull: 160. Grant Heilman, © Alan Pitcairn: 165. Taurus Photos, © Eric Kroll: 166. Photo Researchers, Inc., © Bruce Roberts: 167TL. Click, Chicago, © Donald Smetzer: 167BL. Bruce Coleman Inc., © M. P. L. Fogden: 169R. Woodfin Camp and Associates, © Momatiuk/East-cott 1981: 170. Woodfin Camp and Associates, © Robert Frerck: 175B. © Momatiuk: 177. John Elk III: 180T. Contact, © David Burnett: 189TR. Stock, Boston, © Donald Dietz: 190TL. © Tom Tracy: 190R. After-Image, © Dale R. Thompson: 192. © Peter B. Kaplan
(Continued on page 438.)

Printed in the United States of America

ISBN 0-15-373204-0

Table of Contents

Maps and Globes

Charts, Graphs, Diagrams, and Timelines

INTRODUCTION

Where do you live? This question sounds simple. To answer it, many people would give their street address. There is more than one way to answer this question, though. Each person lives in many kinds of places.

One place where you live is a **community.** Towns, cities, and suburbs are communities. What is the name of your community?

You also live in a **state.** Your community, and many others, are part of your state. In which state do you live?

Your state is one of 50 states in our **country,** the United States of America. The United States is one of the largest countries in the world.

Look at the photograph of our world, Earth. Beneath the swirling clouds are areas of land and bodies of water. You will read about Earth and its **geography** in this book. Geography means the study of the Earth.

In this book you will also find out about our country's land and its people. You will find out about your own state and other states. Then you will take a look at countries and people around the world. A good place to begin your study of geography is in your own community.

The World Around You

Imagine your neighborhood without any houses, streets, or streetlights. What can you say about the land? Is it flat? Are there hills or mountains nearby? These shapes of the land are called **landforms.**

Do you live near any **bodies of water**? Bodies of water include rivers, lakes, and oceans. We need water in order to live. Oceans and some lakes contain salt water, which humans cannot drink. However, oceans provide us with fish and other seafood. Most lakes and rivers contain fresh water, which we can use for drinking and growing crops.

Now think about the weather where you live. What is the weather like year after year? Is it usually cold in winter, or is it warm all year? Does it rain a lot or a little? The usual weather in a place is called **climate.**

The area where you live also has some **natural resources.** The word *natural* means found in nature, not made by humans. A resource is something that people can use. People use natural resources to help them make a living. Water, forests, and good soil are resources. What natural resources are in your area?

1

As you can see, you already know some of your community's geography. You know about its landforms, bodies of water, climate, and natural resources. These are its **natural features,** the things that humans have not made.

How People Use Natural Features of the Land

To learn about the geography of a place, you need to know what its natural features are and how people use them. People change natural features when they use them. When people plant crops or build homes, for example, they change the land. When people build roads and tunnels, they change the land. When people cut down trees, they change the land.

How do people use the natural features of your area? Are there farms or mines? Are there railroads or bridges?

The photograph below shows part of the city of San Francisco, California. Study the photograph. Look for some of the natural features of the land. What are they? How many changes made by people can you find?

One hundred and fifty years ago this land was only hills and beaches dotted with scrubby bushes. Now it holds the city of San Francisco.

REVIEWING MAPS AND GLOBES

When you study geography, you can read about the land, water, climate, and natural resources of a place. As you read you will need to use two tools of geography, maps and globes.

Maps

A map is a kind of drawing that shows many things about a place. In a map you are seeing a place from above. Look at the map on this page. On this map you see **symbols.** Symbols are signs or markings that stand for real things. At the bottom of the map is a **map key.** A map key shows what the symbols on a map stand for.

Some map symbols are pictures or colors. Dots often stand for towns and cities. Different kinds of lines show roads and **borders.** A border is the outside edge of a place. On a map, borders are shown as lines. Look at the other symbols in the map key. On this map, what is the symbol for railroad?

Now suppose you are going from the park to the railroad. To get there, you need to know the **direction,** or which way to go. North, south, east, and west are

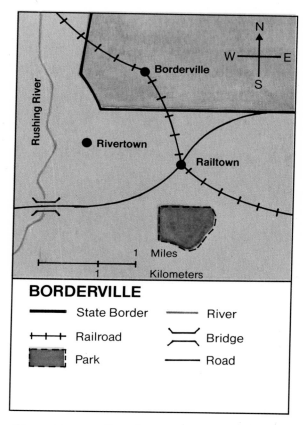

directions. Look at the top of the map for a **compass rose.** A compass rose shows the directions. *N* means north, *S* means south, *E* means east, and *W* means west. Here the compass rose shows the railroad is north. Now find the arrow in the compass rose. The arrow points to the direction that is north on the map.

Maps can show a small area or the whole world. Everything is much smaller than it really is on the Earth. However, you can figure out how far places are from

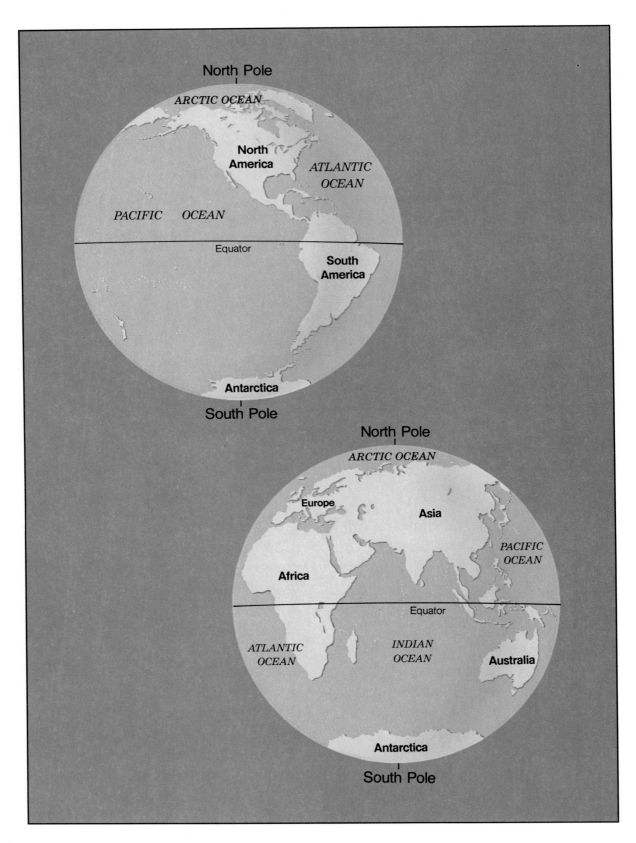

4

one another. To do this, you will need to use the map's **distance scale.**

Find the distance scale in the corner of the map on page 3. On this map, 1 inch stands for 1 mile on the Earth. You can use the scale to find miles and kilometers. Find out how far the bridge is from the park. Use a ruler to measure the distance in inches. How many inches did you measure? Use the distance scale to find out how many miles.

Globes

To see where a place is in the world, you could use a **globe.** A globe is a model of Earth. It is in the shape of a **sphere,** or ball.

As you look at these drawings of a globe you can see the seven continents. They are North America, South America, Europe, Asia, Africa, Australia, and Antarctica. Our country is in North America. Europe and Asia are on the same land mass, but they are separated by mountains. Australia is the only continent that is also one country.

Water covers three-fourths of the Earth. The Earth's largest bodies of water are the oceans. They are the Atlantic, Pacific, Indian, and Arctic Oceans. The Pacific Ocean is the largest; the Arctic Ocean is the smallest.

Although the globe is a model of Earth, it shows some things that are not really on the land or water. For example, people who make globes add the **North Pole** and **South Pole.** The North Pole is the farthest north you can go on Earth. The South Pole is the farthest south. They are the coldest places in the world.

Look at the map on page 3 again. Find north in the compass rose. If you kept going north from this map, you would be at the North Pole. The compass arrow shows the direction toward the North Pole. If you kept going south, where would you end up?

The **equator** is a make-believe line on the globe. It is exactly halfway between the North Pole and the South Pole. The weather near the equator is the warmest in the world.

You will use maps and globes many times this year. Be sure you know all the key words and places in this section. They are the keys to success in geography.

Questions to Answer

1. What does a map key show?
2. What is a compass rose?
3. What does a distance scale tell you?
4. What are some things you can find out about the Earth by looking at a globe?

USING YOUR TEXTBOOK

Your textbook is divided into several parts. Knowing about these parts will help you use this book.

The Table of Contents

The **Table of Contents** tells what the book is about. It also tells where to find the book's different parts.

The Table of Contents begins on page V. Notice that it lists the book's **units** and **chapters.** After each name is a page number. That is the first page number of the unit or chapter. The Table of Contents lists other parts of the book, too.

Find Unit 1 in the Table of Contents. What is it called? This unit tells about the land and the people of the United States. Unit 1 has two chapters. What are the names of these chapters? On what page does Chapter 1 begin?

Chapters and Lessons

Each chapter is divided into small lessons. Each lesson begins with a number and a title. For example, the first lesson in Chapter 1 is **1. Americans Come from Many Places.**

Below the title is a section called **To Guide Your Reading.** A list of important words and names follows. This list includes **Key Words, People,** and **Places.** After these important words are three or four questions. You will find answers to these questions in the lessons.

You will see the words and names again as you read the lesson. They are printed in dark, or **boldfaced,** letters. Sometimes a boldfaced word is followed by a different spelling. You will see it in parentheses ( ). This spelling tells you how to say the word. For example, the word *plateau* will be followed by (pla•TOH).

Pay attention to these bold-faced words. When you see a boldfaced word, look for its meaning. Find each boldfaced place on a map in the chapter you are studying. Knowing these words will help you understand the lesson. They can help you find the answers to questions, too.

The Glossary

If you do not remember the meaning of a key word while you are reading, look for it in the **Glossary.** You will find the Glossary near the back of the book. The Glossary lists the key words in ABC order. It gives their meanings and tells you how to say them.

The Index

At some time you may need to review something, or you may want to read more about it. The quickest and easiest way to find any subject in your book is to use the book's **Index.** The Index begins on page 431, near the end of the book. The Index lists everything in the book in ABC order. It also gives the page numbers where the information is found.

Suppose you want to find information about the Rocky Mountains. You can find the Rocky Mountains listed in the Index in two ways. You can look under *R* for *Rocky,* or you can look under *M* for *Mountains.* Look at the Index now. On what pages will you find information about the Rocky Mountains?

The back of this book has two more important parts. One part is an **Almanac,** which gives many facts about each of the states in our country. The **Atlas** provides you with maps of the United States and the world.

There is one more important thing to know about your text-

You can use the Index to find any subject in this book.

book. Treat it with care. *Never* write in it. Your book should be as clean for another student next year as it is for you this year.

Questions to Answer

1. What is Unit 4 about? On what page does it begin?
2. Find the first lesson in Chapter 2. What is the name of this lesson?
3. How can you find the meaning of the key word *geography*? Give two ways.
4. On what pages will you find information on Missouri?
5. What does the Atlas of this book include?

OUR PEOPLE, OUR LAND

The United States has many different kinds of land. You can find rocky beaches as well as rich farmland. Hot deserts, great forests, and mountains topped with snow are all part of our country. The American people, too, are different in many ways. Our families have come from countries around the world. Our land and our people make this a special country.

In this unit you will read about our people and our land. As you read, you will see why Americans are proud of their country.

CHAPTER 1

The American People

The United States is a country made up of many different people. We are all Americans. You, your family, and your friends are also part of the American people.

In this chapter you will read how the United States came to have so many different people. You will see why freedom is so important to all Americans. You will find out that Americans are different from each other, but you will also discover that Americans have many things in common and share something special.

1. AMERICANS COME FROM MANY PLACES

╔═══╗
To Guide Your Reading

Look for these important words:

Key Words
- customs
- nation
- immigrants
- ancestors

- Vikings
- Pilgrims
- slaves
- slavery

People
- Christopher Columbus

Look for answers to these questions:

1. What groups of people came to live in America?
2. Why did people come to America?
3. Why do people still come to the United States today?
╚═══╝

Cowboy hats, Easter eggs, Halloween pumpkins, the English language. Each of these things is different. Yet all of them have something in common. People brought them to our country from other places.

Americans came to the United States from all over the world. They brought their special ways of doing things. These special ways of doing things are called **customs** (KUHS•tuhmz).

Many American customs come from around the world. For example, do you carve pumpkins at Halloween? This custom comes from Europe, where Halloween began. Do you color eggs at Easter? People from Poland and Russia brought their custom of painting eggs to America.

Many of the things we use come from other places, too. The Mexican *sombrero* (som•BRAIR•oh), for example, became our cowboy hat. Different kinds of music and dance also came here from elsewhere. Even our language, English, was brought by early settlers in America.

People have moved to this country, or **nation,** for hundreds of years. For this reason, the United States is often called a nation of **immigrants** (IM•ih•grints). Immigrants are people who move to a new country. Each year, many immigrants still come to start new lives in our country.

11

The first Americans traveled from Asia and went on to settle in different areas all over North and South America.

The First Americans

Thousands of years ago, a piece of land joined Asia to North America. People walked across this land from Asia. They were the first people to come to North America. These people were the **ancestors** (AN•ses•tuhrz), or early families, of the American Indians.

The First European Explorers

People from Europe reached North America much later. About 1,000 years ago, the **Vikings** reached North America. These explorers from Northern Europe only stayed a few years. In 1492 **Christopher Columbus** sailed here from Spain. He was trying to reach China and Japan. There he hoped to trade for gold, spices, and silk. Columbus thought he could reach China by sailing west from Europe. Instead he found North America. He gave the name "Indians" to the people he met. Columbus believed he had reached the islands called the Indies.

Columbus returned to Spain with gold. Hearing his stories, other Spanish explorers crossed the Atlantic Ocean. Among these explorers was an Italian living in Spain, Amerigo Vespucci (veh•SPYOO•chee). Vespucci said that he explored parts of what is now North and South America. He

12

believed he had reached a "new world," not Asia. A German mapmaker thought the new land should be named after Vespucci. Soon all of Europe was calling the new land America.

The French and the English

Because of these early explorers, the Spanish later settled in southern and western North America. They were not the only ones interested in America, though. Columbus's discovery also brought the French and the English.

Traveling by river, the French explored the north and the center of our country. They saw beaver and other animals with valuable furs. Soon the French were buying furs from the Indians to sell in Europe.

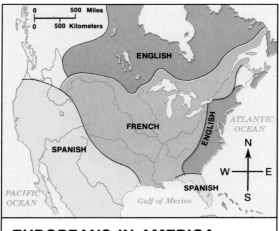

EUROPEANS IN AMERICA, EARLY 1700s

In the 1600s groups of English people settled in the eastern part of America. Some groups, like the **Pilgrims,** came here to find freedom. They wanted to have their own religion. In Europe they were not free to do so.

Many other people from Europe came to America. They wanted to find better lives for themselves. They wanted a chance to own land. They were willing to work hard to keep what they earned.

Slavery Begins and Ends

When our country was young, few people lived here. Needing workers for their large farms, some people bought **slaves.** A slave was a person owned by another person. Slaves could be bought and sold. They had no freedom.

Slaves came from Africa. In Africa, black people were taken from their homes and put in chains. Then they were locked up in ships. The ships carried them to many parts of North and South America. There they were bought by people who needed workers.

For years many Americans were troubled about **slavery**, or the owning of slaves. Though many people felt it was wrong, Americans were not sure how to end slavery. Finally, they fought

13

Most of these immigrants from Asia are studying English and learning about American customs.

a terrible war among themselves. During this war, slavery was ended for all time. Freedom was now the right of all Americans.

The Land of the Free

Freedom is important to Americans. Through the years, the hope of freedom brought many people to America. They came from Europe, Africa, and South America. They came from Asia and Australia. Many came from other parts of North America.

Today, immigrants still come to live here. Like the immigrants long ago, they hope to find better lives in America. They hope to share in America's freedom.

Reading Check

1. Name two things that immigrants brought to America.
2. Who were the first people to come to North America?
3. Why did Christopher Columbus sail to the new world?
4. Why have people come to America?

14

AMERICAN FOODS

The popular hot dog and hamburger

Pizza

Indian corn

What are your favorite foods? Do you know where these foods came from?

Some of our favorite foods were brought to America from other lands. Other favorites were first grown or invented in this country.

When people came here from other places, they cooked foods they had liked to eat in their old countries. Other Americans tasted these new foods and liked them. Soon Americans were eating foods from all over the world.

Hamburgers got their name from Hamburg, a town in Germany. Another food we eat from Germany is named after the town of Frankfurt, Germany. The Germans eat these sausages with sauerkraut (SOWR·krowt). We put them in buns and call them hot dogs. What, do you think, is another name for them?

From Italy came other foods Americans enjoy. Immigrants brought pizza along with spaghetti, macaroni, and ravioli. Spanish explorers planted the first orange trees in America. English settlers came here with apple seeds. Later immigrants brought us Mexican tacos and tortillas (tawr·TEE·uhs), Jewish bagels, Polish sausage, Swiss cheese, and much more.

Not all our food came from other countries, however. The American Indians showed the Pilgrims how to steam clams and plant corn. Beans, tomatoes, and pumpkins are Indian foods, too. So are turkey and cranberries. You can have quite a feast, whether you eat foods from other countries or from our own!

2. AMERICANS ARE DIFFERENT IN MANY WAYS

To Guide Your Reading

Look for these important words:

Key Words

- manufacturing
- goods
- service

Look for answers to these questions:

1. In what ways are Americans different from one another?
2. What kinds of jobs do Americans have?
3. How do Americans have fun?

Have you ever noticed how different Americans are? Each of us is different from one another in many ways.

Americans have come from all over the world. We have many different kinds of last names. Armas, Cerone, Lowenstein, Lucas, Jones, Rodriguez, Washington, Wong, Zisk—these are just a few names you might find in a phone book.

Americans are different in how they look and in what they do. Many Americans speak more than one language. We believe in different religions. Each of us has different talents and skills. Some of us are good in sports. Some of us sing well. Some of us know how to build or fix things.

Some Americans live in small towns.

Others make their homes in big cities.

16

Americans live in different kinds of communities. Many Americans live in great cities. Others live in suburbs outside of cities. Still others live on farms or in small towns.

Americans work at many different jobs. Some Americans are farmers. They grow wheat, corn, cotton, fruit, or vegetables. They raise dairy cows for milk or sheep for wool. They raise beef cattle, chickens, or hogs for meat.

Americans have many different jobs in **manufacturing** (man•yuh•FAK•chuhr•eeng). The word *manufacturing* means making **goods.** Goods are things such as clothing, beds, radios, books, and cars.

Americans have many different **service** jobs. A service is some activity that people do for others. When a waitress brings you food in a restaurant, she is providing a service. When your family gets mail, the mail carrier is providing a service. Teachers, doctors, writers, librarians, sales clerks, and truck drivers are just a few more people who provide services to many other Americans.

Americans may live in suburbs close to big cities. Many work in these cities during the day.

Our nation's farms provide food for people in our country's towns, cities, and suburbs.

Music brings together different kinds of people of all ages. Much American music is a blend of music from other places.

Americans enjoy many different ways of having fun. Millions of Americans enjoy sports like baseball, soccer, basketball, or swimming. Millions of others enjoy fishing, hiking, or camping. Some Americans enjoy flying in balloons, while others like movies, the theater, and concerts. Many Americans like taking pictures or reading. These are only a few ways Americans have fun. Each person's choice is different just as each American is different.

The United States is a mix of all these differences. Our people come from many places. We have many different customs and religions. We have different languages and different ways of living and working. All together, these differences make Americans a special people.

Reading Check

1. Name three ways in which Americans are different from one another.
2. Name four kinds of communities.
3. What is the difference between goods and services?
4. In what different ways do Americans enjoy themselves?

18

3. AMERICANS SHARE MANY THINGS

To Guide Your Reading

Look for these important words:

Key Words
- government
- laws
- republic
- voting
- democracy
- rights
- responsibilities
- heritage

Look for answers to these questions:

1. What do Americans have in common?
2. What is the difference between rights and responsibilities?
3. What are some parts of our American heritage?

What is an American? Ask a hundred different people, and you will get a hundred different answers. Yet in some special ways, Americans have much in common.

Americans share their country's past. Together we remember America's past on national holidays. These are days important to all our nation's people.

One of our most important holidays is the Fourth of July. Our country once was ruled by England. On July 4, 1776, America declared its freedom from England. Each July 4, millions of Americans celebrate this holiday. We fly our flag, have parades, and go on picnics.

Our people share a special way of life. We learn about one another from television and newspapers.

On the Fourth of July, fireworks light up the skies over our nation's capital, Washington, D.C., and over cities across the country.

In playing and watching popular sports like baseball, Americans share the fun and excitement of people working together as a team.

Together we play and watch many sports. We eat American foods such as hot dogs and apple pie. All these things help bring us together as a people.

Our Government

One important thing Americans share is their **government.** A government is a group of people who lead a city, a state, or a country. One important job of leaders is to make **laws.** Laws are rules for all to follow.

The United States has a government called a **republic.** In the American republic, people are free to choose their leaders. We choose leaders by **voting** for them. To become a leader, a person must get the most votes. Our leaders must listen to the people who choose them. If our leaders do not do a good job, we can vote for new leaders.

Democracy

Americans share many beliefs, too. Our most important belief is **democracy** (di•MOK•ruh•see). *Democracy* means that people are free to make choices about their lives. They can choose the leaders of their government. They can choose where they live and how they earn a living. They decide what to think, say, and read. In many countries of the world, people are not free to make such choices. Why, do you think, is this freedom important?

Rights and Responsibilities

In America's democracy, people believe in certain **rights** and **responsibilities.** A right is a freedom that belongs to you. We Americans believe in the right to choose our leaders. A responsibility is something that you should do. Americans have a responsibility to obey the laws. We have a responsibility not to harm other people. We have a responsibility to learn about our country.

Some of our rights were written down long ago. You can still read them today.

Our American Heritage

Americans share other beliefs. We believe in hard work and fairness. We believe in working together to solve problems. We also believe in doing the best we can. Americans have always come up with new ideas, new ways of solving problems. These beliefs have made the United States a strong country.

Finally, Americans believe in themselves. We believe in sharing our different ideas. By sharing them, we can find the best ways to solve problems. That is better than if everyone thought the same way.

Our way of life and beliefs make up our **heritage.** Our American heritage comes to us from our country's past. It comes from all the Americans who have ever lived. It is a heritage of which to be proud. It is a heritage that you will add to in the years to come.

Reading Check

1. Name four things that Americans share.
2. Why do Americans celebrate the Fourth of July? How do we celebrate this holiday?
3. What kind of government do Americans have?
4. How do Americans choose their leaders?

SKILLS FOR SUCCESS

EXPLORING THE LIBRARY

Suppose you want to find out about American Indians. You would probably go to a library. Most libraries have a number of books about this **subject.** The subject is what a book is about.

Look at the picture on this page. All these books are about one subject. What is it?

Parts of the Library

Libraries keep their books in three different sections. One section is for **fiction,** one is for **nonfiction,** and one is for **reference** books.

Fiction books are made-up stories. *Hawk, I'm Your Brother* is a fiction book. It is a made-up story about an Indian boy who wishes he could fly like his hawk.

Find this book in the picture. You can see the **spine,** or backbone of the book. The spine shows the book's title, the author's last name, and the letter *B.* The letter *B* is the first letter of the author's last name. What is the author's last name?

Now suppose you are looking for *Hawk* on the shelves. Fiction books are arranged in alphabetical, or ABC, order, by the authors' last names. Does this book come before or after a book by Mary Barton?

Nonfiction books give facts about real people and things. *Indians: The First Americans* is a nonfiction book. It describes how and where different Indian groups lived.

Look at the spine of this book. It shows the book's title, the author's last name, and the number 970. Nonfiction books are arranged in number order. All nonfiction books on the same subject have the same number. For example, 970 is the number used by the library for books about American Indians.

The card catalog lists all of the books in a particular library.

Reference books are collections of facts. Most libraries have encyclopedias, dictionaries, and atlases in the reference section. For example, *Great North American Indians* is a dictionary of Indian leaders.

Reference books have a number and the letter *R* or *REF,* for *reference,* marked on them. You cannot take reference books out. You have to use them at the library.

Finding the Book You Need

The **card catalog** can help you find books in the library. It is a large cabinet of small drawers. The drawers are full of cards. Each book in the library has at least two cards. One is the **title card.** It has the book's title at the top. Another is the **author card.** It has the author's last name at the top.

All the cards are kept in alphabetical order. Suppose you want to find the title card for *Hawk, I'm Your Brother.* You will look in the drawer marked *H.* This letter begins the first word in the book's title. (If the first word is *a, an,* or *the,* use the first letter of the second word.)

Suppose you have read several books by Miska Miles and want to find another one. The author cards will tell you the titles of her books. You use the author's last name to find them. Look at the cards below. What is the title of one book by Miska Miles?

jF   Hawk, I'm your brother.
Baylor, Byrd. Illustrated by Peter Parnall. New York: Scribner, 1976. 48 p. illus.

jF   **Miles, Miska**
    Annie and the old one. Illustrated by Peter Parnall. Boston: Little, Brown, 1971. 44 p. illus.

To find a nonfiction book, you need to know its number. Remember, nonfiction books are kept in number order. The title card will give you the number of a book. The number is in the upper left-hand corner. Find the title card of *The Art of the North American Indian.* What is its number?

970.6
G

The art of the
North American Indian.
Glubok, Shirley. New York:
Harper & Row, 1964.
48 p. illus.

973.1
B

INDIANS — AMERICAN
Baity, Elizabeth (Chesley)
  Americans before Columbus.
Illustrated with drawings and
maps by C.B. Falls and with 32
pages of photographs. New
York: Viking Press, 1961, 1951.
272 p. illus., maps

Subject cards can also help you find books. All nonfiction books in a library have subject cards. You look under "Indians—American" for any books about American Indians. These cards are in the card catalog drawer marked with the letter *I*. Each card has the subject written at the top. Then it gives the author, title, and number. Look at the subject card on this page. What is the book's title?

CHECKING YOUR SKILLS

Answer the questions below. Use the spines of these books to help you.

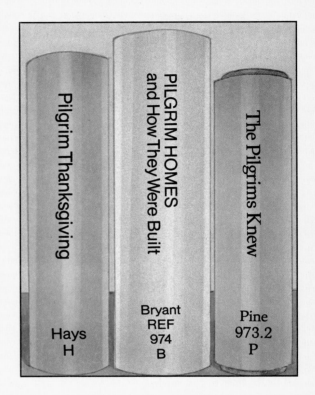

Pilgrim Thanksgiving — Hays H

PILGRIM HOMES and How They Were Built — Bryant REF 974 B

The Pilgrims Knew — Pine 973.2 P

1. What is the subject of these books?

2. Which book is nonfiction?

3. Which book cannot be taken out of the library?

4. Suppose you want to find a nonfiction book called *The Plymouth Thanksgiving.* What information do you need to find this book?

5. Suppose you want to find a book about the Pilgrims. How could you find books about them?

CHAPTER 1 REVIEW

WORDS TO USE

Copy the sentences below. Fill in the blanks with the right words from the list.

democracy   **manufacturing**
government   **right**
immigrants

1. People who move to a new country are ____.

2. Making goods is called ____.

3. People who lead a city, a state, or a country make up a ____.

4. A ____ means that people are free to make choices about their lives.

5. A ____ is a freedom that belongs to you.

FACTS TO REVIEW

1. Which of these is a custom?

   a. carving Halloween pumpkins
   b. making cars
   c. voting

2. Where did the Spanish settle in America?

3. Why have immigrants come to America? Give two reasons.

4. Give an example of a service job.

5. Name two ways that Americans share a special way of life.

6. How do Americans choose their government leaders?

7. What are some choices that Americans can make?

8. What responsibilities do all Americans have? Give three examples.

9. Why is it important for Americans to share their ideas?

10. What is our American heritage?

IDEAS TO DISCUSS

Imagine a place where everyone is the same. Describe it. Would you like to live there? Why or why not?

◯ SKILLS PRACTICE

Using the Library   Use the title card on page 24 to answer these questions.

1. What is the subject of this book?

2. What information will help you find this book in the library?

CHAPTER 2

The American Land

AMERICA THE BEAUTIFUL

O beautiful for spacious skies,
  For amber waves of grain,
For purple mountain majesties
  Above the fruited plain!
America! America!
  God shed His grace on thee
And crowned thy good with brotherhood
  From sea to shining sea!

Katharine Lee Bates

About
this
chapter

You may already know the song "America the Beautiful." It tells of America's wide skies, rich farmlands, and high mountains. In this chapter, you will take a trip across our 50 states. You will discover America's natural wonders for yourself.

1. A LAND BETWEEN OCEANS

To Guide Your Reading

Look for these important words:

Key Words
• boundaries

• Gulf of Mexico
• Great Lakes
• St. Lawrence River

Places
• Rio Grande

Look for answers to these questions:

1. What oceans reach the shores of the United States?
2. Which states do not touch any other state?
3. Which countries are our neighbors?
4. What other bodies of water form part of our borders?

The United States is a country of hot places and cold places, rainy places and dry places. Mountains, forests, and wide, open country stretch across the land. Rivers cut through the land, and oceans pound the shores.

The United States has so many different places because it is so large. It is the fourth largest country in the world. The United States stretches east to the Atlantic Ocean and west to the Pacific Ocean. The oceans are our east and west **boundaries.** *Boundary* is another word for *border.*

The United States has 50 states, but only 48 are joined by their state borders. Each state touches at least one other. Two states, Alaska and Hawaii, stand alone. Alaska is far in the north. It is our largest state. Water surrounds Alaska on three sides. Hawaii, our fiftieth state, is far out in the Pacific Ocean. It is made up of more than 100 islands.

South of the United States is the country of Mexico. Part of our border with Mexico is a river, the **Rio Grande** (REE•oh GRAND). Rio Grande is a Spanish name meaning "Big River."

The Rio Grande flows into the **Gulf of Mexico.** The gulf is a body of water that is actually a part of the Atlantic Ocean.

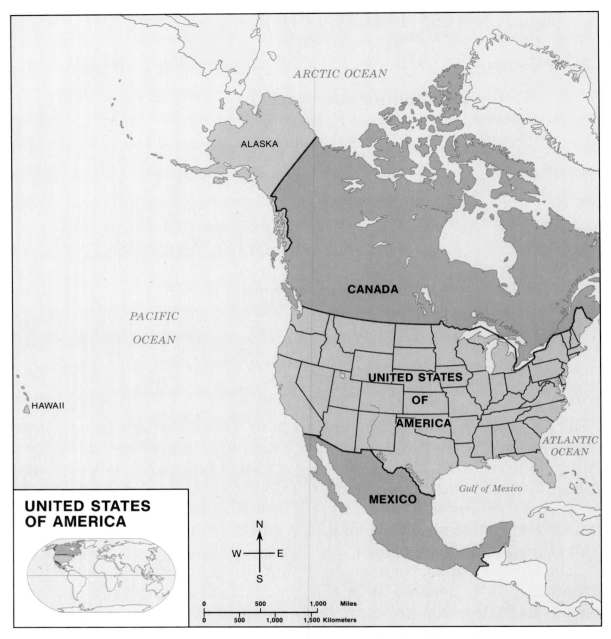

ARCTIC OCEAN

ALASKA

CANADA

PACIFIC
OCEAN

Great Lakes

St. Lawrence R.

UNITED STATES
OF
AMERICA

HAWAII

ATLANTIC
OCEAN

Rio Grande

Gulf of Mexico

MEXICO

UNITED STATES
OF AMERICA

N
W E
S

| 0 | 500 | 1,000 | Miles |
| 0 | 500 | 1,000 | 1,500 Kilometers |

The country of Canada is our northern neighbor. Our boundary with Canada is long. Four of the **Great Lakes** and part of the **St. Lawrence River** come between the countries. Canada also shares a border with our most northern state, Alaska.

Reading Check

1. What are the east and west boundaries of our country?
2. Where are Alaska and Hawaii?
3. What river forms part of our border with Mexico?
4. What forms part of our border with Canada?

28

2. A LAND OF MANY LANDS

To Guide Your Reading

Look for these important words:

Key Words
- skyscrapers
- coast
- capital
- plain
- harbors
- plateaus
- canyons
- desert
- basin
- wilderness

Places
- Coastal Plain
- Appalachian Mountains
- Interior Plains
- Mississippi River
- Rocky Mountains
- Great Basin
- Sierra Nevada
- Cascade Range
- Central Valley
- Coast Ranges

Look for answers to these questions:

1. Where are the plains in our country?
2. What mountains stretch across our land?
3. How are plateaus and plains alike? How are they different?
4. How is the Pacific coast different from the Atlantic coast?

Imagine that you are taking a trip across the United States. You board a plane at an airport in New York City. This is the largest city in the United States. After you take off, you will fly over the **skyscrapers**, or tall buildings, of New York. Then suddenly the land changes. Much of it is low, flat, and sandy. You are flying along the Atlantic **coast**. A coast is land next to an ocean.

Your first stop along the Atlantic coast is Washington, D.C. This city is our nation's **capital.** A capital is a city where leaders make laws. Our leaders make laws for our country in Washington, D.C. This city is in an area called the District of Columbia. The letters *D.C.* stand for the District of Columbia. This area, or district, is not a state. It is a place of government buildings, a workplace for our leaders.

The Coastal Plain

As you fly out of Washington, D.C., you will see that the land around it is low and flat. This land is part of a long **plain** that lies

UNITED STATES OF AMERICA
- National boundary
- State boundary
- ⚝ National capital
- ● Large city
- ▲ Mountain peak

PACIFIC OCEAN

CANADA

WASHINGTON
▲ Mt. Rainier
14,410 ft.
(4,390 m)
Columbia Plateau

Columbia River

OREGON

COAST RANGES
CASCADE RANGE

IDAHO

MONTANA

ROCKY MOUNTAINS

Missouri River

Snake River

WYOMING

INTERIO

Platte

NEVADA

Great Salt Lake

UTAH

COLORADO
▲ Mt. Elbert
14,430 ft. (4,400 m)

SIERRA NEVADA

Sacramento River

Central Valley

CALIFORNIA

▲ Mt. Whitney
14,490 ft.
(4,420 m)

COAST RANGES

Los Angeles ●

Colorado River

Colorado

Colorado Plateau

Grand Canyon

Painted Desert

ROCKY MOUNTAINS

ARIZONA

NEW MEXICO

Sonoran Desert

Gila River

Rio Grande

Gulf of California

MEXICO

PACIFIC OCEAN

HAWAII

0   100 Miles
0   100 Kilometers

SOVIET UNION (USSR)

ARCTIC OCEAN

BROOKS RANGE

Yukon River

ALASKA

Mt. McKinley ▲
20,320 ft. (6,190 m)

CANADA

ALASKA RANGE

Bering Sea

0   250   500 Miles
0   250   500 Kilometers

PACIFIC OCEAN

along the Atlantic Ocean. A plain is a large area of flat, low land. Find the **Coastal Plain** on the map on this page. It begins on the coast of Massachusetts. Then it stretches from New York City to Florida, and on into Texas. In the north it is very narrow. In Florida it is more than 500 miles (about 800 km) wide.

Many important rivers cross the Coastal Plain and spill into

the ocean. Can you name some of them? Three of them are the Delaware, the Potomac, and the Savannah rivers. At many places where rivers meet the sea there are good natural **harbors.** A harbor is a place where ships can dock safely. The land around harbors protects the ships from storms and strong winds. A good harbor is deep so ships can come close to shore.

31

The beautiful Blue Ridge Mountains are part of the Appalachian Mountains.

The Appalachian Mountains

As you travel west across the plain, the land begins to rise. The **Appalachian** (ap•uh•LAY•chee•uhn) **Mountains,** with their low, rounded tops, come into view. These tree-covered mountains stretch through the eastern part of our country.

The Interior Plains

To the west of the Appalachians, the land slopes down. The view ahead seems endless. Here in the center of the United States lie huge plains. They are the **Interior** (in•TIR•ee•uhr) **Plains.** The word *interior* means inside. The Interior Plains are inside our country. They have some of the richest soil in the world. Much of our country's food comes from these plains.

Through the Interior Plains flows the longest river in the United States, the **Mississippi** (mis•uh•SIP•ee) **River.** Other rivers and streams flow into the Mississippi. Some of these are the Missouri, Ohio, Arkansas, and Tennessee rivers.

The Great Lakes are another water treasure of our nation's heartland. Look for these lakes on the map. They are the world's largest group of freshwater lakes. Their waters could cover the whole United States to a depth of 12 feet (about 4 m).

The Rocky Mountains

Your plane is now flying toward the western edge of the Interior Plains. Out of the plains rise the snow-covered tops of the **Rocky Mountains.** These mountains cover much of the western United States. The Rocky Mountains are famous for their scenery. Thick forests, clear blue lakes, and rushing streams attract many visitors every year.

The Rocky Mountains are among the world's tallest mountains. The highest parts of the Rockies are covered with snow all year.

Deserts and Plateaus

Within our western mountain region you can see other land-forms. Besides the mountains, you can find many valleys, **plateaus** (pla•TOHZ), and **canyons.** A plateau is high, flat land, like a table. A canyon is a narrow valley with steep sides.

After you cross the Rocky Mountains, the view changes again. Now the land is mostly dry, with few plants. It is the largest **desert** (DEZ•uhrt) area in our country.

In this desert area you will find the **Great Basin.** A **basin** is low, bowl-shaped land. The Great Basin is one of the driest parts of our country. The Great Salt Lake is here. This lake is very salty.

Mountains and Valleys

As you continue to fly west, you will see more mountains. Just inside California is the **Sierra Nevada.** *Sierra Nevada* means "Snowy Mountains" in Spanish. The snow in these mountains melts to form many lakes, rivers, and streams. To the north, in Washington and Oregon, is the **Cascade Range.**

Ocean waves pound the rough cliffs along California's northern coast.

Snow and ice glitter at the top of Mt. McKinley in Alaska.

To the west of the mountains are large valleys of rich farmland. The largest is the **Central Valley** of California. The word *central* means "in the middle." The Central Valley grows fruits and vegetables for much of the nation.

All along the Pacific Ocean are the **Coast Ranges.** These mountains give much of the Pacific coast a rocky, rugged look.

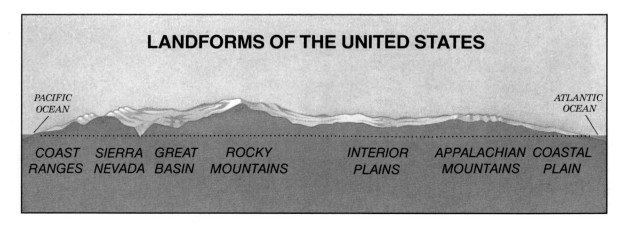

LANDFORMS OF THE UNITED STATES

PACIFIC OCEAN

ATLANTIC OCEAN

COAST RANGES   SIERRA NEVADA   GREAT BASIN   ROCKY MOUNTAINS   INTERIOR PLAINS   APPALACHIAN MOUNTAINS   COASTAL PLAIN

A chain of islands glimmering in the sun, Hawaii lies in the middle of the Pacific Ocean about 2,800 miles (4,480 km) from California.

Alaska and Hawaii

Your plane continues north along the Pacific coast to Alaska. Alaska, our largest state, has huge forests and open plains, wide valleys and high mountains. Mount McKinley, North America's highest mountain, is in Alaska. Snow and ice cover northern Alaska for most of the year. Thousands of animals roam free across this hard land. Much of Alaska remains **wilderness.** A wilderness is land that people do not live in. Alaska has the fewest people of all the states in our country.

Flying south across the Pacific Ocean, you finish your trip in Hawaii. Its many islands are really the tops of mountains rising out of the sea. Hawaii is warm and green all year.

Reading Check

1. What kind of land is east of the Appalachian Mountains?
2. Where are some of the biggest rivers in the United States?
3. What is the Great Basin?
4. How is Alaska different from other states? How is Hawaii different from other states?

3. A LAND OF MANY CLIMATES

To Guide Your Reading

Look for these important words:

Key Words
- weather
- climate
- temperature
- precipitation
- sea level
- growing season

Look for answers to these questions:

1. What is climate?
2. What does temperature depend on?
3. Why is precipitation important?

You probably have heard people ask, "What's the **weather** like today?" They mean, "Is it hot, rainy, cold, or cloudy?"

People do not ask, "What's the **climate** like today?" That's because weather and climate are different. Climate is the weather a place has year after year. If a place is usually hot in summer and rainy in winter, that is its climate. Climate has two main parts, **temperature** (TEM•puhr•uh•chuhr) and **precipitation** (prih•sip•uh•TAY•shuhn).

Temperature

Temperature is how warm or cold a place is. Often temperature depends on where a place is. Alaska is near the North Pole. Northern Alaska is the coldest place in our country. Hawaii is near the equator. It is one of the warmest places in our country. The rest of our country lies between these two places. The northern United States is usually colder than the southern part.

Temperature also depends on how high a place is. We measure height from **sea level.** Land level with the surface of the oceans is

LAND AT SEA LEVEL

sea level

ocean   land

36

at sea level. As land gets higher, its temperature gets cooler. Many mountain tops have snow all year. The weather never gets warm enough to melt the snow.

Precipitation

Precipitation is another important part of climate. Precipitation means rain or snow.

Precipitation is very important to plant life. In fact, no plant can live without some precipitation.

When you know the precipitation and temperature of a place, you can begin to understand what grows there. Places with dry climates have few plants. Unless water is brought to them, hot, dry places are poor farmlands. In warmer, wetter climates, grasses can grow. Trees need a lot of rain, though. Only places with very high precipitation have thick forests.

Many parts of our country have warm summers and cold winters. Most plants cannot grow in very cold or freezing weather. The time when the weather is warm enough for plants to grow is the **growing season.** Some places in our country have warmer or wetter growing seasons than others because every place has its own special climate. Your state's climate is different from any other state's.

These juicy oranges will be shipped to different areas of our country. Oranges and other fruits grow all year in sunny places like California and Florida.

Our country's many climates let us grow many kinds of crops. Most of the foods we eat are grown in the United States. Our different climates help us grow large amounts and many kinds of food.

Reading Check

1. How is climate different from weather?
2. What are the two main parts of climate?
3. Why is precipitation important?
4. Why is the United States able to grow much of its own food?

4. A LAND OF MANY RESOURCES

To Guide Your Reading

Look for these important words:

Key Words
- natural resources
- minerals

- fuels
- products
- irrigation

Look for answers to these questions:

1. What are natural resources?
2. What are the important resources of the United States?
3. Why are natural resources important for our country?

Among the countries of the world, the United States is a giant. Our people have worked hard to make it strong and wealthy. Our **natural resources** (NACH•uhr•uhl REE•sohr•ses) have also made this country strong. Natural resources are things in nature that people can use.

The land itself is an important resource. Many parts of our country have rich soil. Our climate and soil help us grow huge amounts of food. Our land also has many **minerals** (MIN•uhr•uhlz) and **fuels** (FYOO•uhlz). Sand, stone, and iron are minerals. We use these minerals to make machines and buildings. Coal, oil, and natural gas are fuels. We use fuels to make heat and to run many kinds of machines.

Forests are another important natural resource. Our forests are among the world's largest. Forests cover about a third of our country. From them come lumber, paper, and other **products.** A product is something that people make or get from nature.

The United States has good water resources. Our rivers, lakes, and streams provide water for drinking, farming, and manufacturing. They also provide many kinds of fish. Some rivers are used to make electric power.

Some areas in our country have good soil but little rain. People must bring water to them. This is called **irrigation.** Through irrigation we have turned many of our deserts and dry places into valuable farmland.

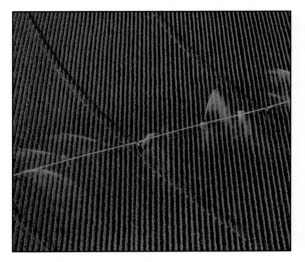

A huge irrigation sprinkler on a farm in Nebraska rolls around a field in a circle. Without irrigation this area would be too dry to farm.

From trees we make many things we need, such as writing paper, cardboard boxes, and lumber for building houses.

Stone is one resource needed for building skyscrapers.

Our land, our forests, and our water are resources we need in order to live. They make the United States a strong country and a place of beauty. It is everyone's responsibility to use our resources wisely. If we do not, our country will not have as many. Future Americans will need these resources, too. The way we use them today will shape our country's future.

Reading Check

1. What are the main natural resources of the United States?
2. How do we use fuels?
3. What is irrigation?
4. Why should we use our resources wisely?

SKILLS FOR SUCCESS

USING SPECIAL-PURPOSE MAPS

Landform Maps

Some maps are called **special-purpose maps.** One such map is the map below, a **landform map.** Landforms are shapes of the land. The four main landforms are **mountains, hills, plateaus,** and **plains.** Landform maps show these different shapes of land. The map key shows what colors they are on the map. Find the brown color in the key. It tells you that mountains are brown on the map. What mountains are in the eastern United States? in the western United States? in Alaska?

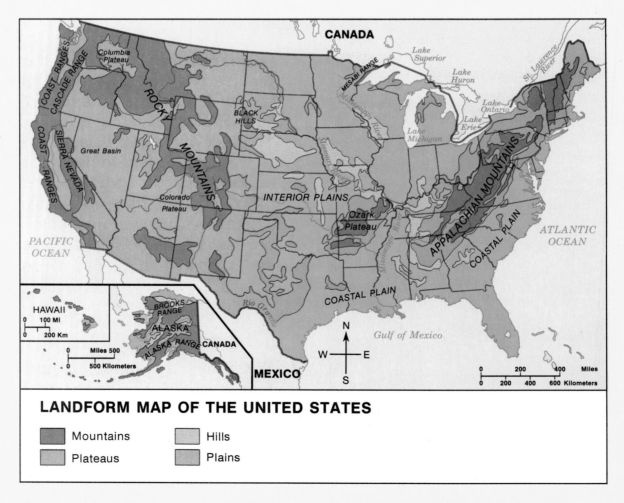

LANDFORM MAP OF THE UNITED STATES

- Mountains
- Hills
- Plateaus
- Plains

Now look at the center of the landform map. Most of it is green. Look for this color in the key. What kind of land does this area have? Is the land flat or hilly? Where do you find plateaus in our country?

This map also can tell you other things about the land. You know that mountains and plateaus are high. You know that hills and plains are low. So this map also shows the higher and lower parts of the United States. Where are the low parts of our country?

Temperature Maps

Below is a **temperature map.** It shows the summer and winter temperatures in the United States.

The map key shows the temperatures in summer and winter. For example, it tells you that green areas have warm summers and cold winters. Most of the map is colored green. What kind of temperatures does Chicago have? Now look at Hawaii. It is colored orange. What does the key tell you about Hawaii's temperatures?

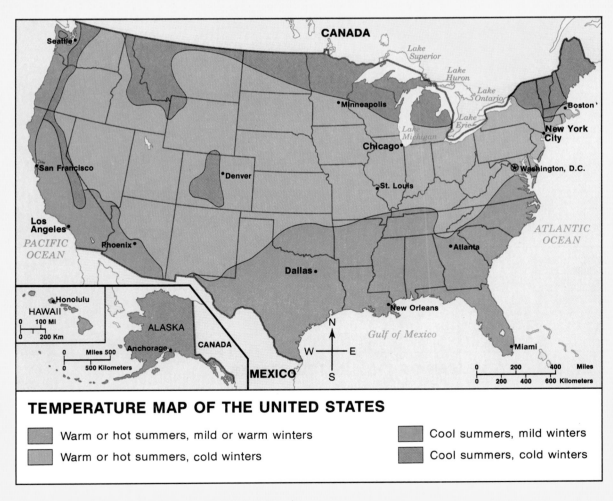

TEMPERATURE MAP OF THE UNITED STATES

Warm or hot summers, mild or warm winters	Cool summers, mild winters
Warm or hot summers, cold winters	Cool summers, cold winters

Precipitation Maps

Another kind of map shows precipitation. The map below shows the usual precipitation in the United States. It tells how much rain or snow falls in an average year.

Find Boston on the precipitation map. Boston is in an area colored light blue. This means Boston receives more than 40 inches (about 100 cm) of precipitation a year. What other cities on this map get the same amount?

Now find Phoenix on this map. How much precipitation does Phoenix have in a year? You can see that Phoenix is in a dry area. Only scattered grasses and small bushes grow here. Find Chicago on this map. How much precipitation does Chicago have in an average year?

Some areas in the south and the west receive more than 60 inches (150 cm) of precipitation a year. What cities are in those areas?

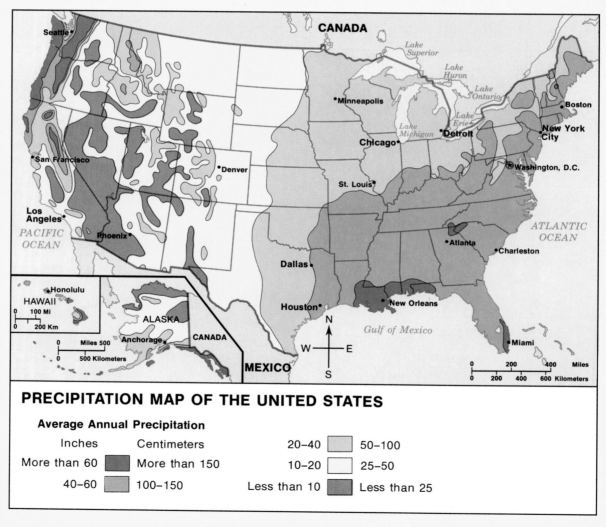

PRECIPITATION MAP OF THE UNITED STATES

Average Annual Precipitation

Inches	Centimeters			Inches	Centimeters
More than 60	More than 150			20–40	50–100
40–60	100–150			10–20	25–50
				Less than 10	Less than 25

Resource and Product Maps

The map below is a **resource and product map.** This map shows the main natural resources and products of our country.

A map like this uses symbols and colors to show different resources and products. The map key explains what the symbols and colors mean. For example, what does ⬛ mean? Now find the symbol for oil in the map key. Near what cities is the symbol for oil? In these places, oil, an important resource, is found.

Now find the color for wheat and other grains. Find the major wheat-growing areas on the map. In these areas growing wheat is important.

Look at the map key. Find the color for undeveloped land. Undeveloped land is land that people are not using yet. Now look at the map. Where are large areas of undeveloped land found?

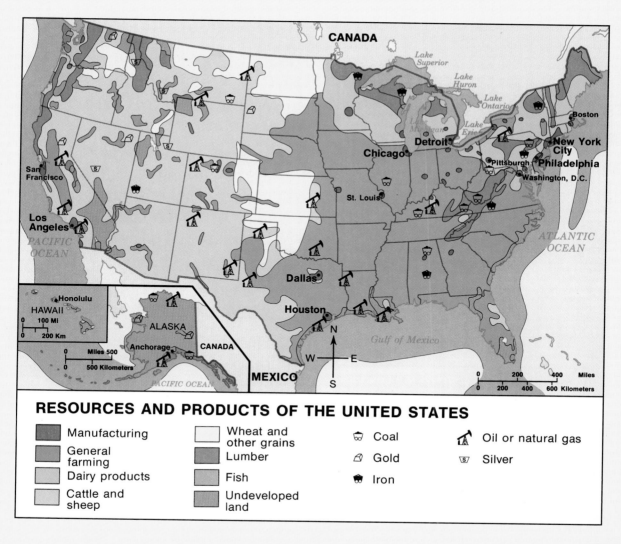

RESOURCES AND PRODUCTS OF THE UNITED STATES

▨ Manufacturing	☐ Wheat and other grains	⌣ Coal	🛢 Oil or natural gas
▨ General farming	▨ Lumber	◭ Gold	Ⓢ Silver
☐ Dairy products	▨ Fish	⬛ Iron	
☐ Cattle and sheep	▨ Undeveloped land		

43

Inset Maps

Look back at Alaska and Hawaii on the maps in this lesson. These states are not shown where they really are. Hundreds of miles separate them from the other 48 states. To show the whole area, all parts of the map would have to be much smaller. Instead, Alaska and Hawaii are each shown in an **inset.** The box around each shows that it is an inset.

An inset often has a distance scale. The scales of an inset and the main map may be different. Below is part of the map on page

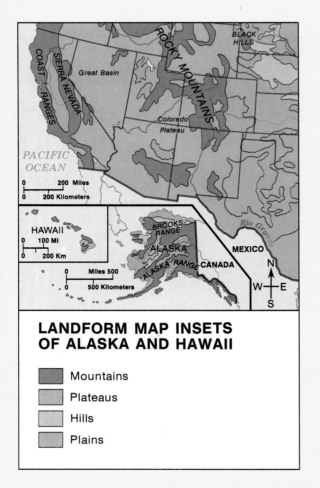

LANDFORM MAP INSETS OF ALASKA AND HAWAII

- Mountains
- Plateaus
- Hills
- Plains

40. Look at Alaska. On the Earth, Alaska is more than twice the size of Texas. Here Alaska appears only one-fourth as large as it really should. Notice that the scales of the inset and the main map on page 40 are different.

Look at the inset of Hawaii on this page. All together, the Hawaiian Islands are a little larger than the state of Connecticut. Do the insets for Hawaii and Alaska have the same scale?

CHECKING YOUR SKILLS

Answer these questions. Use the maps in this lesson to help you.

1. Which map shows the high and low parts of our country?

2. Orange trees grow best in warm, sunny weather. They cannot live through cold winters. Which map tells you where oranges can grow?

3. Oil is an important natural resource. Which map tells you where oil comes from?

4. Find the inset of Hawaii on each map.

    a. What kinds of land does Hawaii have?

    b. What is its yearly temperature and precipitation?

    c. What map shows farming and manufacturing in Hawaii?

CHAPTER 2 REVIEW

WORDS TO USE

Copy the words numbered 1 to 10. Next to each word write its meaning.

1. **basin**
2. **boundary**
3. **canyon**
4. **fuels**
5. **interior**
6. **plain**
7. **plateau**
8. **precipitation**
9. **sea level**
10. **wilderness**

a. Border
b. Inside
c. Low, flat land
d. Land where no people live
e. Amount of rain or snow
f. Level of the surface of the oceans
g. What we use to make heat and to run machines
h. Low, bowl-shaped area
i. High, flat land, like a table
j. Narrow valley with steep, high sides

FACTS TO REVIEW

1. Name four bodies of water that are United States boundaries.

2. What is the largest group of freshwater lakes in the world?

3. What is the difference between climate and weather?

4. What are minerals used for? Give two uses as examples.

5. Why can the United States grow large amounts of food? Give three reasons.

IDEAS TO DISCUSS

1. You read that the United States has many different landforms and climates. Now imagine our country with flat land and a cold climate everywhere. How would flat land and a cold climate change your life?

2. Why is it important for our country to have many different kinds of land, climates, and resources?

◯ SKILLS PRACTICE

Using Special-Purpose Maps Use the maps on pages 40 to 44 to help you answer these questions.

1. What kinds of land does Alaska have?

2. What kinds of temperatures does Alaska have?

3. About how much precipitation does Anchorage get?

4. Where is gold found in Alaska?

CLOSE-UP

GEOGRAPHIC DICTIONARY

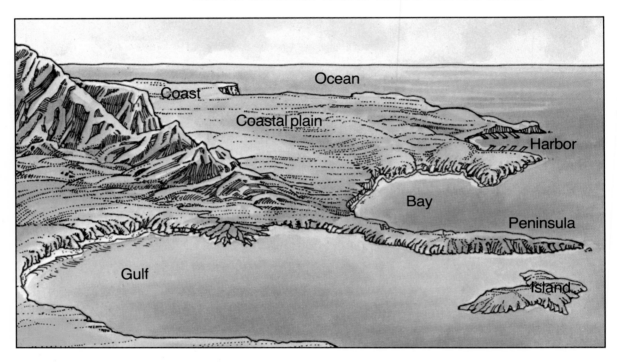

On the following pages are descriptions of important natural features. Study these words. You will meet them again in your reading.

bay a small area of ocean partly surrounded by land

coast land next to an ocean

coastal plain low, flat land near an ocean

continent one of the Earth's main bodies of land

gulf a large area of ocean partly surrounded by land

harbor a place on a coast where ships can dock safely

island land completely surrounded by water

ocean a large body of salt water

peninsula a piece of land with water on three sides of it

sea a large body of salt water surrounded by land

46

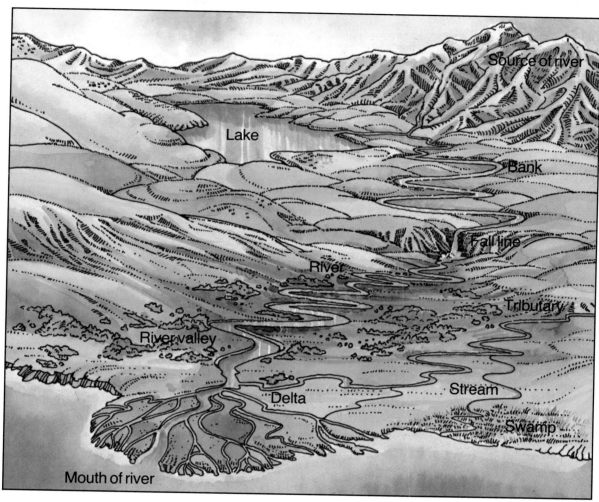

bank the land on each side of a river

branch a stream or river that flows into a larger one

delta soil laid down at the mouth of a river, usually shaped like a triangle

fall line a chain of waterfalls formed by rivers dropping down to lower land

lake a body of fresh or salt water surrounded by land

mouth of river the place where a river empties into a larger body of water

river a large stream of water

river basin all the land drained by a river and its branches

river valley low land through which a river flows

source of river a stream or another body of water from which a river begins

stream a small body of running water

swamp low, wet land

tributary a small river that flows into a larger one

waterway body of water ships can use

47

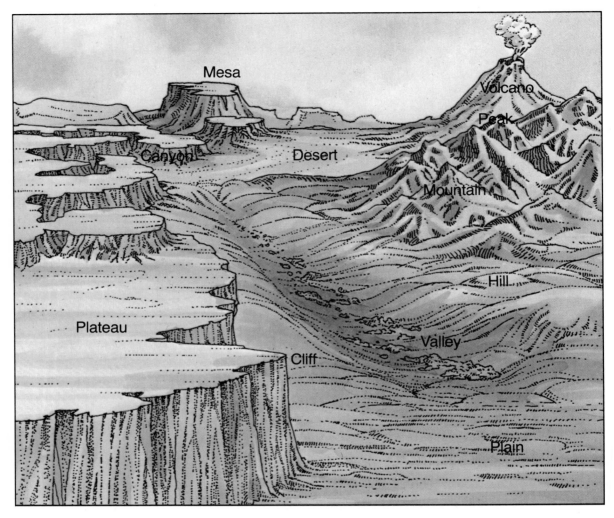

basin a low, bowl-shaped area

canyon a narrow valley with high, steep sides

cliff a high, steep wall of rock

desert dry land where few plants grow

foothill a low hill at the base of a mountain

hill a small, raised part of the land, lower than a mountain

mesa a flat-topped hill with steep sides, common in dry areas

mountain a large, high part of the land with steep sides

mountain range a group or chain of mountains

peak the pointed top of a mountain

plain a large area of flat or gently rolling land

plateau an area of high, flat land

sand dune a hill of sand piled up by the wind

slope the side of a mountain or hill

valley low land between mountains or hills

volcano an opening in the Earth that throws out melted rock and gases

UNIT 1 REVIEW

WORDS TO REMEMBER

Copy the sentences below. Fill in the blanks with the right words from the list.

climate
democracy
goods
heritage
immigrants

irrigation
minerals
natural resources
republic
voting

1. We are a nation of _____.

2. We manufacture many kinds of _____.

3. Our government is known as a _____.

4. We choose our leaders by _____ for them.

5. We believe in _____, or that people are free to make choices about their lives.

6. Americans are proud of their way of life and beliefs, America's special _____.

7. Temperature and precipitation are important parts of _____.

8. The United States is rich in almost all _____, such as water, soil, and minerals.

9. Copper and iron are _____ that help us make machines and buildings.

10. Through _____ we can grow food in dry areas.

FOCUS ON MAIN IDEAS

1. Why is the United States often called a nation of immigrants?

2. Name at least three ways in which people make a living in the United States.

3. In what ways are Americans different from one another? How are they alike?

4. Name a way in which Americans share in their government.

5. What are some responsibilities that Americans have? Give two examples.

6. What are three beliefs that Americans share?

7. Name each of these places:

   a. A group of lakes between Canada and the United States

   b. Mountains in the eastern United States

c. Large plains inside our country

d. A state made up of islands

8. Why is the northern United States usually colder than the southern part?

9. What are some natural resources of the United States? Tell what each resource is used for.

10. Why do we need to use natural resources carefully?

ACTIVITIES

1. **Research/Oral Report** What part of the world did your family come from? Do you know of any special customs from there? Do Americans follow these customs too? Share what you find out with the class.

2. **Remembering the Close-Up** Make a poster showing the four main landforms: mountains, hills, plateaus, and plains. Be sure to show how they are different from each other.

◯ SKILLS REVIEW

1. **Using the Library** Use the subject card on page 24 to answer the questions.

   a. What is the title of this book?
   b. In what section of the library will you find this book?

c. What information do you need to find this book in the library?

2. **Using Special-Purpose Maps** Use this map to help you answer the questions.

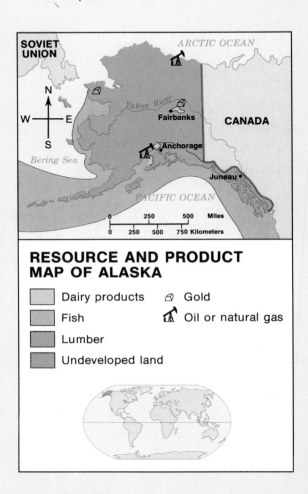

RESOURCE AND PRODUCT MAP OF ALASKA

a. What kind of map is this?
b. Near what river has gold been found?
c. Where is natural gas found— in the north, south, or center of Alaska?
d. Near what city in Alaska are dairy products found?

50

YOUR STATE

You will read about many places in this book. At the same time, you will learn about your own state. You will find a Your State section after each unit in this book. Here you will find a number of activities that you can do. These activities will help you learn about your state.

In many activities you will be doing research. **Research** means finding out facts and information. In doing research, you will use this book and library books. Newspapers, television, and other people will also help you.

LEARNING ABOUT GEOGRAPHY

1. Where is your state? Find your state on a United States map and on a globe. On a piece of paper, write the states, the country, or the bodies of water next to your state. In what part of our country is your state (north, south, east, or west)?

2. Find your state on a map. Measure the longest part of your state. Then measure the widest part. Use the map scale to find out the real distances.

3. What is the climate of your state like? Use the maps on pages 41 and 42 to find out. Draw winter and summer pictures to show what this climate is like.

LEARNING ABOUT GOVERNMENT

4. Every state has a state government. A state government makes laws for the people of the state. Your state's leaders make laws in your state's capital city. Draw a simple map of your state. You can use the maps in this book to help you. Find and label the capital city. Use a star to show the capital. Label the large cities and bodies of water in your state.

LEARNING ABOUT RESEARCH

5. What books about your state are in your school library? Use the subject cards in the card catalog to find out. Make a list of some of the books. Write down the titles of the books and their authors' names.

THE SHAPES OF THE LAND

The geography of our country is made up of many things. The shape of the land and the ways people use it are two important parts of geography. When we study geography, we also look at the water, climate, and other natural resources of a place.

Each chapter of this unit explores a different **natural region.** Natural regions are large areas that have something natural in common. Mountain regions have mainly high, rocky land. Desert regions have dry lands. Plains regions are low and flat, with few trees. The United States has each of these kinds of regions. Rivers cross all these regions, connecting them as well as changing them in some way.

CHAPTER 3

Rivers

Like streets and highways, rivers wind their way across our country. Fast or slow, great or small, rivers change the land as they move along. In turn, people change rivers as they use them.

This chapter describes how rivers are formed and how people use rivers. You will find out that a river's water can be used for more than farming. You will also find out about America's most important rivers. You will read how these rivers change our land and how we change rivers.

54

1. RIVERS, LAND, AND PEOPLE

To Guide Your Reading

Look for these important words:

Key Words
- source
- riverbed
- banks
- branches
- tributaries
- drains
- river basin
- silt
- sandbars
- mouth

Look for answers to these questions:

1. Why did people live near rivers long ago?
2. Why are rivers important today?
3. How does a small stream become a big river?
4. How do silt and sandbars change a river?

Rivers have always been important to people. Rivers were a good place to find food. Their clean, sparkling water brought deer and other animals to their shores. People could also fish in rivers.

People first learned to grow crops near rivers. The land next to rivers is often good for farming. The soil is rich, and there is plenty of water for plants.

Many of the world's first cities grew up along rivers. Even today most large cities are near rivers. Rivers not only provide water for drinking and for farms, but also for factories. Rivers, like highways, connect towns. Goods are often shipped from place to place by river.

No two rivers are exactly alike. Some are slow, wide, and deep enough for large ships. Other rivers are narrow, fast moving, and full of rocks. Some rivers are sparkling blue. Others are colored red or brown by the tons of earth they carry. Yet all rivers are alike in two ways. They are formed in the same way and they are made up of the same parts.

How Rivers Are Formed

The place where a river begins is called its **source**. Many rivers begin high in the mountains. Water from rain, melted snow, and underground springs collects at the source. This water begins to run downhill as a stream.

As the stream runs downhill, other streams join it. Rain and melting snow feed the stream. It becomes larger and moves faster.

The fast-moving stream carries bits of sand, soil, and rock from the land. These bits grind a deep, wide path into the earth. The bottom of the path is called the **riverbed.** The sides of the stream are its **banks.**

The rushing stream cuts into the earth and becomes lower than the land around it. Rain and melting snow flow into the stream. Soon the stream is large enough to be called a river.

Smaller rivers and streams, called **branches,** join the river. Branches are also known as **tributaries** (TRIB·yuh·tair·eez).

A river **drains,** or carries water away from, the land around it. The area of land drained by a river and its branches is a **river basin.**

Soil washed into the river is called **silt.** On its journey, the river collects tons of silt, small stones, and sand. When the river reaches flat land, it slows down. The river no longer has the force to carry all of its load. Most of the stones and sand settle to the bottom, making the river shallower in these areas.

In some places the sand piles up to form islands. Sometimes the sand forms small hills called **sandbars.** The islands and sandbars may split the river into smaller parts.

Boats can sometimes be grounded on a sandbar in a river because a sandbar can often be out of sight below the river's surface.

Many rivers begin their journeys to the ocean as shallow streams.

Tributaries are small rivers or streams that flow into a large river.

The water from a river flows out into the ocean.

Sooner or later, most rivers reach the ocean. The place where a river empties into the ocean is called the river's **mouth.** There the river drops its remaining load of silt, and the fresh water of the river mixes with the salt water of the ocean.

Reading Check

1. Why is a river a good place to find food? Why are cities near rivers?
2. In what two ways are all rivers alike?
3. How does a river begin?
4. How does a river end?

SKILLS FOR SUCCESS

READING A MAP GRID

Some scientists are digging up an early Indian village. As they work, they make a drawing like the one below. It will help them remember how the village looked.

Notice the crossing lines in the drawing. This pattern of lines is called a **grid.** Around the grid are letters and numbers. In this grid the **columns** have numbers. Columns run up and down. The **rows** run from left to right. Each row in the grid has a letter.

The columns and rows form boxes. Find the box with the pots in it. Now find the letter to the left of the box. This box is in the row marked *C.* Next, look above the box. The box is also in column *1.* This is box C–1. The scientists found pots in this part of the village. In what box is the arrowhead? In what box is the ax?

Mapmakers use grids to help people find places on a map. On the next page is a map with a grid.

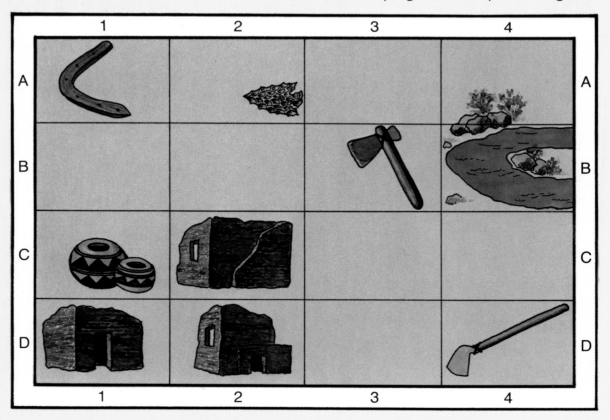

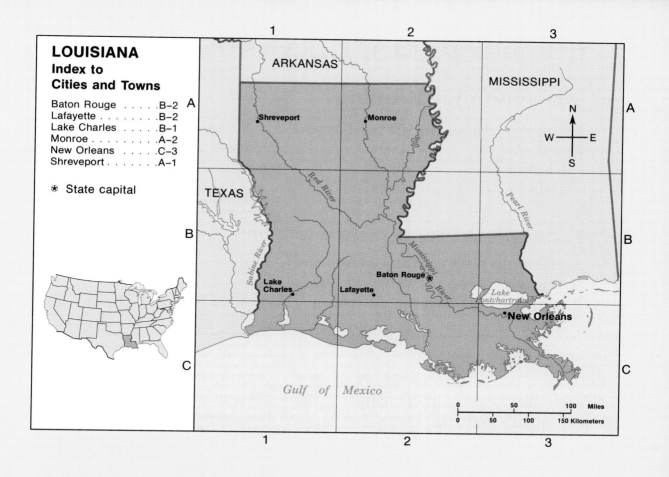

LOUISIANA
Index to
Cities and Towns

Baton Rouge B–2
Lafayette B–2
Lake Charles B–1
Monroe A–2
New Orleans C–3
Shreveport A–1

⊛ State capital

The map shows some cities and towns in the state of Louisiana.

A map with a grid may have an index such as the one you see at the left of this map. The index helps you find the names of places you are looking for. It lists them in alphabetical order. The index also gives the grid letter and number for each place.

This index tells you that New Orleans is in box C–3 on this map. Find row C on the map grid. Place your finger on the letter C. Move it across the map to the column under number 3. This is box C–3. Find New Orleans in box C–3.

Look for Baton Rouge in the index. Baton Rouge is Louisiana's capital. What letter and number do you find for Baton Rouge? Use them to find it on the map.

CHECKING YOUR SKILLS

Answer these questions. Use the map of Louisiana to help you.

1. What lake is in box B–3?

2. What city is in box A–2?

3. In which box is Shreveport?

4. In which box is the mouth of the Mississippi River?

59

2. RIVERS CHANGE THE LAND

To Guide Your Reading

Look for these important words:

Key Words
- delta
- erode
- erosion

- floods
- dikes
- dams

- water power
- polluted

Look for answers to these questions:

1. How do rivers change the land?
2. How do people change rivers?
3. What causes water pollution?

Year after year, a river drops its silt at its mouth. Over the years, the silt begins to build up. It forms a triangular piece of land called a **delta.** Find the Mississippi River delta on the map on page 59. As you can see, it looks like a triangle.

Deltas are good for farming. They are made up of silt, the rich soil that comes from the river's basin. The river is always bringing more silt to the delta. Because of their rich soil, deltas are valuable places to grow crops.

You have seen how rivers build up deltas. However, rivers can also slowly wear away, or **erode,** the Earth's surface. This slow wearing away of large areas of the land is called **erosion** (i•ROH•zhuhn).

When rivers erode the land, they may form deep canyons.

Water from melting snow and spring rains can cause rivers to flood.
This house, once on the river bank, is in danger of being swept away.

Floods can also change the land. A river that overflows is a flood. Heavy rains and melting snow can cause a flood. A flood can be like a gigantic firehose, tearing away huge pieces of land. It can sweep away houses and trees. The rushing waters knock down everything in their path.

Flooding rivers can also build up the land. When rivers overflow slowly, the water gently spreads out. When the flood waters flow back to the river, they leave silt behind. After many floods, the silt builds up into rich, black soil. This rich soil is very good for farming.

People Change Rivers

People can change rivers in a number of ways. For example, people have learned how to control small floods. The next time you are at a river, look at the banks. Do they look like walls? If they do, people may have built **dikes** there. Dikes are high banks that help stop flooding.

People also build walls, or **dams,** across rivers. A dam holds back a river. People let the water flow through the dam as slowly or as quickly as they want.

Dams have other uses, too. Dams store water for drinking and irrigation. The picture on this

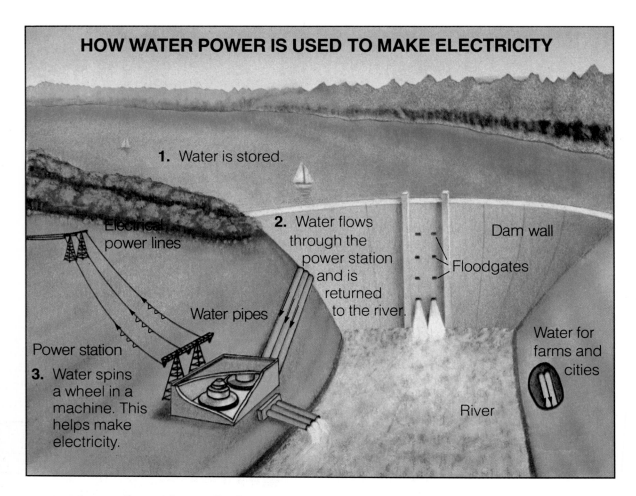

HOW WATER POWER IS USED TO MAKE ELECTRICITY

1. Water is stored.

Electrical power lines

2. Water flows through the power station and is returned to the river.

Dam wall

Floodgates

Water pipes

Power station

3. Water spins a wheel in a machine. This helps make electricity.

Water for farms and cities

River

page shows how dams help make **water power.** The rushing river water spins a wheel very quickly to make electricity.

People change rivers in other ways. They build bridges across them. They make rivers wider and deeper so that ships can travel on them.

People have changed rivers in many useful ways. Yet people have also made some harmful changes. Cities and factories dumped their wastes into rivers. Some rivers became dirty, or **polluted.** Polluted water is a danger to all who

use it. Water pollution is still a problem in American rivers today. However, many cities now clean waste water before returning it to the rivers. By doing this, Americans are working to control pollution.

Reading Check

1. What is a delta?
2. Name two ways that rivers change the land.
3. How can people control floods?
4. Name three ways that people change rivers.

3. RIVERS IN THE UNITED STATES

To Guide Your Reading

Look for these important words:

Key Words
- waterway
- barges
- ports
- industries
- steel mills
- transportation
- current

Places
- St. Lawrence Seaway
- Grand Coulee Dam

Look for answers to these questions:

1. What are six of the largest rivers in our country?
2. Why are ports useful?
3. How do we use our rivers?

The United States has several large rivers. Do you live near one of them? How does this river help you?

The Mississippi River

Mississippi means "Great River" in the language of the Ojibway (oh•JIB•way) Indians. They named this river well because the Mississippi is the longest river in the United States. It begins at Lake Itasca in northern Minnesota. From there it flows 2,348 miles (3,780 km) south to the Gulf of Mexico.

The Mississippi is also called "Old Muddy." When the muddy Missouri River meets it, the Mississippi becomes muddy, too.

The Mississippi is the longest, and in some parts the widest, river in our land.

63

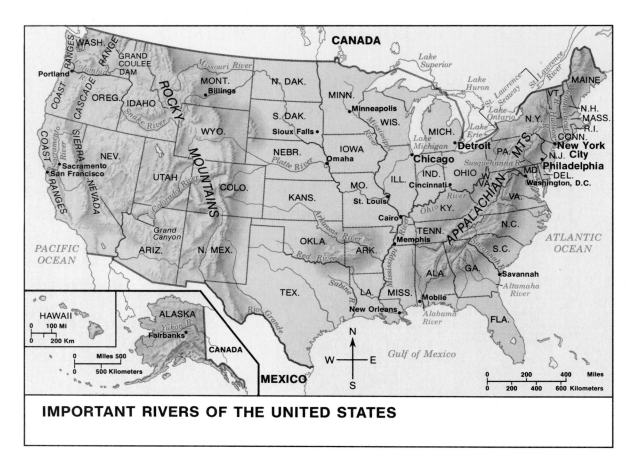

Tugboats push barges carrying grain up the Mississippi.

Besides providing water for farming and manufacturing, the Mississippi provides a route for ships. This great river is the main **waterway** within the United States. A waterway is a body of water that ships can use.

Many of the boats on the Mississippi are **barges.** Barges are large, flat-bottomed boats that are pushed by tugboats. You can often see long strings of barges being pushed up and down the river. Barges carry goods from one part of our country to another. They are the cheapest way to ship heavy goods such as machinery.

At many ports in our country, supply ships unload iron and coal for the manufacture of steel.

Ships load and unload goods at **ports** along the Mississippi. A port is a city with a large, busy harbor. St. Louis, Missouri, and Memphis, Tennessee, are two major Mississippi River ports. From a port, goods are sent by train, plane, or truck to other places.

The Mississippi empties into the Gulf of Mexico near New Orleans, Louisiana. This city is our country's largest port. Many of our products leave New Orleans for other countries. In turn, many countries bring their products to New Orleans to be sold throughout the United States.

The Ohio River

The Ohio River is an important branch of the Mississippi. Two rivers meet to form the Ohio River in Pittsburgh, Pennsylvania. The Ohio joins the Mississippi at Cairo, Illinois.

Along the Ohio are many important **industries.** Industries are kinds of manufacturing. The steel industry, for example, manufactures steel. Barges bring coal down the Ohio from Pennsylvania, West Virginia, and Kentucky to cities like Cincinnati, Ohio. There the coal is burned in **steel mills,** where steel is made.

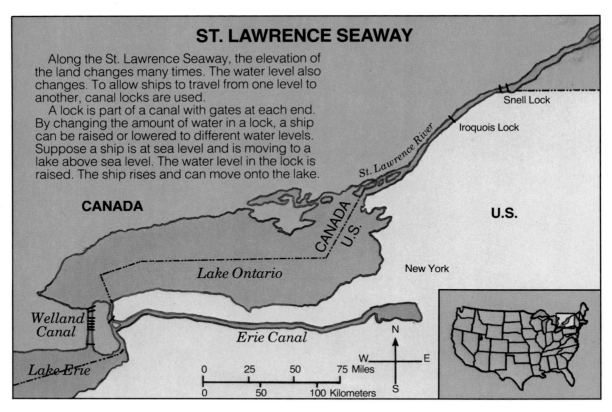

ST. LAWRENCE SEAWAY

Along the St. Lawrence Seaway, the elevation of the land changes many times. The water level also changes. To allow ships to travel from one level to another, canal locks are used.

A lock is part of a canal with gates at each end. By changing the amount of water in a lock, a ship can be raised or lowered to different water levels. Suppose a ship is at sea level and is moving to a lake above sea level. The water level in the lock is raised. The ship rises and can move onto the lake.

CANADA

U.S.

Snell Lock

Iroquois Lock

St. Lawrence River

CANADA
U.S.

Lake Ontario

New York

Welland Canal

Erie Canal

Lake Erie

| 0 | 25 | 50 | 75 Miles |
| 0 | 50 | 100 Kilometers |

N
W — E
S

HOW A SHIP MOVES THROUGH A LOCK

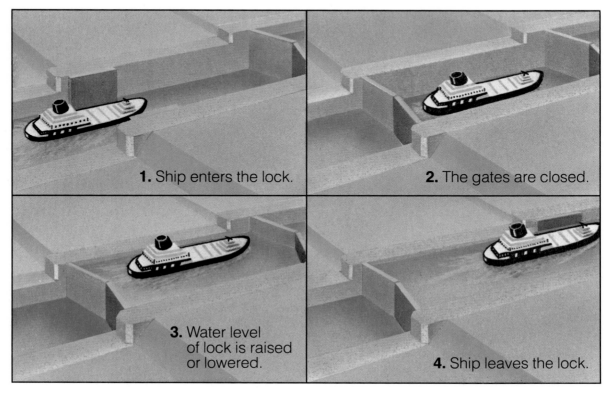

1. Ship enters the lock.

2. The gates are closed.

3. Water level of lock is raised or lowered.

4. Ship leaves the lock.

The St. Lawrence River

The St. Lawrence River forms part of our border with Canada. It begins at Lake Ontario in New York and flows east to the Atlantic Ocean. Part of this river is the **St. Lawrence Seaway.** This waterway connects the Great Lakes with the Atlantic Ocean. Ocean ships from our country and other countries use the Seaway to reach the Great Lakes cities. At ports along the Great Lakes, the ships are loaded with grain, machinery, and car parts. The ships then go east by the St. Lawrence Seaway. From there they carry these products to places around the world.

The Rio Grande

The Rio Grande (REE•oh GRAND) also forms part of the United States border. It separates Texas and Mexico for more than 1,240 miles (about 1,996 km). The Rio Grande begins in the Rocky Mountains and ends at the Gulf of Mexico.

On its journey to empty into the Gulf of Mexico, the Rio Grande carved steep canyons along the Texas border.

The powerful Grand Coulee Dam provides irrigation for many farms and controls flooding along the Columbia River.

The river passes through much dry land on its journey south. Like Indians long ago, farmers of today still use the Rio Grande for irrigation. Power plants now also use the river's flow to make electricity. Irrigation and power plants use a lot of water. Parts of the Rio Grande can dry up by late summer. Rain and melting snow later renew the river's water supply.

The Columbia River

The Columbia River begins in the Rocky Mountains of Canada. From Canada the river flows south into the states of Washington and Oregon. Along the way, it passes through the Cascade Range. Its mouth is on the Pacific Ocean.

Much of our country's water power comes from the Columbia. Water power can be used to make electricity. The most important electric power plant on the Columbia is the **Grand Coulee** (GRAND KOO•lee) **Dam.** It makes more electricity than any other American dam. The dams on the Columbia have helped manufacturing to grow in this part of the United States.

The Colorado River widened and deepened its course over millions of years. Cutting through layers of rock, it carved out the Grand Canyon.

The Colorado River

You have seen that rivers have many uses. They are important in **transportation,** or moving people and things from place to place. Rivers provide water power, fishing, and water for irrigation. They also serve as boundaries between states and between countries. The Colorado River is useful in many of these ways.

The Colorado River brings water from the Rocky Mountains to the driest part of our country. Southern California, Arizona, and Nevada depend on the Colorado for water and electricity.

The Colorado River also flows through the Grand Canyon. The river's **current,** or flow, slowly carved out the deep canyon. Today, thousands of people come to admire the Grand Canyon's amazing beauty.

Reading Check

1. What is a waterway?
2. Which is the longest river in our country?
3. How does coal get from Pennsylvania to Ohio?
4. How was the Grand Canyon formed?

SKILLS FOR SUCCESS

USING ELEVATION MAPS

In this chapter you followed the route of many rivers. Some rivers start in the mountains, but others do not. Many empty into oceans, but some do not. All rivers do have one thing in common, though. They all flow from a high land down to a lower land.

The map on this page is called an **elevation map.** It shows high and low land. Different colors show the **elevation,** or height, of the land. The map key tells what the colors mean.

In this map key the elevation of land colored medium green is from

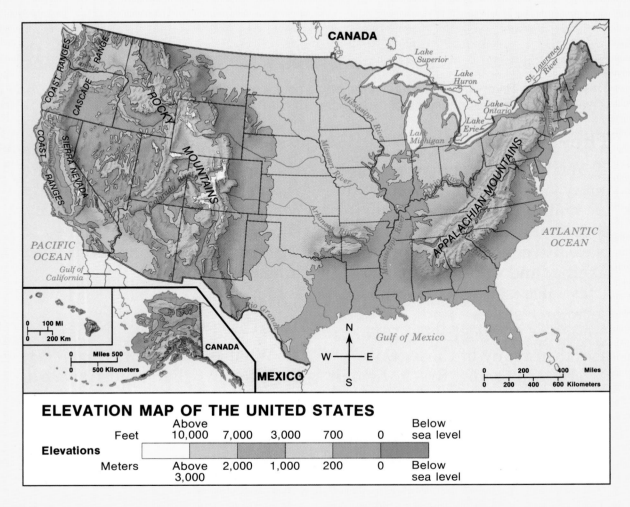

ELEVATION MAP OF THE UNITED STATES

Elevations	Above 10,000	7,000	3,000	700	0	Below sea level
Feet	Above 10,000	7,000	3,000	700	0	Below sea level
Meters	Above 3,000	2,000	1,000	200	0	Below sea level

0 to 700 feet (about 200 m) above sea level. As you have read, land at sea level is the same height as the oceans. The next color shows the elevations of land between 700 to 3,000 feet (about 200 to 1,000 m) above sea level. All places colored light green reach heights between those elevations.

Find the source of the Rio Grande. The source is in the Rocky Mountains. Notice that the land around the source is colored yellow. Find this color in the map key. Yellow stands for land above 10,000 feet (about 3,000 m). The Rio Grande's source is high in the mountains.

Now find the mouth of the Rio Grande. The land around the mouth is colored medium green. What does this color stand for? This is low, flat land. The Rio Grande flows from very high land to low, flat land.

Which Way Do Rivers Flow?

A river always flows in one main direction. You can use an elevation map to find out which way a river flows.

Find the source of the Rio Grande on the map again. Move your finger south down the Rio Grande to the Gulf of Mexico. Your finger is moving **downstream.** Downstream means toward the river's mouth. Now trace the river back up to its source. Your finger is moving **upstream.** Upstream means against the flow of the river.

The word *downstream* tells how a river flows. Water always flows downhill. Rivers can flow from north to south like the Rio Grande. They can flow from east to west like the Columbia. In fact, rivers flow in all directions. Yet their main flow is always downhill from source to mouth. The source is always higher than the mouth.

The source of the Columbia River is in the Rockies. Trace the river to its mouth. What is the elevation of the land there? In which direction does the river flow?

CHECKING YOUR SKILLS

Use the elevation map to help you answer these questions.

1. Which way do rivers flow?

2. What are the elevations of the land around the Missouri River's source and its mouth?

3. The source of the Hudson River is in the Appalachian Mountains. Its mouth is in the Atlantic Ocean.

   a. What are the elevations of the land around the Hudson River's source and its mouth?

   b. In what direction does the Hudson River flow?

71

NANCY OHAMA, ENGINEER

Mrs. Ohama studies her map.

Mrs. Ohama and a highway engineer

Bridge being built

Mrs. Ohama walks through the thick brush at the river's edge. She carefully studies her map. Soon she finds the place she is looking for. Mrs. Ohama is an engineer. An engineer draws plans for buildings, roads, and equipment. Right now Mrs. Ohama is planning a bridge.

Before she begins, Mrs. Ohama explores the area where the bridge will be built. Then she looks at soil from the river bottom. From several samples she can tell where the ground is solid. That way she knows where to put the thick posts that will hold up the bridge.

Later, Mrs. Ohama talks with a highway engineer. They discuss how many cars and trucks will use the bridge each day. The highway engineer explains how large the bridge should be.

Mrs. Ohama decides to use concrete and steel to build the bridge. The bridge must be strong for the cars and trucks that drive over it. The bridge must also be strong to stand against the force of water if the river floods.

There is much to do before the bridge can be started. Highway workers build a road on each side of the river. Other workers dig out deep holes and fill them with concrete. The bridge will rest on these concrete-filled holes, called footings. After this, the workers begin to build the bridge. They start at the river banks and work toward the middle.

In two years the bridge will be finished. Drivers can then save time and fuel by using the bridge. Children will be happy, too. They will have a safe bike path across the new bridge.

CHAPTER 3 REVIEW

WORDS TO USE

Copy the paragraph below. Fill in the blanks with the right words from the list.

branches   **silt**
erodes   **source**
mouth

The place where a river begins is its (____)(1). Other rivers and streams, called (____)(2), join it. As the river flows, it wears away, or (____)(3), the land around it. The river carries away soil, or (____)(4), sand, and rocks. A river ends at its (____)(5).

FACTS TO REVIEW

1. Why were rivers important to people long ago?

2. Why have many cities grown up along rivers? Give at least three reasons.

3. How are deltas formed?

4. How do floods change land? Give two examples.

5. How are dams and dikes different from each other?

6. Why are dams useful? Give two reasons.

7. How have rivers become polluted?

8. What is a port? Name one city that is a port.

9. What river joins the Mississippi River?

10. On what river can goods go to the Atlantic Ocean? What river empties into the Gulf of Mexico?

IDEAS TO DISCUSS

1. Look at the atlas map on pages 420–421. What cities are built on or near rivers? Which of these cities are also on the ocean?

2. Why is water pollution dangerous? What might be some ways to protect rivers?

○ SKILLS PRACTICE

Using Elevation Maps   Answer these questions about the Savannah River. Use the map on page 70 to help you.

1. The Savannah River begins in the Appalachian Mountains. How high is the land there?

2. Does the river flow from north to south or from south to north?

CHAPTER 4

Mountains

"As solid as a rock . . ." "As old as the hills . . ."
Have you heard these sayings? They mean that
something is strong and lasting, like a mountain.
Did you know, though, that mountains change all
the time? Day after day, forces below and above
the earth change mountains.

This chapter describes how mountains are
formed and how they are changed. You will find
out how important mountains are to climate and
what natural resources they provide. You will also
find out about some jobs people have in a mountain region today.

1. MOUNTAINS OLD AND NEW

To Guide Your Reading

Look for these important words:

Key Words
- volcanoes
- lava
- peaks
- altitude
- mountain ranges

Places
- Appalachian Mountains
- Rocky Mountains

Look for answers to these questions:

1. How are mountains formed?
2. How are old mountains different from new mountains?
3. Which are the newer mountains of North America?
4. Which are the older mountains of North America?

In a way, mountains have a lifetime. They are formed, they grow older, and they wear down. Some of these changes are so slow that it is hard to see them. Others can be quick and violent.

The Shaping of Mountains

Most mountains are so old that we can only guess how they were formed. One idea is that mountains grew slowly. Little by little, forces deep within the Earth pushed up parts of the Earth's surface. Ripples and ridges formed on the surface, slowly forming mountains.

Mountains can also be formed quickly. **Volcanoes** (vahl•KAY•nohz) form mountains in a quick and sometimes explosive way. A volcano begins as a crack in the Earth's surface. Through the crack comes hot, melted rock. This melted rock is called **lava** (LAH•vuh). The lava flows over the land like oatmeal boiling over in a pot. As the lava cools, it hardens. The land around the crack is built up. Over the years, the volcano explodes again and again. Gradually the volcano's lava forms a mountain shaped like a cone. Volcanoes formed many of the mountains in California, Oregon, Washington, and Hawaii.

Some of them are still making lava.

When they are new, many mountains have high, sharp tops, or **peaks.** After many years, mountains start to show their age. Rain, ice, blowing sand, and heat begin breaking up the rock. Water and wind carry away the bits of broken rock. Through such ero-sion, the shape of a mountain changes. Its peak gets lower and rounder. Erosion is wearing down the mountains you see today.

Mountains of Our Country

The United States has two large areas of mountains. In one, the mountains are old, low, and

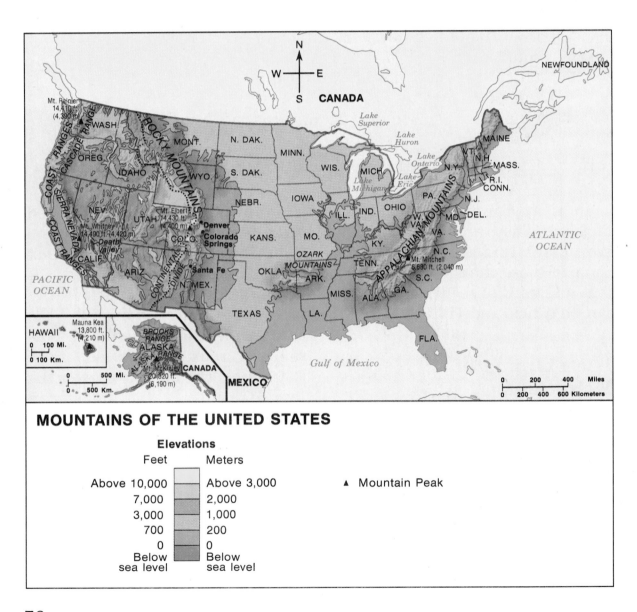

MOUNTAINS OF THE UNITED STATES

Elevations

Feet	Meters	
Above 10,000		Above 3,000
7,000		2,000
3,000		1,000
700		200
0		0
Below sea level		Below sea level

▲ Mountain Peak

The gently sloping Appalachian Mountains are 230 million years old.

The Teton Range in the Rocky Mountains has snow-capped peaks.

rounded. In the other, the mountains are new, high, and steep. Look at the pictures on this page. Which mountains are old?

Now look at the map on page 76. Find the **Appalachian Mountains.** These are the older mountains. They cover much of our country's eastern side. The Appalachians begin in Newfoundland (NOO•fuhnd•luhnd), Canada, and end in northern Alabama. They stretch almost 2,000 miles (about 3,220 km).

The newer, taller mountains are in the West. These are the **Rocky Mountains.** The Rocky Mountains begin in Alaska and end in New Mexico. The Rockies are much higher than the Appalachians. Peaks in the Rockies can reach 14,000 feet (4,267 m).

The height of a mountain is called its **altitude.** Altitude is another word for elevation. We measure altitude from sea level, just as we do for elevation.

Mountains are usually in chains or groups, known as **mountain ranges.** The Appalachians and the Rockies have many mountain ranges. What other mountain ranges can you find on the map?

Reading Check

1. How does a volcano form a mountain?
2. Where are the two largest areas of mountains in the United States?
3. What is altitude?
4. What is a mountain range?

2. WHY MOUNTAINS ARE IMPORTANT

To Guide Your Reading

Look for these important words:

Key Words
- moisture
- barriers
- passes

Look for answers to these questions:

1. How do mountains influence climate in the United States?
2. What happens when winds from the Pacific Ocean meet mountains?
3. How are mountains barriers to travel?

You may live hundreds of miles from the nearest mountains. Yet mountains are important to you wherever you live. How wet or dry a place is often depends on mountains. Mountains cause some of the wettest and driest climates in the world.

Mountains and Climate

Look at the drawing on page 79. It shows how important mountains are to climate.

Winds blow from west to east across the Pacific Ocean. Winds are moving air. As the winds blow, the air picks up **moisture,** or water, from the ocean. The winds blow across the Pacific Coast. When they meet mountains, the winds move upward. As they rise, the air grows colder and clouds form. Cold air cannot hold very much moisture. The moisture in the clouds falls as rain. Rain falls mainly on the western side of the mountains. Because of the rain, forests grow thick and green here.

When the air crosses over the mountains, it holds little moisture. The eastern side of the mountains gets little rain. The Cascade Range makes eastern Washington and Oregon dry. The Sierra Nevada in California makes Death Valley, California, one of the hottest, driest places in the United States.

Mountains are important to climate in another way. Like walls, high mountains block

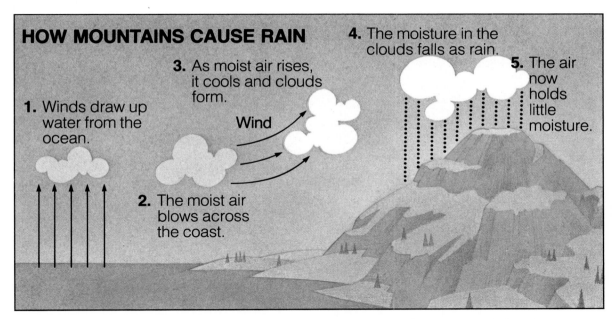

HOW MOUNTAINS CAUSE RAIN

1. Winds draw up water from the ocean.

2. The moist air blows across the coast.

3. As moist air rises, it cools and clouds form.

Wind

4. The moisture in the clouds falls as rain.

5. The air now holds little moisture.

strong winds. Where no mountains block the winds, the weather can get very cold. The center of Canada and the United States have no mountains. In winter, cold winds from the North Pole sweep south. Many states like North and South Dakota and Nebraska have cold, snowy winters.

Mountains and Travel

Long ago, mountains were **barriers** to travel. A barrier blocks the way of something. Mountains blocked the movement of people and goods from place to place. People feared the high, rugged slopes. They had no roads to travel. They were not sure what lay beyond. To get across a mountain range, people had to find **passes,** or narrow ways between mountains.

Even if they did find a pass, mountain travelers had to face the weather. Sudden snow storms and rock and snow slides threatened people's lives. Mountains made it hard for Americans to move west.

Today people cross mountains more easily. Airplanes fly over mountains. Roads cross them. These roads are often steep, narrow, and full of curves. Even today, mountain travel is not easy.

Reading Check

1. What kinds of climate do mountains cause?
2. Which mountain range makes eastern Washington and Oregon dry?
3. Why do North and South Dakota have cold, snowy winters?
4. What are mountain passes?

SKILLS FOR SUCCESS

USING LATITUDE AND LONGITUDE

Lines of Latitude and Longitude

Look at this map of Colorado. Run your finger across the northern border of Colorado. The border is right on the line marked 41°N. This line is called *41 degrees north.* Find the southern border of Colorado. What number is beside this line?

These two lines are **lines of latitude,** or **parallels.** All lines of latitude go across a map, from east to west.

Now find Denver on the map. It is close to the line marked 105°W. This line is called *105 degrees west.* The line goes from top to bottom. Another such line is next to the city of Delta. What is the line called?

These are **lines of longitude,** or **meridians.** Lines of longitude go north and south on a map. Find Durango on the map. Between which two lines of longitude is Durango located?

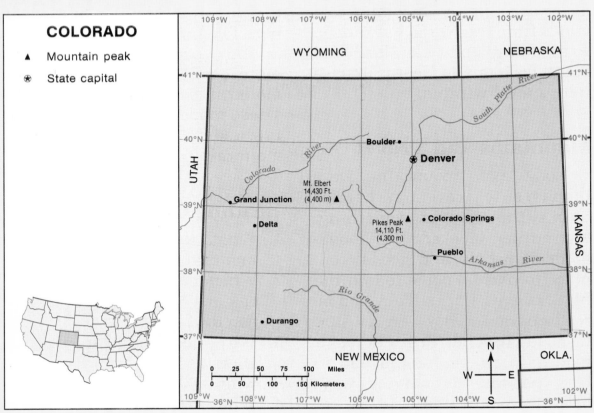

Lines of Latitude and Longitude on a Globe

Lines of latitude also run east and west on a globe. Lines of longitude still run north and south.

Some lines of latitude and longitude have names. The equator is a line of latitude. It divides the Earth into **hemispheres.** A sphere is a ball or globe. A hemisphere is half of a ball or globe. The northern half of the Earth is the **Northern Hemisphere.** The southern half is the **Southern Hemisphere.**

Notice on the drawing of the globe that the lines of latitude are numbered from the equator. The equator is 0° (zero degrees). The lines in the Northern Hemisphere are labeled *N,* for north. The North Pole is labeled 90°N.

The Northern Hemisphere has two important lines of latitude. They are the **Tropic of Cancer** and the **Arctic Circle.** Find the Tropic of Cancer at 23½°N. Find the Arctic Circle at 66½°N.

The lines in the Southern Hemisphere are labeled *S,* for south. How is the South Pole labeled?

Two lines of latitude in the Southern Hemisphere also have names. At 23½°S is the **Tropic of Capricorn.** At 66½°S is the **Antarctic Circle.**

Find the area between the Tropics of Cancer and Capricorn. These lands usually have warm weather. Now look north of the Arctic Circle and south of the Antarctic Circle. These areas are usually cold the year round.

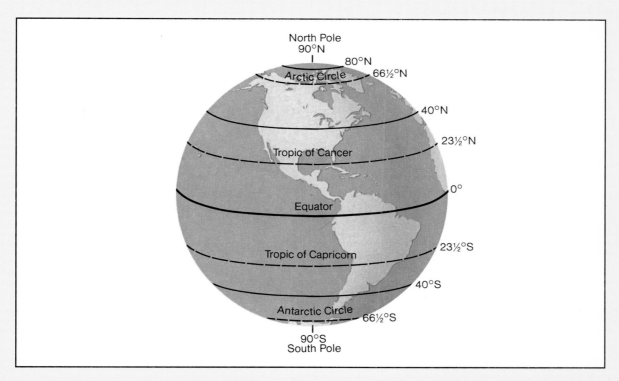

81

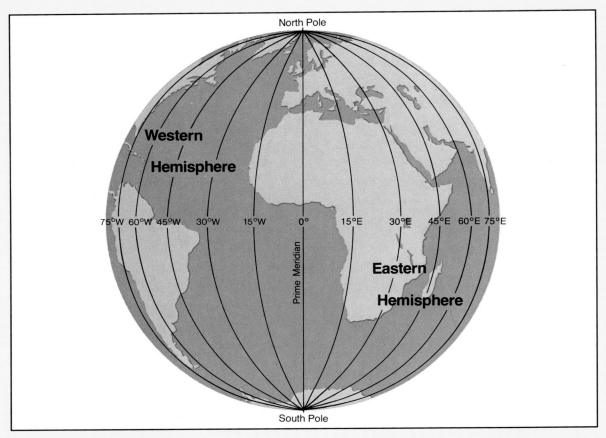

North Pole

Western

Hemisphere

75°W 60°W 45°W 30°W 15°W 0° 15°E 30°E 45°E 60°E 75°E

Prime Meridian

Eastern

Hemisphere

South Pole

The **Prime Meridian** is a special line of longitude. Like the equator, it divides the Earth in half. The eastern half is the **Eastern Hemisphere.** The western half is the **Western Hemisphere.**

Notice that lines of longitude are numbered from the Prime Meridian. The Prime Meridian is 0° (zero degrees). The lines in the Eastern Hemisphere are labeled *E,* for east. The lines in the Western Hemisphere are labeled *W,* for west.

CHECKING YOUR SKILLS

Answer these questions. Use the map of Colorado to help you.

1. What line of latitude is near the city of Denver?

2. What line of longitude is near the western border of Colorado?

3. What three cities are near 105°W?

Use the drawings of the globes to answer these questions.

4. If a town is near 10°N, is it in the Northern Hemisphere or the Southern Hemisphere?

5. Is a town near 10°N likely to have warm weather or cold weather? How does the globe help you know this?

3. MOUNTAIN REGIONS TODAY

To Guide Your Reading

Look for these important words:

Key Words
- fossils
- swamps
- range

- graze
- brand
- fleece
- shear

- recreation
- national parks
- state parks
- conservation

Look for answers to these questions:

1. Why are mountains valuable regions?
2. How was coal formed?
3. What are some jobs people have in mountain regions?
4. Why do people like to visit the mountains?

If you took a trip through our country's mountain regions, you would find few large communities and little farming. The sloping land makes it hard to build roads and homes for towns. Little farming is possible because the soil is thin and rocky. The year-round cold climate in some parts of the mountain regions makes farming difficult. Also the land is too steep for large farm machines. Only in valleys and on plains and plateaus will you find farms, ranches, and towns.

Yet mountains are valuable regions. They provide needed resources to other parts of our country. Getting these resources is the job of many people in mountain communities.

Mining

Large amounts of coal are mined in the Appalachian Mountains. Coal provides fuel for making steel and electricity. About one-half of all our electricity is made with coal. Many people in the Appalachian Mountains make their living as coal miners.

Coal is a fuel that comes from **fossils.** Fossils are what remains of plants and animals that died millions of years ago.

Coal was formed mainly in **swamps.** A swamp is low, wet land. Plants in swamps lived and died, building up into thick layers. Later, layers of sand and soil covered the dead plants. After many millions of years, the layers of sand and soil turned into

Coal, a valuable fuel, is found deep in the mountains. Miners must wear lighted hats to go underground. Once dug, coal is loaded onto trains and brought to plants to be cleaned.

rock. The layers of rock squeezed the plants into coal. It took a layer of plants about 20 feet (about 6 m) thick to make a 1 foot (about 30 cm) thick layer of coal.

After the coal was formed, some of the earth was pushed up to form mountains. Today the mountains contain the layers of coal formed so long ago.

Though coal is found in the United States today, we must be careful not to waste this important resource. The Earth is not making more coal. We must save some coal for the future.

Like the Appalachians, the Rocky Mountains are rich in coal. Buried within them are other valuable fuels—oil, natural gas, and uranium. The Rocky Mountains are also rich in metals, like copper, silver, and lead.

Forests

When the first European settlers came to eastern America,

forests covered much of the land. As towns grew, some forests were cut down to build houses and stores. Many trees were also cut down to clear the land for farms.

Today, forests cover about a third of our country. Many of our largest forests are in mountain areas and in Alaska.

Trees in forests are cut down for lumber. Most lumber is used for building. Lumber is used to build homes and schools. The wood from trees is also used to make other products, like paper. The United States makes more paper than any other country in the world.

Forest areas need much rainfall. Forests grow well in areas with about 40 inches (about 102 cm) of precipitation a year. The map below shows the main forest areas of our country.

Like coal, trees are an important resource. Unlike coal, however, trees can be replaced. People can plant new trees where others were cut down. By replanting forests, people can make sure they will have enough wood for the future.

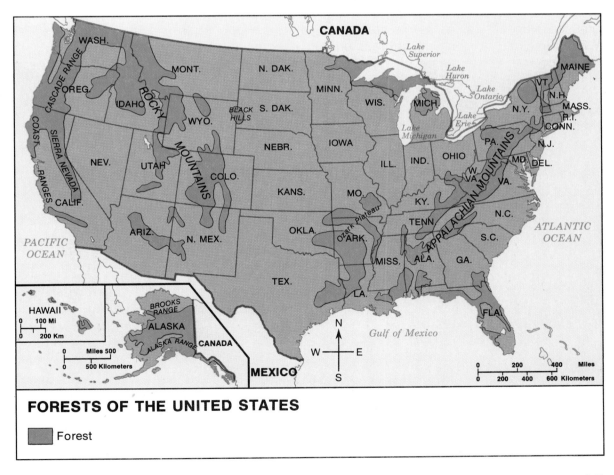

FORESTS OF THE UNITED STATES

Forest

Ranching

Beef cattle and sheep do well in a dry climate with few trees and some grass. For this reason, people in some mountain regions are ranchers. Their cattle and sheep wander over miles of grassland, called the **range.** The animals eat, or **graze** on, the thin grass. It takes many acres of land as well as some hay or grain to feed a herd.

Calves are born in the spring. After about two months, the ranchers **brand,** or mark, the calves. The brand shows who owns the calves. During spring and summer the herd grazes on the range. When the cattle can find little grass, ranchers may have to move their herd. Sometimes they must bring water and food out to the herd. Ranchers also raise hay and grain for the herd to eat in the winter.

Sheep ranchers get wool and meat from their animals. The sheep's woolly coat is called **fleece.** In the spring, ranchers **shear,** or cut, the sheep's fleece. Spring is also the time when lambs are born. Soon they are

In spring and summer, cattle roam the open range to eat mountain grasses. Ranchers must make sure their cattle have enough feed. When the cattle can find little to graze on, ranchers move the herd.

A skier skims down a snowy slope in the Rocky Mountains of Wyoming.

following their mothers on the range. Sometimes, though, a lamb wanders off. A rancher may spend hours looking for a lost lamb.

Recreation

Millions of people visit mountain regions each year. The mountains provide **recreation** (rek•ree•AY•shuhn), or things people do for enjoyment. People enjoy the splendid scenery in the mountains. During the summer, people go to the mountains to camp. They hike, fish, boat, and mountain climb. During the winter, people can ski, ice skate, and play in the snow.

National and State Parks

Many places in our country remain wilderness today. Our national and state governments have set aside some of this land for parks. **National parks** and **state parks** are found in mountain regions as well as other parts of the country.

Every visitor to our parks has a responsibility to protect them. Fire safety is especially important. People can start forest fires. Carelessness with matches or campfires easily starts a fire. Each year fires destroy thousands of acres of forests. It can take a hundred years for a burnt-down forest to grow back.

Our national and state parks are a valuable natural resource. Protecting our natural resources is called **conservation** (kahn•suhr•VAY•shuhn). *Conservation* means saving something by using it wisely and carefully. If we protect our parks, we can enjoy them for years to come.

Reading Check

1. Why do mountain regions have few large communities?
2. What are some resources found in mountains?
3. Why are beef cattle and sheep raised in mountain regions?
4. What kinds of recreation do mountains provide?

87

MARK KATZ, FOREST RANGER

Entrance to the park

Lookout towers help rangers spot fires.

Preventing a forest fire

Do you think of skyscrapers when you think of New York? Most people do. The city of New York has many tall buildings. The whole state of New York, though, does not.

Forests cover about half of New York State. Many of New York's forests are within its more than 140 state parks. Its largest state park is the **Adirondack** (ad•uh•RAHN•dak) **Forest Preserve.** It is larger than the state of Delaware. Inside the park's forests are bears, deer, coyotes, and wildcats.

Mark Katz is a forest ranger in one of New York's state parks. He and the other forest rangers have two important jobs. They protect the forests and the wildlife. They also look after the people who visit the park. The forest rangers help make the parks safe and enjoyable for everyone.

Ranger Katz worries most about fires. From high in a lookout tower he watches for smoke. More and more rangers use planes to watch for fires. Sometimes rangers have to put out fires. Large fires can burn for days, destroying thousands of trees and animals.

Mark Katz and other forest rangers help park visitors. They show campers how to put up tents. They answer questions about what to see and do and clear trails for hiking. Forest rangers make sure campers obey the park's rules, also.

Rangers help people discover the wonders of nature. Ranger Katz enjoys his job. He likes the clean air of the mountain park. Most of all, he likes to work in the forest. There the only skyscrapers are the tall, towering trees.

SKILLS FOR SUCCESS

USING CROSS-SECTION DIAGRAMS

If you cut an orange in half, this is what you see. This view of the inside is called a **cross section.** Cross sections show the insides of things.

The cross section below shows a view of the inside of a mountain. You can see the layers of stone and soil inside it. Certain places, like the Appalachian Mountains, have layers like these.

The top layer of the mountain below is **topsoil.** Topsoil is the soil that people walk on. Many mountains are rocky, with little topsoil.

Below the soil on this mountain is **sandstone** and below that is **shale.** Sandstone is made up of sand. Shale is made up of clay.

The next layer in this cross section is **limestone.** Limestone is rock made up of mud and shells from long, long ago.

Coal lies below the limestone. Coal may also be found just below the topsoil or in large cracks on the sides of mountains.

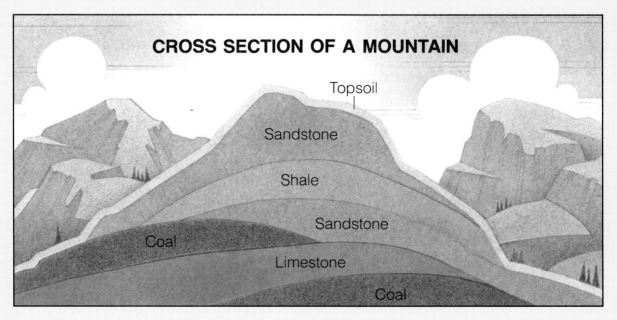

CROSS SECTION OF A MOUNTAIN

Topsoil

Sandstone

Shale

Sandstone

Coal

Limestone

Coal

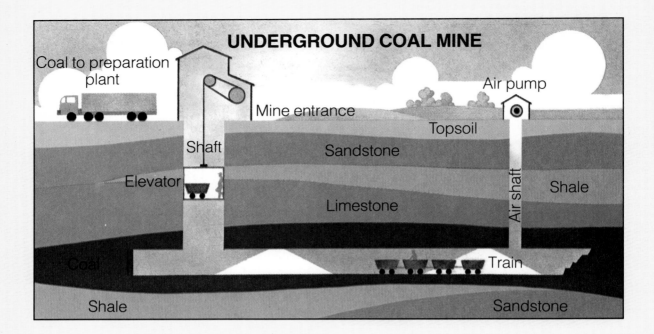

UNDERGROUND COAL MINE

Coal to preparation plant

Mine entrance

Air pump

Topsoil

Sandstone

Shaft

Elevator

Limestone

Air shaft

Shale

Coal

Train

Shale

Sandstone

In the Appalachians, coal often lies deep in the earth. Look at the cross section of an underground mine on this page. To get to the coal, people must drill a deep hole called a **shaft.**

An elevator carries miners to and from the coal. The elevator also brings the coal out of the mine.

The miners sometimes use explosives to dig tunnels. They also use drills to break the coal into chunks.

Small train cars carry the coal to the elevator. Find the train cars in the diagram. Do they move back and forth or up and down?

Harmful gases in the earth sometimes get into a mine. These gases must be pumped out of the mine. Find the air shaft on the cross-section diagram. At the top of the shaft is an air pump. The air

pump helps pull these harmful gases out of the mine.

In the mine, coal is mixed in with rock and dirt. The mixture must then go to a preparation plant. There the rock is removed. Now the coal is ready to be shipped.

CHECKING YOUR SKILLS

Answer these questions. Use the cross-section diagram to help you.

1. The mine shaft must go through four layers to reach the coal. What are these layers?

2. How is coal brought to the elevator?

3. What takes harmful gases out of a mine?

4. Where does the coal go when it leaves the elevator?

90

CHAPTER 4 REVIEW

WORDS TO USE

Write a sentence for each word. Your sentences should explain the meanings of the words.

1. **volcanoes**
2. **mountain range**
3. **fossils**
4. **recreation**
5. **conservation**

FACTS TO REVIEW

1. What are two ways that mountains may have been formed?

2. How does erosion change the shape of a mountain?

3. Name some differences between the Appalachian and the Rocky mountains.

4. How do mountains make places wet or dry?

5. Why are mountains barriers to travel?

6. What two important resources are found in mountain regions?

7. How can people make sure there is enough wood for the future?

8. Why must ranchers move their herds from place to place?

9. What can people do for recreation in mountain regions?

10. Why has land been set aside for national and state parks?

IDEAS TO DISCUSS

1. You have read that erosion changes mountains. People also change mountains to make travel easier. What are some of the changes people have made?

2. Why is it important to conserve forests? In what ways can people save trees? Have you been to a state or a national park? What did you do there?

3. What are some jobs done in mountain regions only in warm weather? What jobs can be done in good or bad weather?

◯ SKILLS PRACTICE

Using Latitude and Longitude
Answer these questions. Use the map and the drawing on pages 80 and 81 to help you.

1. Near what line of latitude is Mount Elbert?

2. Which is closer to Colorado, the Tropic of Cancer or the equator?

CHAPTER 5

Deserts

Some people think all deserts are the same. They think all deserts are hot, dry, terrible places with nothing but sand. Some deserts are like that. Other deserts, however, have many places where people, plants, and animals can live.

In this chapter you will find out what deserts are like. You will see that deserts can be useful as well as beautiful. You will read about the jobs people have in deserts. You will also read how people solve their most important problem in a desert—finding water.

1. NORTH AMERICAN DESERTS

To Guide Your Reading

Look for these important words:

Key Words
- evaporate
- sand dunes
- flash flood
- cactus

- mesquite

Places
- North American Desert

- Great Basin Desert
- Mojave Desert
- Sonoran Desert
- Chihuahuan Desert

Look for answers to these questions:

1. How are deserts different from each other?
2. How do wind and water change deserts?
3. Why are some plants and animals able to live in a desert?

Deserts can look quite different from one another. Some deserts have mountains and high cliffs. Other deserts are flat. Some deserts have drifting sand and few plants. Other deserts have fairly good soil where flowers and other plants grow and bloom.

Dry Lands

Deserts are alike in one way. They get little rainfall. All deserts receive less than 10 inches (about 25 cm) of rainfall a year.

A very large desert called the **North American Desert** stretches across some of the western part of our country. This desert can be divided into four major areas: the **Great Basin**

Desert, the **Mojave** (moh•HAH•vee) **Desert,** the **Sonoran** (suh•NOH•ruhn) **Desert,** and the **Chihuahuan** (chuh•WAH•wahn) **Desert.** The map on page 94 shows these desert areas. The Sonoran and the Chihuahuan deserts stretch from the United States into Mexico. The Great Basin Desert is the largest of all four. It lies between the Sierra Nevada and the Rocky Mountains.

Deserts are places of very high and very low temperatures. During the day, temperatures may reach as high as 120°F (about 49°C). When rain falls, it can sometimes **evaporate** (i•VAP•uh•rayt), or dry up, before it reaches the earth.

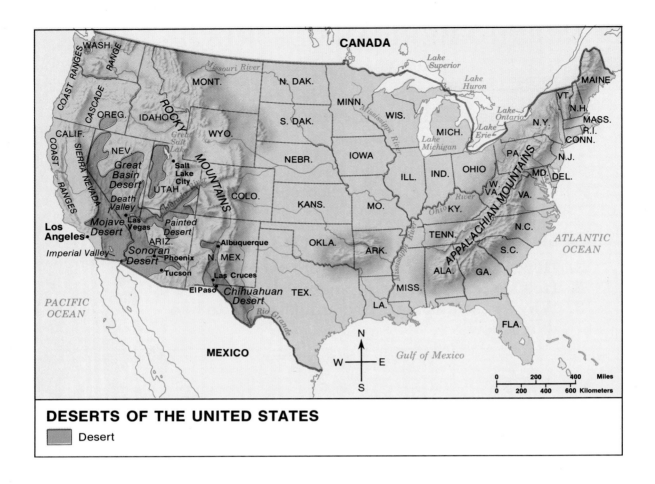

DESERTS OF THE UNITED STATES

[ ] Desert

Desert air contains little moisture, so few clouds pass over these dry lands. The sun beats down, baking the ground. The air stays hot all day.

At night temperatures drop quickly. Nights in the desert are often cold.

Wind and Water

Strong winds often blow across deserts. In some deserts the winds blow sand into piles. These rounded piles of sand, or **sand dunes,** take many shapes.

Water changes the desert even more than wind does. A sudden storm may drop half the year's rainfall in just a few minutes. The rain does not sink into the hard, baked ground. Instead, the rain causes a powerful **flash flood.** The racing water streams across the desert, cutting into the land. Flash floods are often caused by storms that remain in one place for a while.

Year after year, such floods change the shape of the land. They leave behind amazing rocks of every size and shape.

Monument Valley, above, is a desert in Utah. Red sandstone towers 1000 feet (300 meters) high overlook the landscape.

Plants and Animals of the Desert

Though life in a desert may seem impossible, many plants and animals live there. Each kind has developed ways to survive in the dry, hot lands.

One of the well-known American desert plants is the **cactus.** The cactus plant stores water in its thick, fleshy stem. When the earth is dry, the cactus lives on the stored water. Sharp spines keep animals from eating the plant.

Some American desert plants have long roots. One such plant

Prickly pear cactus grows well in desert areas. Its fruit is good to eat.

A mesquite's roots may grow 60 feet (about 18 m) underground for water.

The tiny kangaroo rat uses its strong back legs to leap across the desert.

is the treelike bush called **mesquite** (muh•SKEET). The long roots of the mesquite help it to reach underground water.

The mesquite grows pods that look like green beans. When the pods open, the seeds drop to the ground. Wind covers the seeds with sand and soil. These seeds may lie buried for a long time. When the rains do come, the seeds grow and blossom. The young plants turn the desert into a carpet of flowers.

Snakes, lizards, rabbits, and mice are some animals that live in the desert. During the day they stay cool in holes or under plants. At night they come out to eat insects, plants, or other animals.

Small desert animals get water from the food they eat. Such small animals are eaten by larger desert animals, like coyotes (ky•OH•teez) and foxes. Coyotes and foxes must get water from springs or waterholes.

Some deer and antelope also make the desert their home. They live mostly on grass. They too must find water to drink at springs or waterholes. There they may also find their enemies. To escape, they run. The pronghorn, a kind of antelope, is the desert's fastest runner. It can run for short periods as fast as 60 miles (about 96 km) per hour.

Reading Check

1. How much rainfall do deserts get?
2. What is the largest desert region in the United States?
3. What is a flash flood?
4. What are some animals that live in deserts?

MARIA MARTINEZ

Maria Martinez

Maria Martinez and a few of her finished pots

A shiny pot of desert clay

You are visiting a museum in an American city. In one room you notice a glass case. Something small and round glistens behind the glass. You look closely. It is a beautiful black pot.

The person who made this pot was a Zuni Indian. Maria Martinez lived in the desert of New Mexico. She learned to make pots when she was a young girl.

In the early 1900s, a scientist visited Maria's village. He showed Maria some shiny pieces of pottery. The pieces were from pots Maria's ancestors may have made. They were about 700 years old. The scientist asked Maria if she could make a pot with the same shine. After many tries, Maria learned to make her pots shiny and black.

The materials Maria used were simple. She dug clay where she lived. To shape the clay, her hands were her tools.

To make a pot, Maria started by rolling the soft clay into a long coil. Then she wound the coil into the shape of a pot. Maria scraped the pot inside and out. She rubbed it smooth with a stone. Sometimes Maria painted designs on her pots. Her paintbrush was made of yucca (YUK•uh) leaves. Maria baked the pots in a very hot fire. The heat made the desert clay turn black.

Maria's pots became famous. Museums all over the world collected them. Maria continued to make her pots in New Mexico for the rest of her long life. She taught her family to make beautiful pots also. Though Maria died in 1980, at the age of 94, her family now makes the shiny, black pots.

SKILLS FOR SUCCESS

USING BAR GRAPHS

Terry is writing a report about climates in four desert cities. First, she gets some information from the library. It looks like this.

Average Annual Precipitation	
City/State	Precipitation in Inches
Phoenix, Arizona	7
Winnemucca, Nevada	8
Albuquerque, New Mexico	8
Roswell, New Mexico	10

Terry wants her report to be simple and easy to understand. She decides to put the information in a **graph.** A graph is a drawing that shows numbers. Terry's graph is called a **bar graph.**

The names of the cities are across the bottom of the bar graph. The numbers on the left are inches of precipitation.

Look at the bar above the name *Albuquerque, New Mexico.* Find the top of the bar. Look across to the number at the left. The bar goes

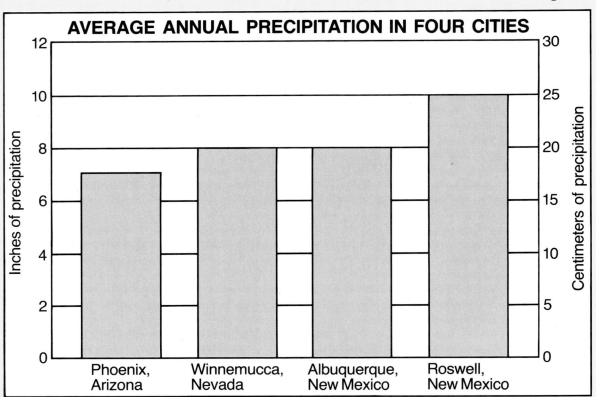

98

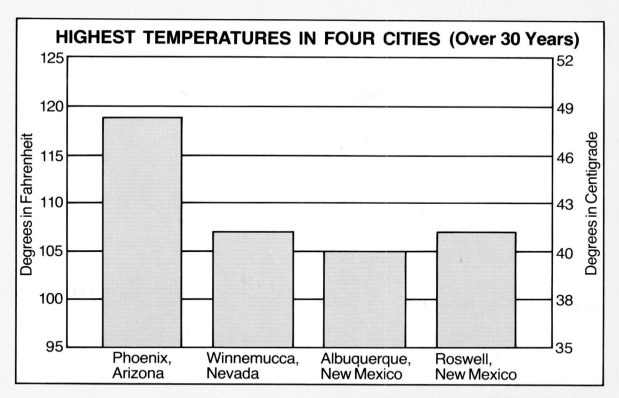

HIGHEST TEMPERATURES IN FOUR CITIES (Over 30 Years)

up to the number 8. This means that Albuquerque has about 8 inches of precipitation a year. Look at the bar for Roswell, New Mexico. Find the top of the bar. Look across to the left. About how many inches of precipitation does Roswell get?

Sometimes the bars stop below or above the lines. Look at the first bar. It shows precipitation in Phoenix, Arizona. The bar goes past the 6 but stops below the 8. This means that Phoenix has more than 6 inches of precipitation.

A bar graph makes it easy to compare numbers. Look at all the bars in the graph. Which city has the highest precipitation? Which city has the lowest precipitation?

CHECKING YOUR SKILLS

Use the graph above to help you answer the questions.

1. What was the highest temperature in Albuquerque?

2. What was the highest temperature in Winnemucca?

3. Which city had the higher temperature, Roswell or Albuquerque?

4. Which city had the highest temperature? Which city had the lowest temperature?

5. Which two cities had high temperatures that were about the same? What was that temperature?

2. DESERT REGIONS TODAY

To Guide Your Reading

Look for these important words:

Key Words
- fertilizer
- canals

Places
- Imperial Valley

Look for answers to these questions:

1. What natural resources do deserts provide?
2. How is water brought to deserts?
3. Why is the Imperial Valley good for farming?
4. How are our deserts changing?

In some deserts, you can travel miles without seeing a house. The heat and lack of water make living there hard. In other desert areas, however, towns and cities grow larger every year. Today thousands of people are moving to some desert areas.

Desert regions can be good places to live. Many people enjoy their clear, clean air, hot weather, and sunshine. Air conditioners are machines that cool buildings. They have helped make desert living comfortable.

Deserts are also good places to work. Many people come to desert areas for jobs. Desert regions have valuable minerals. Mining these minerals and manufacturing products from them are two important desert industries that provide jobs for people.

Though surrounded by desert, many people in Arizona live in cities.

Minerals

Some deserts contain important fuels and minerals such as oil, copper, and uranium. The salt on your table may have come from

100

The Great Salt Lake is much saltier than any ocean. When its water level is low, its islands and the land around it are white with salt.

a desert, too. Large patches of salt are found near the Great Salt Lake. The Great Salt Lake is part of the Great Basin Desert. Another valuable mineral in desert areas is potash. Potash is used as a **fertilizer** (FUHR·tuh·ly·zuhr). Fertilizers are materials that help plants grow.

Water

People need water to use the desert's resources. Factories and homes need water. Water is used in mining. With enough water, deserts can be good places for farming. Deserts often have good soil and weather for growing crops.

Irrigation now brings water to many desert areas. Giant pipes and pumps carry water from mountains hundreds of miles away. In some places people dig deep wells to reach underground water.

Irrigation changed a valley in the Colorado Desert into one of the world's richest farmlands. This valley in southern California is the **Imperial Valley.** It was once a dry and empty land. Irrigation turned it into America's

101

Canals bring water to the Imperial Valley and turn desert into rich farmland.

"salad bowl." The Imperial Valley grows more lettuce than any other place in the country.

The Imperial Valley gets its water from the Colorado River. Miles of **canals** bring the water to the farmlands of the valley. A canal is a stream or river built by people.

The desert soil and the climate of the Imperial Valley are perfect for farming. With irrigation, farmers can grow crops all year long.

The Changing Desert

Some desert areas still look as they did many years ago. Others, however, are quickly growing and changing. Irrigation has helped these places grow. Each year, more people come to live in desert areas.

Growing numbers of people, farms, and industries need more and more water. Most rivers and streams are being tapped for their water. Water is pumped from underground wells faster than rain can replace it. Many people living in desert areas worry about lack of water. Without water, desert cities may not keep growing. Some people, however, believe that more water will be found.

In the past, people thought that deserts were useless. Today, we know that is not true. As we explore our deserts, we find more oil, gas, and minerals. With irrigation, the desert soil can be used for farming.

We must use our desert resources wisely, however. If we do, our desert lands will provide for our needs now and into the future.

Reading Check

1. Why are deserts good places to live and work?
2. What minerals are found in deserts? Give two examples.
3. From where does the Imperial Valley get its water?
4. Why is the Imperial Valley an important farming area?

SKILLS FOR SUCCESS

USING TABLES

The word *table* can be used to talk about different things. A table is a piece of furniture. A book has a table of contents. A table can also be a way to show information.

The table below shows a number of facts about four states. The names of the states are at the left of the table. What are they?

Across from each state name is a row of boxes. All of the first row is about Arizona. What state is the second row about?

The boxes that go down a table are columns. At the top of each column is a title that tells the kinds of information in the table. The first column tells the state names. What do the other columns tell?

Suppose you want to find the nickname of California. Look down the left side to find the row for California. California is the second row, the one colored orange. Now look across the top of the table. Find the column for nicknames. Look

TABLE A

State	Nickname	State Bird	State Flower
Arizona	Grand Canyon State	cactus wren	saguaro cactus blossom
California	Golden State	valley quail	golden poppy
Nevada	Sagebrush State	mountain bluebird	sagebrush
New Mexico	Land of Enchantment	roadrunner	yucca

TABLE B

State	Capital	Population (1983)	Area (in square miles)
Arizona	Phoenix	2,963,000	113,909
California	Sacramento	25,174,000	158,693
Nevada	Carson City	891,000	110,540
New Mexico	Santa Fe	1,399,000	121,666

down this column to find the orange row. In the orange row is the name *Golden State.* California's nickname is the "Golden State." What is Arizona's nickname?

A table often shows numbers. Table B gives more information about Arizona, California, Nevada, and New Mexico. Once again, the state names are in the first column. The second column gives the capital of each state. The third column gives the **population** of each state. Population is the number of people who live in a place. What is the population of Nevada?

The last column tells each state's **area.** Area is amount of land. Look at the row for New Mexico. What is its area?

At the back of this book is an Almanac. This section has a long table called "Facts About the States." In this table you will find some information about all 50 states.

CHECKING YOUR SKILLS

Answer these questions. Use the tables in the lesson to help you.

1. What is the state flower of Arizona?

2. What is the nickname of Nevada?

3. What is the population of Arizona?

4. What is the area of California?

104

CHAPTER 5 REVIEW

WORDS TO USE

Copy the sentences below. Fill in the blanks with the right words from the list.

cactus   **flash flood**
canals   **fertilizers**
evaporates

1. Hot desert air dries up, or _____, rain water.

2. A _____ cuts into desert land, changing its shape.

3. The _____ stores water in its thick stem.

4. Materials that help plants grow are _____.

5. Miles of _____ bring water to the farmlands of the Imperial Valley.

FACTS TO REVIEW

1. Between what mountains is the Great Basin Desert?

2. How does the mesquite plant get water?

3. Why are people moving to desert regions? Give two reasons.

4. Why are some deserts good for farming?

5. Why are more people today worried about lack of water in desert areas?

IDEAS TO DISCUSS

1. How do people use the natural resources of deserts? In what ways might we use desert resources in the future?

2. How is living in the desert different from your way of living? How is it the same?

○ SKILLS PRACTICE

Using Bar Graphs Use the graph to answer these questions.

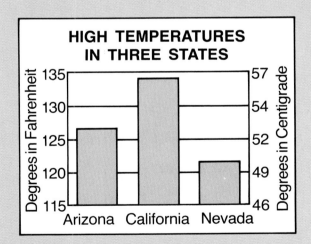

HIGH TEMPERATURES IN THREE STATES

1. Was the temperature higher in Arizona or Nevada?

2. Which of the states had the highest temperature?

CHAPTER 6

Plains

About
this
chapter
Much of the United States is plains. In some places, these flat lands stretch as far as the eye can see. Farms with large, flat fields dot the land. Cattle roam on sprawling ranches. Not only farms and ranches are here, however. Some of the largest cities in our country are also found on plains.

In this chapter you will read about two large plains regions in our country. You will read how people make their living in plains regions. You will find out why weather on plains can help or cause problems for people. You will also find out what part cities play in life on the plains.

1. THE COASTAL PLAIN

To Guide Your Reading

Look for these important words:

Key Words
- Fall Line
- flour mills
- sawmills

- fertile
- raw materials
- finished products

Places
- Coastal Plain

Look for answers to these questions:

1. What features of the land make the Coastal Plain important?
2. What old and new industries are found on the Coastal Plain?
3. Why can goods easily be moved in and out of cities on the Coastal Plain?

A large plain stretches along the Atlantic Coast to the Gulf of Mexico. This low, flat land is the **Coastal Plain.** The Coastal Plain begins as a narrow strip of land in the north. As it stretches south, it gets wider and wider. At Florida the plain swings west.

Some of our largest cities are on the Coastal Plain. New York City, Philadelphia, Boston, Miami, Houston, and Dallas are a few of these large cities. Our nation's capital, Washington, D.C., is also on the Coastal Plain.

The Fall Line

If you look at a map, you will see that many large cities form a line along the Coastal Plain's western edge. These cities are close to what is called the **Fall Line.** The Fall Line comes between the Appalachian Mountains and the Coastal Plain. At the Fall Line, the elevation of the land drops suddenly. Rivers with their sources in the mountains have waterfalls here. Their waters drop to the plain below and from there continue across the Coastal Plain. At their mouths they empty into the Atlantic Ocean.

Early settlers in the east could not travel by water beyond the Fall Line. Instead, they stayed near the Fall Line, building **flour mills** and **sawmills.** Flour mills are factories where wheat is made

MILL WHEEL

Mill

Flow of river

Direction wheel turns

Wheel

Post that turns mill machinery

Water empties onto the top of the mill wheel and is caught in bucket-like blades.

The water's weight moves the mill wheel, which turns wheels in the mill.

into flour. Sawmills are buildings where logs are cut into lumber. The waterfalls provided power for these mills.

In a water-powered mill, the rushing water turned waterwheels. The waterwheels turned other wheels and machines within the mill. Towns grew up rapidly around the mills and factories on the Fall Line. Products from the factories could be shipped on the rivers to cities on the Atlantic Coast.

Today, the waterfalls provide electric power to cities on the Fall Line. Look at the map on the next page. Find the cities on the Fall Line on this map.

Farming on the Coastal Plain

Do you eat peanut butter sandwiches for lunch? Peanuts grow in the southern part of the Coastal Plain. Your jeans and shirts may have been made from the cotton that grows there, too.

Much of the Coastal Plain has rich, **fertile** (FUHR•tuhl) soil. Fertile soil is full of minerals that make plants grow. You may remember that some of the best farmland is near rivers. Many rivers begin in the Appalachian Mountains and flow across the Coastal Plain. On their way to the ocean, the rivers add to the soil the silt carried down from the mountains. The Coastal Plain's climate is good for farming also. Most parts of the plain get plenty of rain. Usually from 40 to 60 inches (about 100 to 150 cm) of rain fall each year.

South of Maryland, the summers are hot and long. In some places, certain crops can be grown all year long. The winters to the south of Maryland are cool and mild.

The weather is different north of Maryland. There the Coastal Plain has cold winters and shorter, warm summers. The climate, however, is still somewhat milder than the land farther west. In the summer, ocean winds help cool the coast. In the winter, ocean winds help keep it warm.

Coastal Ports

Some of the large cities of the Coastal Plain are ports. Our busiest port, New Orleans, Louisiana, lies on the Gulf of Mexico at the mouth of the Mississippi River. Our second largest port is New York City, New York. New York City is at the mouth of the Hudson River. At New York City,

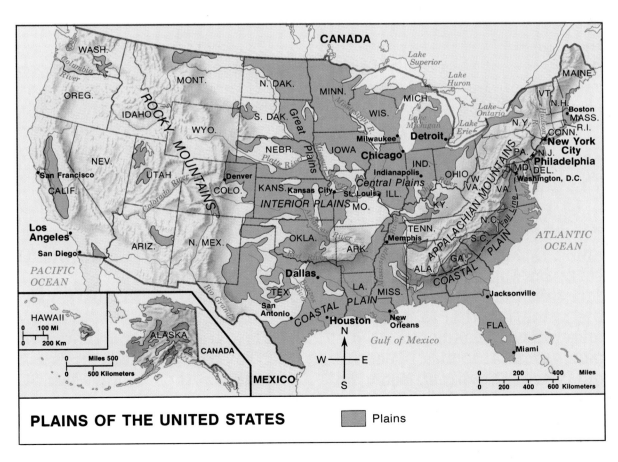

PLAINS OF THE UNITED STATES Plains

New York City is a major world seaport on our country's East Coast. From here, ships carry goods to ports around the world.

the Hudson River flows into the Atlantic Ocean. Hundreds of ships can dock in the harbor around New York City.

Manufacturing and Travel

The cities of the Coastal Plain manufacture many products. Ships bring **raw materials** to ports on the plain. Ships also carry **finished products** from the ports to other places. Raw materials are materials used to make something else. Wool, cotton, wood, and oil are some raw materials. Finished products, such as clothing and furniture, are made from raw materials.

Trucks, trains, and planes also carry goods to and from cities on the Coastal Plain. Highways and railroads criss-cross the plain. Every year, airplanes carry millions of people and many goods into and out of cities.

Reading Check

1. Name three large cities on the Coastal Plain.
2. How were waterfalls important to settlers in America? How are they important now?
3. Name three products grown or made on the Coastal Plain.
4. Why is the Coastal Plain a good farming area? Give two reasons.

110

2. THE INTERIOR PLAINS

To Guide Your Reading

Look for these important words:

Key Words
- prairie
- Corn Belt
- feedlots

- Wheat Belt
- drought

Places
- Interior Plains
- Central Plains
- Great Plains

Look for answers to these questions:

1. What are the Interior Plains?
2. Why are the Interior Plains good for farming?
3. What is the difference between the Central Plains and the Great Plains?
4. Why are the Central Plains and the Great Plains important to Americans?

Our largest plains region is "inside" our country. This region, the **Interior Plains,** covers thousands of square miles. The Interior Plains lie between the Appalachian and the Rocky mountains.

There are ten states in the Interior Plains region. Some of our largest and richest farmlands are in these states. They have flat land, fertile soil, and long, sunny summers for growing crops. The Interior Plains provide most of the food and meat for our country. Most of the land in this region is used for growing crops and raising animals.

The Interior Plains are two plains really. They are called the **Central Plains** and the **Great Plains.** The Central Plains start in central Ohio. They reach as far west as the middle of Kansas. The Great Plains begin in Kansas, Nebraska, North Dakota, and South Dakota. They end at the Rocky Mountains.

The Central Plains

Long ago, the Central Plains were called the **prairie.** Seas of tall grass and flowers covered the prairie. When the grass died, it rotted and became part of the soil. This made the prairie soil fertile. The fertile soil and the rain of the Central Plains helped new grass and flowers grow.

The tall, waving prairie grass is now almost gone. Settlers came and farmed the rich, fertile soil, planting wide fields of corn. Much of the Central Plains is now called the **Corn Belt.** The map on page 114 shows this wide area.

Three-fourths of all our corn comes from the Corn Belt. Corn grows better here than anywhere else in the country. Corn, in fact, is a kind of tall grass. Farmers in the Central Plains use more land for corn than for any other crop. They feed most of the corn to the hogs, cattle, and chickens they raise. Only a small part is grown for people to eat.

Today, most prairie land is covered with fields of tall corn.

Early settlers saw the prairie as a "sea of grass," tossing like ocean waves in the wind. Below is some tall prairie grass still found in northern Kansas.

112

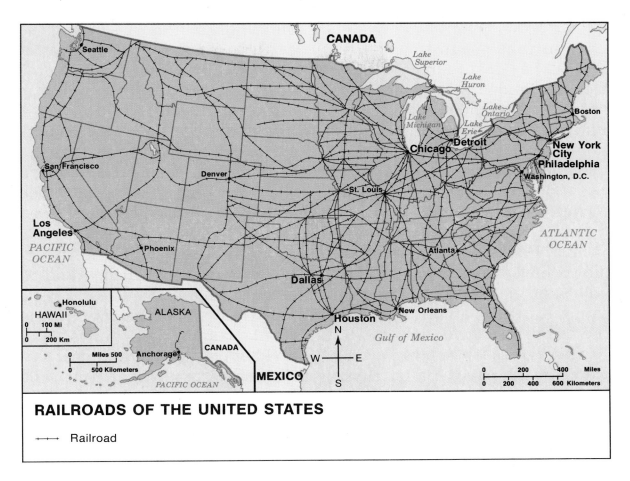

RAILROADS OF THE UNITED STATES

⊢——⊣ Railroad

Factories and Cities

Not many people live on the farmlands of the Central Plains. Instead, most people live in big cities. Among the largest cities on these plains are Chicago, Detroit, Milwaukee, Kansas City, St. Louis, and Cincinnati.

Many kinds of factories are in these cities. Some make tractors and other farm machines. Some manufacture paper, rubber, and steel products.

Your breakfast cornflakes do not come straight from the field either. People in Central Plains cities turn corn into cornflakes and other foods. Factories there also make cereals, cold cuts, and frozen and canned vegetables.

From the factories, trucks, trains, and planes carry products to and from the Central Plains. The broad, flat land of the plains is ideal for highways, airports, and railroads. The map on this page shows the main railroads in the United States. Notice that many railroads meet in the Central Plains region. Chicago, Illinois, is one of the most important transportation centers.

113

The Great Plains

In contrast to the Central Plains, the Great Plains are a dry, treeless land. In the past, short grass grew on much of the Great Plains. Only short grass could grow because of the lack of rain. Look at the map on page 42. The Great Plains have less than 20 inches (about 50 cm) of precipitation a year. Now look at the Central Plains on the map. These plains have from 20 to 40 inches (about 50 to 100 cm) of precipitation a year. Can you tell why the tall prairie grass grew well?

Short grass still grows in many places on the Great Plains. Herds of cattle on large ranches graze on the grass. Before sending the cattle to market, however, ranchers usually feed their herds grains. The cattle are rounded up and brought to **feedlots.** Feedlots are large pens. In feedlots cattle are fed corn and grain to fatten them for market. When they are ready for market, the cattle are shipped by train or by truck.

Many people in the Great Plains work on ranches and at feedlots. People in Great Plains cities may work at meat-packing plants. Hamburger, steaks, veal, and hot dogs come from beef cattle. Leather, soap, medicines, and fertilizers come from cattle, too.

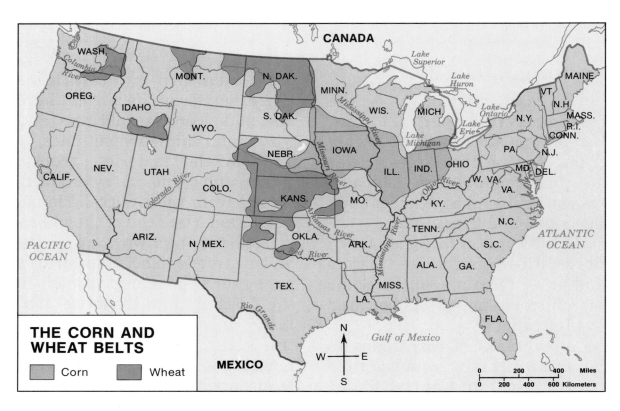

THE CORN AND WHEAT BELTS

Corn   Wheat

Farming on the Great Plains

Wheat is the main crop on most farms in the Great Plains. Wheat grows so well here that the Great Plains are often called "the breadbasket of the world." After corn, wheat is the largest crop in our country. Wheat is in many of the foods we eat each day. Bread, cereal, and noodles are just a few foods made from wheat.

Most of our wheat grows in the area called the **Wheat Belt.** The map on page 114 shows the Wheat Belt of the Great Plains.

The sunny, dry climate of the Great Plains is best for growing wheat. Yet farmers do face problems in this climate. The weather here changes often and suddenly. Huge storms develop quickly on the plains.

One of the farmers' greatest worries is **drought** (DROWT), a time of little or no rainfall. A drought can kill a wheat crop. Droughts are dangerous on the Great Plains for another reason. If the soil gets too dry, it can blow away. These problems make irrigation all the more important.

Cattle weighing up to 900 pounds each (about 400 kg) eat grain in feedlots.

When this wheat is harvested, part of the kernel will be used for animal feed.

During a drought, farmers are in danger of losing their farm soil to dust storms. Strong winds can carry the soil for miles.

Farmers on the Great Plains face other dangers, too. Too much rain can ruin a wheat crop. If winter lasts too long, farmers cannot plant at the right time. If winter comes too soon, it may also kill the wheat. Fire is another danger on the Great Plains.

Farmers on the Great Plains raise much of the food we eat. Their work is difficult, but millions of Americans depend on the crops of the Great Plains. We depend on these crops for jobs as well as for food. Many people besides farmers make a living from food. Some work in the factories that make bread and other food products. Others work at jobs that move food and food products from place to place. Others are butchers, bakers, grocers, and workers in supermarkets and restaurants. What other jobs have to do with food?

Reading Check

1. Where are the Interior Plains?
2. What is the Corn Belt?
3. What are some of the goods manufactured in the Central Plains?
4. Why are the Great Plains important to many people in the United States?

SKILLS FOR SUCCESS

USING REFERENCE BOOKS

Most of America's grain is grown in the Interior Plains. Suppose you were writing a report about grain. How would you find the information you need?

Your library has different kinds of **reference books** to help you. Reference books are books full of facts. Many reference books are easy to find and use.

Using an Encyclopedia

An **encyclopedia** is a good place to look for information. An encyclopedia has articles on many subjects. The articles are arranged in alphabetical order. For example, an article about *water* comes before an article about *wheat*.

An encyclopedia can be one large book. More often, though, an encyclopedia has about 25 separate books, or **volumes.**

An encyclopedia may have one volume for each letter of the alphabet. The letters are shown on the books' covers. You would find the article about wheat in volume *W.* What volume would have an article about corn?

Some encyclopedias have **guide words** instead of letters on

The encyclopedia contains information on nearly every subject.

the covers. For example, a volume might have the guide words *Virginia-Zurich.* This volume would have articles that come between *Virginia* and *Zurich* in alphabetical order. You would find an article about wheat in this volume.

Suppose you want to find information about barley. If a volume has the guide words *B-Butter,* would you find information about barley in this volume?

main [mān] *adj.* Most important; principal; major.

main·land [mān′land] *n.* The major part of land, not an island or peninsula.

maize [māz] *n.* Corn; the plant or its seeds; also called Indian corn.

maj·es·ty [maj′is·tē] *n.* A title for a king or a queen; a way to address royalty.

Using a Dictionary

Now suppose you are reading about corn. You come across a word you have never seen before. To understand what you are reading, you need to know what the word means.

A **dictionary** can help you learn new words. A dictionary tells you what words mean and how to spell and say them.

Dictionaries list thousands of words in alphabetical order. Above is part of a dictionary page. Find the word *maize* on the page.

The letters in parentheses ( ) tell you how to say the word. The *n.* tells you that *maize* is a noun. A noun is a word that names a person, place, or thing. Next comes the meaning of the word.

You can find words quickly in a dictionary. The top of every page has two guide words. The guide words are the first and last words on the page. The words on a page come between the guide words in alphabetical order. Look at the dictionary page above. What are the guide words on it?

Using an Atlas

Suppose you need to know where grain grows in North America. You can find information about places in an **atlas.** An atlas is a book of maps. Some atlases have road maps. Some atlases have maps of countries around the world. Atlases may include maps showing crops, population, products, and many other things.

Using an atlas as a guide, this student draws a map of the state of Florida.

The maps in an atlas are listed in its Table of Contents. The Table of Contents also gives the page numbers of the maps.

Here is part of an atlas's Table of Contents. On what page is a wheat map of the United States?

Suppose you want to find out where a city or a country is. Many atlases have an index of place names. The index lists the names of places in alphabetical order. It tells on what page of the atlas to find a place. Often, the index will tell where to look on the map grid.

Using an Almanac

Grain grows in certain places year after year. However, the *amount* of grain that grows in a place may change. When you need the latest information, the best reference is an **almanac.** Almanacs are books of facts and figures. They are brought up to date every year.

An almanac often shows information in tables and charts. However, the subjects are not in alphabetical order. The almanac's index will help you find what you are looking for. It lists the subjects in alphabetical order. Look at this index from an almanac:

Wheat, Amount of tells how much wheat was grown in a year. To find this information, you would look on pages 126 and 127. On what page will you find information about wheat prices?

CHECKING YOUR SKILLS

Answer these questions about reference books.

1. You are using an encyclopedia to find out about sawmills. Would you look in volume *S-Smith* or *Smithsonian-Szechwan?*

2. What are three things a dictionary can tell you about a word?

3. The guide words *Wexford* and *wheedle* appear on a dictionary page. Which words—*well, wheat, world,* or *wharf*—will be found on the page?

4. To find out the price of corn in a recent year, which kind of reference book would you use?

CLOSE-UP

Wild turkeys, once found across North America, still live in wilderness areas.

At one time, huge herds of buffalo rumbled over the Great Plains.

ANIMALS IN OUR COUNTRY

When America was a wilderness, herds of animals roamed free. Many kinds of wildlife filled the forests and rivers.

Some, like the deer, black bear, and beaver, still live in many places. Others, like the buffalo, were almost killed off as people settled in America. Today there are few grizzly bears or condors, our largest bird. These animals live in lonely places far from towns and cities.

Yet each region of our country is still home to many animals. Some of you have seen squirrels, raccoons, deer, and hawks. A lucky few have seen the bighorn sheep of the Rocky Mountains. On these pages are a few of the unusual animals of our country.

The Alligator

How would you like to find an alligator in your backyard? That has happened to people in Florida. Alligators live in swamps and rivers in the southern states. Many swamps are being drained to make way for houses and farms. When alligators lose their homes, they sometimes turn up in funny places.

Alligators are related to snakes and lizards. An alligator floating in water looks like a bumpy, greenish-gray or black log. All you can see is the top of the alligator's head.

Alligator babies are black and yellow when they hatch from their eggs. They are only 9 inches (about 23 cm) long. They may be 12 feet (about 4 m) long when they grow up.

Alligators eat fish, frogs, raccoons, snakes, and birds. Alligators only hurt people who get too close to them. Alligators stay away from people when they can.

Alligators sometimes lie on river banks or hide in their dens.

121

As a symbol of our country, the bald eagle is pictured on United States money. What bills or coins picture the eagle?

The Bald Eagle

The fierce-looking bald eagle is a symbol of our country's freedom. Yet the bald eagle is not as free as it used to be.

Bald eagles live near lakes, rivers, or the sea. They build their nests in the tops of tall trees. In many places the trees have been cut down. Water pollution has killed fish that the eagles eat. Water pollution has made other fish poisonous to the birds. Now the bald eagle is rare in most states.

The bald eagle is not really bald. It has white feathers on its head and tail. The rest of its feathers are brown. The wings of the bald eagle spread seven feet (about 2 m) across. The bald eagle is the second-largest American bird.

Bald eagles choose a partner for life. They come back to the same nest each year to raise a new eagle chick. Every year the parent eagles add more grass and twigs to their nest. The nest can grow very large. One eagle nest weighed two tons!

The Black Bear

A family is camping in a national park. They see a black bear nearby. The bear sits up on its back legs. It seems to be begging for food.

"Oh, the bear is so cute!" a boy says. "Can I feed it? Can I pet it?"

The correct answer is no! Black bears may look cute, but they are not pets. They are wild animals. Most black bears will not look for a fight. Yet they can be quick, strong, and dangerous.

Black bears are the most common bears in the United States. They live in the mountains and

122

forests of our country. They eat mostly berries, roots, acorns, and grass. They may also eat fish, insects, and birds. For a special treat, a bear sometimes steals honey from a bee nest.

Black bears are better left alone.

Rattlesnakes usually rest during the day and search for food at night.

Rattlesnakes

The rattlesnake gets information about the world around it in interesting ways. It can smell with its forked tongue. It can sense heat with the two pits below its eyes.

A rattlesnake eats small animals such as birds, rats, and mice. These animals have warm blood, as you do. The rattlesnake's pits sense that warmth. They help the snake find its food even in the dark.

A rattlesnake has two long front teeth called fangs. These fangs are hollow inside. When the

123

snake bites an animal, poison flows through the fangs into the animal's body.

Rattlesnakes are found in deserts, swamps, woods, and mountains. When walking where rattlesnakes live, wear heavy boots. Look where you step.

The rattlesnake gets its name from a rattle on its tail. When angry or afraid, the snake shakes this rattle. It makes a dry, hissing kind of sound. Rattlesnake bites can be very dangerous. If you see or hear a rattlesnake, get away from it.

Caribou

The caribou (KAIR·ih·boo), a North American reindeer, lives in Alaska. It is well fitted for its cold home. Its feet have broad, split hooves that help it walk on snow. Its brown coat is thick and

People in Alaska still hunt caribou for food and for hides.

124

warm. Both the male and female caribou have antlers. They use their antlers and hooves to dig holes in the snow to find food.

Few animals can live in the plains of northern Alaska. The caribou is one of the animals that can. In the plains of northern Alaska, the ground is frozen all year. In spring it thaws just enough for grasses and small bushes to grow. The caribou feeds on these plants.

As winter approaches, herds of caribou travel hundreds of miles south. They are going to the pine forests. There they dig beneath the snow for their food, called reindeer moss. In spring they will return to the Alaskan plains.

The prairie dog prefers grasses and plants for its food.

The Prairie Dog

A prairie dog sits near the opening of its **burrow,** or hole. Suddenly a shadow silently passes over it. An enemy—maybe a hawk—is flying overhead.

The prairie dog makes a short, sharp barking sound. The bark means "Danger!" Then the animal dives into its underground home. All around, other prairie dogs disappear into their own burrows.

That doglike bark gave the prairie dog its name. The prairie dog is really a squirrel, however. Prairie dogs have brown bodies, small ears, and short tails.

Prairie dogs dig their burrows near one another. Some of the burrows are connected. Large groups of burrows make up prairie dog towns. Prairie dog towns used to be common in all the Great Plains states. Many can still be found there.

CHAPTER 6 REVIEW

WORDS TO USE

Copy the words below. Write the meaning of each word or words.

1. **fertile**
2. **raw materials**
3. **prairie**
4. **feedlots**
5. **drought**

FACTS TO REVIEW

1. What is the Fall Line?

2. What are our country's two largest ports?

3. What is the difference between raw materials and finished products? Give an example of each.

4. Why are plains good for farming?

5. What two plains make up the Interior Plains?

6. What is the corn grown in the Central Plains used for?

7. How are goods shipped to and from our plains regions? Name two ways.

8. What are some products made from beef cattle?

9. What are two problems farmers have on the Great Plains?

10. Name at least three jobs that have to do with food.

IDEAS TO DISCUSS

1. Why are cities on plains important? Why do people in cities on the plains depend on ranchers and farmers?

2. What are some crops grown on the Coastal Plain? What are some crops grown on the Interior Plains? What are some ways you use these crops? Where do you get your food?

3. How is the weather on the Coastal Plain different from the weather on the Interior Plains?

○ SKILLS PRACTICE

Using Reference Books Which kind of reference book would you use to find out each of these things?

a. Last year's rainfall in Omaha, Nebraska
b. What the word *prairie* means
c. How beef cattle are raised
d. Where beef cattle are raised

UNIT 2 REVIEW

WORDS TO REMEMBER

Copy the sentences below. Fill in the blanks with the right words from the list.

conservation   **prairie**
erosion   **range**
fertilizers   **raw materials**
industries   **transportation**
port   **water power**

1. The wearing away of land is called ____.

2. Dams help make ____ ____.

3. New Orleans, Louisiana, is our largest ____.

4. Coal mining and steel manufacturing are important ____.

5. Ships, trains, and planes are kinds of ____.

6. Cattle in the mountain regions graze on the ____.

7. Protecting our natural resources is ____.

8. ____ help plants to grow.

9. Wool, cotton, wood, and oil are kinds of ____ ____.

10. Tall ____ grass and flowers at one time covered the Central Plains.

FOCUS ON MAIN IDEAS

1. Where are most large cities? From the list, pick two answers, and explain your choices.

   a. mountain regions
   b. desert regions
   c. plains regions
   d. near rivers

2. Name two ways in which people use

   a. rivers
   b. mountains
   c. deserts
   d. plains

3. Why are port cities good for manufacturing? Give two reasons.

4. How does erosion change mountains and deserts?

5. In what regions are our largest forests?

6. Why is irrigation important to desert regions?

7. How is the climate of desert regions in our country different from the climate of the Coastal Plain?

8. Why are so many cattle raised in the Great Plains?

127

9. What two large crops are grown in the United States? Where are most of these crops grown?

10. Why is weather important to farmers on the Great Plains?

ACTIVITIES

1. **Art/Making a Model** Make a model of a plains, a desert, or a mountain region in a shoebox. Use colored paper, rocks, sand, and clay to show the region's important features.

2. **Research/Writing** Use a reference book to find out about a river near your community. Write a few paragraphs about this river. Include a description of the river's source and its mouth. Write down the length of the river and its main uses.

3. **Writing/Making a List** Mountains, plains, deserts, and rivers have natural resources that make each place special. Make a list of some natural resources found in each. Tell why these resources are important.

4. **Research/Art** What are some of the jobs people do in your community? Cut out magazine pictures showing people doing these jobs. Make a mural for your classroom bulletin board.

⦿ SKILLS REVIEW

1. **Using Elevation Maps** Use the map to answer these questions.

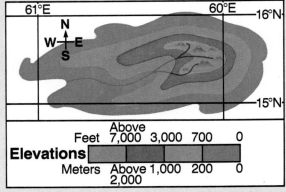

a. Is this island in the Northern or Southern Hemisphere?
b. Does the river in the map flow from east to west or from west to east? How can you tell?
c. Which line of longitude passes near the mountains?
d. What is the elevation of the mountains?

2. **Cross-section Diagrams** Use the cross section below to answer these questions.

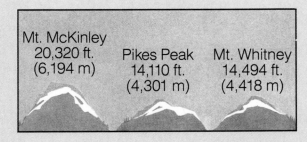

a. What is the elevation of Pikes Peak?

b. What is the highest mountain shown here? What is its elevation?

YOUR STATE

In this unit you have explored the main natural regions of the United States—mountains, deserts, and plains. You have learned about rivers, climates, and landforms that are found in these regions. Now look at your own state's land and learn more about it.

LEARNING ABOUT GEOGRAPHY

1. Look at a map of your state. Look for mountains, deserts, plains, and large rivers. Next, draw a large outline map of your state. Draw the mountains and rivers you have found and label them. Use different colors to show deserts or plains.

LEARNING ABOUT USING RESOURCES

2. In an atlas or encyclopedia, find a resource and product map that shows your state. Then list the ways people in your state use the land and water. Make up symbols to show how people use resources. For example, a fish can stand for fishing. A tree can stand for logging.

Draw these symbols on the outline map of your state.

LEARNING FACTS ABOUT YOUR STATE

3. Look at "Facts About the States" on page 424. Find the information about your state. Make a chart or poster showing some of the information. If you wish, draw pictures of your state bird, flower, and flag.

LEARNING ABOUT STATE AND NATIONAL PARKS

4. Using an encyclopedia or an atlas, find out about a park in your state. What kinds of landforms are in the park? What are people doing to keep the park beautiful? If you have visited this park, tell your class about it.

LEARNING ABOUT RECREATION

5. Make a poster that shows a popular outdoor activity in your state. Write a short paragraph about this activity. How does the land in your state make this activity possible?

OIL
CO.

ST. NICHOLAS

UNIT THREE

REGIONS OF THE UNITED STATES

How do people make a living in your state? Do you know what natural resources your state has? Every state has different kinds of land and natural resources. What people do for a living depends on the land and resources of their state.

In this unit our 50 states are divided into seven parts, or regions. We call these parts the Northeast, the Southeast, the Great Lakes, the Plains, the Southwest, the Mountains, and the Pacific regions. Each region is different from the others. You will read about the people who lived and worked in our regions long ago. You will see, too, how people today make a living in these regions.

CHAPTER 7

The Northeast

About this chapter

When our country began, it had only 13 states. Nine of these states are in the Northeast region. Today almost one-fourth of all Americans live in the Northeast.

As you read this chapter, you will find out why the Northeast is an important farming and manufacturing area. You will read about the Pilgrims, Squanto, and Ben Franklin. You will see why the Northeast is important to our country.

1. THE LAND AND ITS RESOURCES

To Guide Your Reading

Look for these important words:

Key Words
- glaciers
- river valley
- bays
- humid
- needleleaf
- broadleaf
- ore

Places
- Coastal Plain
- Appalachian Mountains
- Hudson River
- New York City
- New York State Barge Canal System
- Connecticut River
- Delaware River
- Massachusetts Bay
- Delaware Bay
- Chesapeake Bay

Look for answers to these questions:

1. What are major landforms of the Northeast?
2. Why are waterways important here?
3. How is the climate in the Northeast different from the rest of the country?
4. What are the important natural resources of this region?

The Northeast is the smallest region in the United States. Yet it has more people than any other region.

Most people in the Northeast live on the **Coastal Plain,** the flat land next to the Atlantic Ocean. The coast there has many large cities with busy harbors. A string of cities runs along the coast from Boston, Massachusetts, to Baltimore, Maryland.

To the west of the Coastal Plain lie the **Appalachian Mountains.** These low mountains cover much of the Northeast region. Among the mountains are rolling hills and green valleys. Large forests cover the mountain slopes in nearly every part of the Northeast.

Land features of the Northeast were formed long ago when the climate turned very cold. **Glaciers** (GLAY•shurz) covered the northern part of this region then. Glaciers are large masses of ice that move slowly. The glaciers scraped away soil and wore down the Appalachian Mountains. They made deep cuts in the land. Later the climate warmed. When the glaciers melted, the cuts filled with water. Today they are rivers and lakes.

Bodies of Water

The **Hudson River** is one of the most important rivers in the Northeast. At its mouth the Hudson flows into the Atlantic Ocean. It forms a large natural harbor. **New York City,** our country's largest city, has grown up around this harbor. The harbor has helped make New York City one of our leading ports.

Starting at the mouth of the Hudson River, a ship can travel

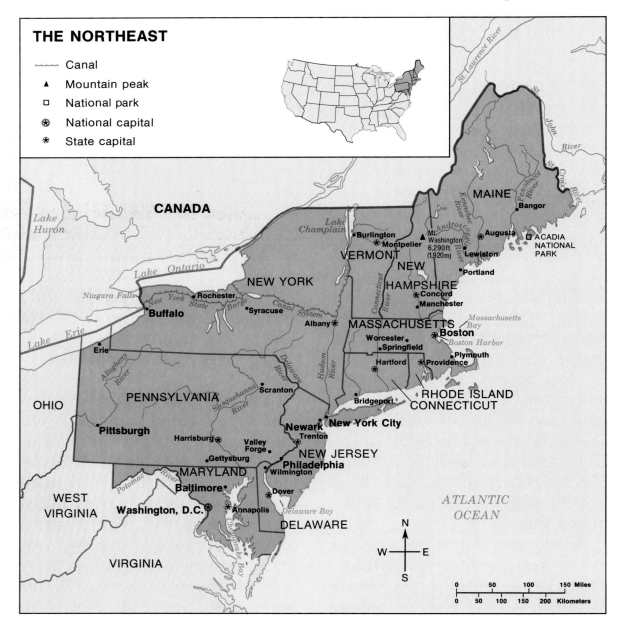

THE NORTHEAST

- ‑‑‑‑‑ Canal
- ▲ Mountain peak
- □ National park
- ⊛ National capital
- ✳ State capital

from New York City to the Great Lakes. First the ship moves north up the Hudson River. At Albany, New York, it turns west. There it enters the **New York State Barge Canal System.** The system is made up of four canals built to move freight across New York. At the end of these canals, the ship reaches Lake Erie. From Lake Erie the ship can go through the other Great Lakes. It can go all the way west to Minnesota!

Another important river in the Northeast is the **Connecticut River.** Some of Connecticut's best farmland lies in the Connecticut River Valley. A **river valley** is the low land through which a river flows.

Farther south the **Delaware River** is an important transportation route for goods of all kinds. The city of Philadelphia (fil•uh•DEL•fee•uh), Pennsylvania, is on the Delaware River.

Several large **bays** lie along the coast of the Northeast. A bay is water partly surrounded by land. **Massachusetts Bay, Delaware Bay,** and **Chesapeake Bay** lead to major ports.

Almost two million people live on the island of Manhattan. Skyscrapers, pleasant parks, and New York Harbor make it the most famous part of New York City.

"There's a house *somewhere* under all this snow!" Northeast snowstorms bring a few problems for some people.

Climate

In some parts of our country the climate does not change much all year. In most of the Northeast it really does change! The four seasons are quite different from one another.

Most of the region has cold, snowy winters. Parts of New York State, for example, have heavy snows. Cities like Buffalo and Syracuse (SIR•uh•kyoos) may get more than 100 inches (254 cm) a year.

The land comes to life in spring. Trees bud and flowers bloom. Summers are warm and **humid** (HYOO•mid). Humid air has a lot of moisture in it. Autumn brings cool, crisp days to the region. Leaves turn gold, orange, and red. Everywhere the trees blaze with color.

Natural Resources

Water is one of the most valuable resources of the Northeast. The region's farms, industries, and large cities use great amounts of fresh water. The entire region gets enough rain and snow to meet its needs, however.

The Atlantic Ocean is another valuable water resource. Millions of fish are caught along the coast each year. Much of this catch is sold all over the United States.

Great forests stretched across the Northeast long ago. Some of that great forest land remains today. These forests are made up of **needleleaf** and **broadleaf** trees. All needleleaf trees have long, sharp leaves like needles. The leaves often stay green all year long. Cedar and pine are two kinds of needleleaf trees.

Broadleaf trees have wide, flat leaves. They often shed their leaves in fall. Oak and maple are two kinds of broadleaf trees.

Good soil is a natural resource of the region's southern part. Farmers grow many kinds of crops in its sandy soil.

The forests that cover much of Vermont show off their fall colors—yellow for birches, bright red for maple trees.

Niagara Falls is between Canada and New York. Though most famous for its falls, the Niagara River is also a source of electric power.

The most important fuel resource in the Northeast is coal. Only Pennsylvania has great amounts of it. Most coal is used for making electricity. It also goes to steel mills. Steel is made by heating coal, limestone, and iron **ore** (OHR). Ore is rock that has a mineral in it.

Reading Check

1. Where do most people of the Northeast live?
2. How can products from the Great Lakes reach New York City?
3. Why is the Atlantic Ocean an important natural resource in the Northeast?
4. Which part of the Northeast has good farmland?

137

SKILLS FOR SUCCESS

USING INTERMEDIATE DIRECTIONS

A fishing boat is sailing east from Boston. Suddenly over the boat's radio comes a message. "Warning! There is a storm ahead of you. Head northeast right away!"

Quickly the boat changes its direction. Which way is northeast though?

You already know that the four main directions are north, south, east, and west. These four main directions are called **cardinal directions.**

Besides the cardinal directions, there are four "in-between" directions. They are **northeast,** **southeast,** **northwest,** and **southwest.** They lie between the four main directions. These in-between directions are called **intermediate directions.** *Intermediate* is another way of saying in-between.

The compass rose on the map will help you understand intermediate directions. Find the line that passes halfway between north and east on the compass rose. It points to northeast. The letters *NE* stand for northeast. That is the direction the boat turned. The line passing between south and west points to

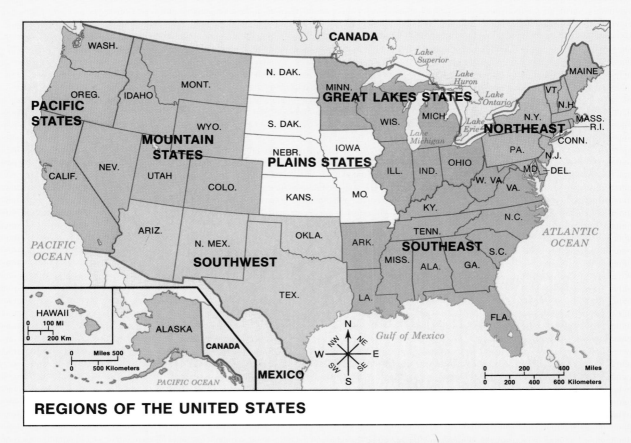

REGIONS OF THE UNITED STATES

the southwest. The letters *SW* stand for southwest. Which direction is between south and east? between north and west?

This unit discusses seven regions of our country. Four of them are named after an important body of water or landform. They are the Great Lakes, Plains, Mountain, and Pacific regions. Three of the regions have names that are intermediate directions. They are the Northeast, Southeast, and Southwest regions.

Look at the map again. Where is the Northeast region? You can find it quickly if you know how to use the compass rose.

CHECKING YOUR SKILLS

Use the map and the compass rose to answer these questions.

1. What are the four intermediate directions?

2. In what direction would an airplane fly from New York to Texas?

3. In what direction would an airplane fly from Florida to Wyoming?

4. Which state is farthest to the northeast?

5. What state is just southeast of Utah?

139

2. THE NORTHEAST LONG AGO

To Guide Your Reading

Look for these important words:

Key Words	People	Places
• Mayflower	• Squanto	• Plymouth
• history	• Benjamin	• New England
• colonies	Franklin	• Philadelphia,
• American		Pennsylvania
Revolution		

Look for answers to these questions:

1. What were some of the hardships the Pilgrims faced?
2. Why was Benjamin Franklin important to our country?
3. In what way did America change during Benjamin Franklin's life?

It is a foggy morning in 1620. The tired travelers find a place to land their boat. They are on the rocky shores of what is now called Massachusetts. The travelers call themselves Pilgrims. Their ship is the **Mayflower.**

The Pilgrims arrived in America in November. Though they built a settlement, which they called **Plymouth** (PLIM• uhth), their first winter was very hard. The Pilgrims had little food. They had never felt such bitter cold. About half of the Pilgrims died within the first year.

Help came in the spring. An Indian named **Squanto** came to Plymouth. Squanto taught the Pilgrims how to live in the new land. He taught them how to grow corn and beans. He showed them how to hunt wild animals. None of the Pilgrims might have lived without Squanto's help.

The Pilgrims are important in America's past, or **history.** They were the first Europeans to settle in the Northeast. The Pilgrims came from England to find religious freedom in America.

Soon other people from Europe came to join them. The nearby town of Boston began to grow. Other towns grew up all over the Northeast. Many of them, like

With Squanto's help, the Pilgrims had their first successful harvest.
They invited the Indians to a feast that became the first Thanksgiving.

Boston, grew into cities. Most of the settlers were from England, as the Pilgrims were. They settled in the states called Connecticut, Massachusetts, Maine, New Hampshire, Vermont, and Rhode Island. The English settlers called this area **New England.** Today we often call these states by this name.

By 1750 many more people lived along the Atlantic coast. New England continued to grow. People started new settlements as far south as Georgia. England ruled these settlements as 13 **colonies** (KAHL•uh•neez). Colonies are places that are ruled by another country.

Ben Franklin's America

In 1723 a 17-year-old boy set out from his home in Boston. Young **Benjamin Franklin** had decided to go to **Philadelphia, Pennsylvania.** He hoped to make his fortune there. When he arrived in Philadelphia, Ben had one dollar in his pocket.

Ben found a job working for a printer. He worked hard so that soon he had enough money to open his own printing shop. He wrote and printed a popular book called *Poor Richard's Almanac.* An almanac is a book that is printed once a year. People enjoyed the advice, news, and many wise sayings in *Poor Richard's Almanac.*

Here are two sayings from the *Almanac:*

Don't throw stones at your neighbors, if your own windows are glass.

When the well's dry, we know the worth of water.

Besides being a printer and an author, Franklin was an inventor. One of his inventions was the Franklin stove. His stove was made of iron and burned wood. It heated homes better than open fireplaces. Another of his inventions was bifocals.

Franklin was always thinking of new ideas and new ways of doing things. He showed that lightning was a form of electricity. He started Philadelphia's first fire department and its first hospital.

America began to change in important ways as Franklin got older. People in the colonies were beginning to draw away from England. Franklin tried to get the 13 colonies to work together more closely.

The English passed laws to make the colonies pay new taxes. Many people refused to pay. They believed the English were ignoring their rights. The two sides were close to war.

The **American Revolution** (rev•uh•LOO•shuhn) began when Ben Franklin was in his seventies. A revolution is a large, sudden change in government and in people's lives. Americans began to fight for freedom from English rule. Franklin was one of the leaders in the American Revolution. He served his country until the day he died. Ben Franklin was then 84.

Ben Franklin served our country both during and after the American Revolution.

Reading Check

1. Who were the Pilgrims? Why did they come to America?
2. How did Squanto help the Pilgrims?
3. What are colonies?
4. Who was Ben Franklin?

NEW ENGLAND SAILING SHIPS

The brig *Eliza of Providence*

On board a brig

It is 1770. England rules 13 colonies in America. Few settlers have crossed the Appalachian Mountains. Yet many people from the colonies have already sailed to ports in Europe, South America, and Africa.

These brave sailors crossed the seas in sturdy little ships called brigs. The ships came from New England. The seas of the world were their highways. Brigs brought American goods to other countries. They brought back goods people in the colonies needed.

Sugar, tea, clothing, and iron were just some of the goods they carried. Sometimes they even carried cuckoo clocks. One New Englander got rich shipping blocks of ice to the warm West Indies.

Some New England boys became sailors when they were only 11 years old. Some later became captains of their own ships.

A captain had to be a good sailor, of course, but he also needed many other skills. He was the ship's doctor. He had to be able to navigate, or find his way, on the sea. He had to control his crew. The captain's word was the law on the seas.

When a captain returned from a long voyage, he brought treasures for his house. Seashells, precious gems, carved chests, and silk were favorite choices. Some New England families still own these treasures brought back from many distant lands.

Brigs were also used as fighting ships during the American Revolution. The ships remained popular well into the 1800s.

SKILLS FOR SUCCESS

USING A TIMELINE

A **timeline** shows a period of time and important events of that period. The events are marked in order on the timeline. The timeline below shows some important events in Theresa Sastre's life.

This timeline covers ten years in Theresa's life. Notice the marks on the line. The space between two marks is equal to one year. The dates on the left are the earliest. The dates on the right come later. The first year on this timeline is 1975, the year Theresa was born.

A timeline helps you see the order in which events happened. The first event on this timeline is Theresa's birth. Look to the right of that event. It shows the next important thing that happened in Theresa's life. It was the birth of her brother, in June 1978. What was the next important event? When did it happen?

You may want to know how many years passed between two events. A timeline can help you figure this out. Let's find out the time between Theresa's birth and her family's move to Delaware. The timeline shows that she was born in 1975. The family moved in 1982. Subtract 1975 from 1982. The difference is seven. Theresa's family moved about seven years after she was born.

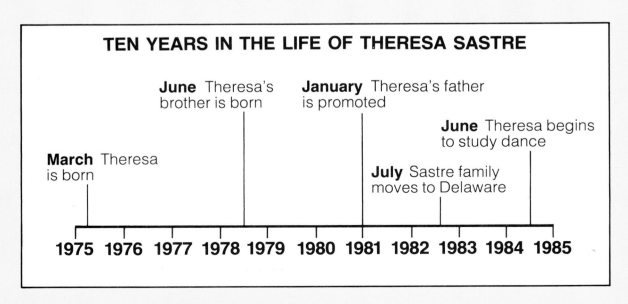

TEN YEARS IN THE LIFE OF THERESA SASTRE

June Theresa's brother is born

January Theresa's father is promoted

June Theresa begins to study dance

March Theresa is born

July Sastre family moves to Delaware

1975 1976 1977 1978 1979 1980 1981 1982 1983 1984 1985

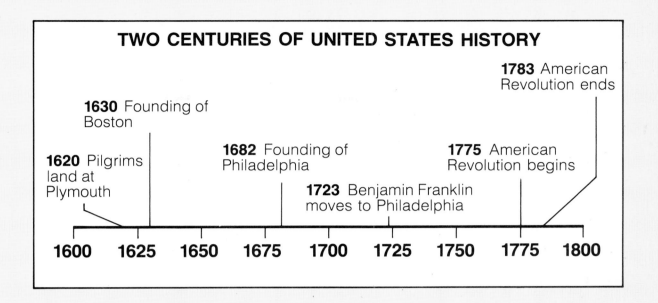

TWO CENTURIES OF UNITED STATES HISTORY

1783 American Revolution ends

1630 Founding of Boston

1682 Founding of Philadelphia

1775 American Revolution begins

1620 Pilgrims land at Plymouth

1723 Benjamin Franklin moves to Philadelphia

1600   1625   1650   1675   1700   1725   1750   1775   1800

Our Country's History on a Timeline

A timeline can also show a period in history. Of course, many years must be shown on the line. This timeline shows some important events in United States history.

Look to the left of the timeline. The timeline begins with the year 1600. Look to the right of the time-line. What is the last year shown?

This timeline is different from Theresa's timeline. It does not show every year. Instead the marks are 25 years apart. The first year is 1600. The second year is 1625. What is the next year shown?

This timeline shows 200 years. A period of 100 years is called a **century** (SEN•chuh•ree). Thus, this timeline shows two centuries. You might also say that it shows the 1600s and the 1700s. This is just another way in which people talk about centuries. The 1600s are the years from 1600 to 1699. The 1700s are the years from 1700 to 1799.

You read this timeline just as you read Theresa's timeline. The earliest event is the Pilgrims' landing at Plymouth. This event took place in 1620. What is the next event shown?

CHECKING YOUR SKILLS

Use the history timeline to answer these questions.

1. What event took place between 1675 and 1700?

2. Was Philadelphia founded before or after Boston?

3. What event came after Ben Franklin's move to Philadelphia?

4. When did the American Revolution begin? When did it end?

3. THE NORTHEAST TODAY

To Guide Your Reading

Look for these important words:

Key Words
- trawler
- food processing
- poultry
- trade

Places
- United Nations

Look for answers to these questions:

1. What jobs might people have in the Northeast?
2. Why is good transportation important for manufacturing?
3. Why do people in the Northeast have such different backgrounds?

In some ways the Northeast has not changed all that much since the days of Ben Franklin. Buildings from the 1700s still stand in many places. Many of the newer buildings are made to look like the older colonial ones. People of the Northeast still even work at some of the same jobs.

Fishing

In Ben Franklin's day many people earned their living by fishing. Today many Northeasterners still get food from the sea. Millions of pounds of lobsters, oysters, clams, cod, and other fish are caught in the Atlantic Ocean.

A day aboard a **trawler** (TRAW•luhr), or fishing boat,

Some of the best lobsters in the world come from the waters of the Northeast.

New England supplies much of the nation's cod, flounder, haddock, herring, and scallops. A day's catch is often sold at auction.

starts early in the morning. The boat leaves the harbor. The captain and crew find a good fishing spot. They lower a huge net into the water and tie the net's long ropes to the boat. The boat drags the net along the bottom of the ocean. Fish such as cod or herring swim into the net.

When the net is full, a machine pulls it up. The crew quickly put the fish in refrigerators so the fish stay fresh.

The day's catch is sold to markets near the harbor. Most of the fish is canned or frozen. Factories in Boston and other cities freeze, cook, or can fish, as well as other foods. **Food processing** (PRAHS•uhs•ing) is therefore important, too. After the fish is canned or frozen, markets sell it to stores all over the United States.

Farming

Today most people in the Northeast live in cities. Yet farming is still important to the region. Dairy products, such as milk, cheese, and eggs, come from all the states of the Northeast. Fruits and vegetables grow in New York, New Jersey, Pennsylvania, Maryland, and Delaware.

Farmers in these states also raise cattle and **poultry** (POHL•tree). Chickens and turkeys are the main kinds of poultry.

Beyond New York, in the New England states, the stony soil and colder climate make it hard to grow most crops. Unlike the rest of the Northeast, New England has short summers and sudden cold weather. Many farmers raise dairy cows here.

Some Northeastern states grow special crops. New Jersey, the "Garden State," is known for tomatoes and blueberries. Do you eat cranberries at Thanksgiving? They may come from Massachusetts, the leading cranberry grower. Maple syrup is one of Vermont's main products. Do you like grape juice? Much of it comes from New York State, a leading grower of grapes.

Manufacturing

The Northeast is an important manufacturing area for several reasons. It has coal for making steel and electricity. It has plenty of water. It has excellent

Duck, chicken, and turkey farms in the Northeast supply poultry for many customers in our country.

Workers drive metal spouts into sugar maples and collect the sap in buckets. The sap is boiled into maple syrup.

148

transportation for carrying goods from place to place. The Northeast also has many people there who make or buy these goods.

Look around your classroom and you may see some products made in the Northeast. Your paper may come from Maine, the "Pine Tree State." The steel in your desk may come from Pennsylvania. Some of your books may have been written in Massachusetts. Your clothing may have been made in New York. Perhaps the American flag was made in New Jersey, home of our country's largest flag factory.

Harbors on the Delaware River, like this one in Philadelphia, handle nearly 3,000 ships a year.

Trade and Transportation

The Northeast is an important center of **trade.** Trade is the buying and selling of goods. Each year tons of goods are bought and sold in the Northeast's cities. Goods leave the Northeast's ports for all parts of the world. Goods from other countries also arrive in these cities.

In order to carry on trade, the Northeast must have good transportation. You may already know that the region's rivers are important transportation routes. Boston, New York City, Philadelphia, and Baltimore, Maryland, are a few of the many port cities that make trade easy. Railroads, highways, and airports are also important for trade.

People of the Northeast Today

People from all over the world have settled in our country. The Northeast is a mix of all these people. They come from many different backgrounds. Many people can trace their ancestors to some of the first settlers from England. Many others have ancestors from Ireland, Italy, Poland, and Germany. People with Latin American, African, and Asian backgrounds have also settled in the Northeast region.

149

People from other states and other countries live, work, and play in the cities of the Northeast.

You will find a variety of these people in the northeastern cities, especially a large city like New York City. More people live in New York City than in any other American city. There you can hear people speaking many languages besides English. Newsstands sell newspapers in different languages. Neighborhood grocery stores sell foods people enjoyed in the "old country." Many people in these neighborhoods also celebrate the holidays of other countries as well as such American holidays as the Fourth of July.

New York City has a special building, the **United Nations.** There people meet to talk and settle problems among their nations.

Reading Check

1. What are some foods that come from the Northeast? Give three examples.
2. What manufactured goods are made in the Northeast? Give three examples.
3. Why is the Northeast an important manufacturing region? Give three reasons.
4. Why are newspapers in different languages sold in New York City?

150

CHAPTER 7 REVIEW

WORDS TO USE

Write a sentence for each word. Your sentence should explain the meaning of the word.

1. **bay**
2. **colonies**
3. **glaciers**
4. **humid**
5. **ore**

FACTS TO REVIEW

1. Why did many cities grow up on the Coastal Plain?

2. Name two ways glaciers changed the Northeast long ago.

3. Why are rivers and canals important in the Northeast?

4. Why is autumn a beautiful time of year in the Northeast?

5. Why is water an important resource for the Northeast?

6. How are needleleaf trees different from broadleaf trees?

7. Give one reason the Pilgrims are important.

8. Give three reasons the Northeast is an important manufacturing region.

9. Why is the Northeast a center of trade?

10. Why is Boston important?

IDEAS TO DISCUSS

1. Most of the Northeast has a climate that changes a lot during the year. Do you prefer a climate that is much the same all year or one that has changes? Give reasons for your answer.

2. Why is the Northeast important to people all over our country?

◯ SKILLS PRACTICE

1. **Using Mixed Directions** Use the map on page 139 to answer these questions.

   a. A plane is flying from Massachusetts to Missouri. In what direction is it traveling?
   b. What state is northeast of Maryland?

2. **Using a Timeline** Use the timeline on page 145 to answer these questions.

   a. How many years are shown on the timeline?
   b. Which event is the earliest?
   c. Which is the latest?

CHAPTER 8

The Southeast

About this chapter

The Southeast region is a mixture of old and new. St. Augustine, Florida, which was built by the Spanish, is the oldest European city in the United States. Jamestown, Virginia, is the home of the first successful English settlement in our country. Today the Southeast is also a gateway to the future. American space shots begin on the launch pad at Cape Canaveral, Florida.

In this chapter you will read how the past and the present mix in the Southeast. You will also find out why the Southeast is one of the fastest-growing regions in our country.

1. THE LAND AND ITS RESOURCES

To Guide Your Reading

Look for these important words:

Key Words
- peninsula

Places
- Coastal Plain
- Mississippi River

Look for answers to these questions:

1. What are some of the landforms of the Southeast?
2. Why are waterways important here?
3. What is the climate of the Southeast?
4. What are the important natural resources of this region?

The Southeast is a large region. It is almost three times the size of the Northeast. There are 12 states in the Southeast region.

The Coastal Plain

Much of the Southeast is low and level. It is part of the **Coastal Plain.** As it stretches south from Virginia, the plain grows wider. It covers almost all of the Florida **peninsula** (puh•NIN•suh•luh). A peninsula is land with water on three sides of it.

The Coastal Plain in the Southeast has large areas of rich farmland. Other areas of good farmland are found in the valleys of the **Mississippi River** and its branches. River floods have given these valleys some of the Southeast's best soil.

Some parts of the Coastal Plain are large swamps. The largest swamp is the Everglades on the southern tip of Florida.

The Piedmont

To the west of the Coastal Plain is the Piedmont (PEED•mont). The Piedmont is a large area of foothills at the edge of the Appalachian Mountains.

The Piedmont is rich in minerals. It has many forests and good farmland. Most of the factories of the Southeast are found in the large cities in the Piedmont, such as Atlanta, Georgia, and Charlotte, North Carolina.

The Blue Ridge Mountains

West of the Piedmont is the part of the Appalachians called the Blue Ridge Mountains. From a distance these forest-covered mountains often look blue. Hickory, maple, oak, and many other kinds of trees abound. The wood from these trees is used to make furniture for the whole country. Small farms lie in the narrow valleys among the mountains.

Bluegrass Country

West of the Appalachians more low land stretches across much of Kentucky and Tennessee. In part of Kentucky many fields are covered with small blue-green flowers. The "Bluegrass" area is known for its racehorse farms. The grass is rich in minerals that make the horses strong.

Major air, railway, and highway routes meet in Atlanta, making it an important transportation center.

Swift thoroughbreds from Kentucky's many horse farms are highly prized throughout the world.

THE SOUTHEAST

▲ Mountain peak

□ National park

⊛ State capital

Waterways

Waterways are important to the Southeast. The region has several large ports. On the Atlantic is Norfolk, Virginia. Mobile (MOH•beel), Alabama, and New Orleans, Louisiana, are large ports on the Gulf of Mexico.

New Orleans is the largest seaport in the United States. New Orleans lies along the Mississippi River about 100 miles (about 160 km) inland from the Gulf of Mexico. Ships from all over the world bring goods up the Mississippi to New Orleans. They leave

At the busy port of New Orleans, ships load and unload grain and goods. From here these goods are carried to places around the world.

with goods shipped to New Orleans from many parts of the United States.

The Mississippi is by far the Southeast's most important river. With its branches it reaches almost every part of the United States between the Appalachians and the Rockies. Each year these rivers carry millions of tons of freight.

The Tennessee Valley Authority

At one time the valley of the Tennessee River was a dangerous place to live. Floods killed people and destroyed homes. Then the national government formed the Tennessee Valley Authority (TVA). Its job was to help people near the river. The TVA built many dams to control floods. It built power plants to make low-cost electric power. The power from these plants has brought industry and jobs to the valley.

Climate

The climate in much of the Southeast is warm and sunny. Summers in most places are long, hot, and humid. Winters are short and often mild.

156

The rainy Southeast climate is ideal for growing rice. Arkansas, Louisiana, and Mississippi lead in rice-growing.

Georgia produces more peanuts than any other state. What are some foods made from peanuts?

All states in the Southeast receive more than 40 inches (about 102 cm) of precipitation each year. The rain and long summers help farmers grow many different crops. Cotton, rice, peanuts, and almost every kind of fruit grow well here.

The high areas of the region have a cooler climate than the lowland areas. The Appalachians often have snow and cold temperatures in winter.

Natural Resources

Some of the Southeast's most important resources are fuels. West Virginia and Kentucky are leaders in the nation's coal industry. Great amounts of oil and natural gas are found along the Gulf of Mexico in Texas and Lou-

isiana. The Southeast also has iron ore and limestone.

The rain and warm weather are also good for growing many kinds of trees. Huge forests of pine as well as oak and hickory trees cover many parts of the Coastal Plain.

The sea is another of the Southeast's important resources. Tons of fish come from the Atlantic and the Gulf of Mexico each year.

Reading Check

1. Which places in the Southeast are best for farming?
2. What is "Bluegrass" country?
3. How has the TVA helped the Tennessee River valley?
4. Why is a mild climate important to the Southeast?

2. THE SOUTHEAST LONG AGO

To Guide Your Reading

Look for these important words:

Key Words
- House of Burgesses
- plantations
- Declaration of Independence

People
- Thomas Jefferson
- George Washington

Places
- Jamestown, Virginia
- Yorktown, Virginia

Look for answers to these questions:

1. What did the House of Burgesses change in America?
2. Why did slavery begin in America?
3. Why was the Declaration of Independence written?
4. In what ways was George Washington a leader of our country?

The Pilgrims were not the first English settlers in America. In 1607 a group of English went to search for gold. Their ship landed on the coast of what is now the state of Virginia. They called their settlement **Jamestown.**

During the first years at Jamestown the settlers almost starved. One winter they had to eat rats and insects to stay alive. Then the settlers discovered that tobacco grew well there. Tobacco became the main crop they traded for food.

By 1619 the English had formed 11 small towns in the colony of Virginia. In that year something very important happened. England allowed the settlers to help run their government. Before this, the colony was ruled by a governor and lawmakers chosen by the English king. Now each town could vote for two men to help run the Virginia government. This group of lawmakers was called the **House of Burgesses** (BUHR•juhs•uhz).

Plantations and Slavery

As more English settlers came to America, they cleared the land and started farms. They soon realized that the rich soil of the

Many large plantations developed in the colonies of the Southeast. Owners became wealthy growing crops such as tobacco and cotton.

Coastal Plain was good for more crops than just tobacco. Many huge farms called **plantations** (plan•TAY•shuhnz) were formed. Tobacco, cotton, and rice became the main crops. Corn and wheat were two other important crops raised on plantations.

Plantation owners needed many workers to grow the crops. Thousands of black people were taken by force from their homes in Africa to work on the plantations. These people were made slaves. They were bought and sold just like goods. They had no rights or freedom.

The American Revolution

As English colonies grew up along the Atlantic coast, troubles with English rule began to grow as well. Lawmakers in England passed new laws and taxes for the colonies. The strict laws and taxes limited freedom and trade in the colonies. The people in the colonies believed these new laws and taxes were unfair. Many refused to obey the English government.

The English government then sent soldiers to make people obey. People in the colonies became even angrier, and fighting broke out. Some people began to talk about breaking away from England. They wanted to fight for their freedom. Some of the people in the colonies wanted to have their own government in America.

Thomas Jefferson

The leaders from the colonies met in Philadelphia in 1776. **Thomas Jefferson** was one of the leaders. Jefferson was a young farmer and lawyer from the colony of Virginia. The leaders asked

Ben Franklin, in the center of this painting, worked with Thomas Jefferson on the Declaration of Independence.

him to write the **Declaration of Independence** (dek•luh•RAY•shuhn uv in•duh•PEN•dens). *Declaration* comes from the word *declare*, which means to say. *Independence* is another word for freedom.

The Declaration explained why the colonies wanted independence. On July 4, 1776, Independence Day, the leaders of the 13 colonies met and voted to pass the Declaration. The Declaration of Independence said that the colonies were now a free nation with its own government. They called themselves the United States of America.

England did not let the American colonies go without a fight. It ordered soldiers to battle with the Americans. For more than five long years England and the United States fought the Revolutionary War.

George Washington

The Americans chose another Virginian to lead their army. His name was **George Washington.**

Washington's job at first seemed almost impossible. England's army was one of the best in the world. The Americans were poorly armed. They didn't even have warm clothes for winter. Still, they wanted freedom and they had a great leader.

George Washington led the Americans to victory during the American Revolution. He then became our first President.

Thomas Jefferson expressed some of our most basic ideas about freedom in the Declaration of Independence.

The worst time was the winter of 1777. The Americans had lost battle after battle. Washington's army was camped at Valley Forge, Pennsylvania, for the winter. It was bitterly cold. The Americans were in rags. Many of them died. Many others were very sick.

Somehow Washington kept his army together. After terrible defeats, the American army finally beat the English in an important battle at **Yorktown, Virginia.** The English gave in. They sent their army home. The United States was free!

We all know whom Americans chose as their first President. It was George Washington. Do you know who our third President was? It was Thomas Jefferson.

Reading Check

1. Where was the first English settlement in our country?
2. What was a plantation?
3. Why was Thomas Jefferson an important American leader?
4. How did George Washington help win the American Revolution?

161

SETTLING THE FRONTIER

Daniel Boone

Cabin raising

At about the time of the American Revolution, America's **frontier** (fruhn•TEER) was the edge of the Appalachian Mountains. It was here that the settled areas ended and the wilderness began. West of the frontier were mountains, forests, and wide, open spaces.

Towns, farms, and cities were already crowding the Atlantic coast. Many people wanted to settle the frontier. Few, however, were able to cross the mountains. It was a long, hard trip.

Then a pass through the mountains was discovered. It was called the **Cumberland Gap.** The famous **Daniel Boone** and other guides led settlers through the pass.

Many families headed for the frontier. They took very little with them. A family's belongings may have been only a sack of corn and a few tools and pots.

When a family found a place to settle, they built a cabin from logs. They cleared land for fields. After this, it was time to plant.

Frontier families lived far apart, but they helped one another. Neighbors got together to build a new cabin. After the corn was harvested, a family might ask neighbors to a **husking bee.** The leaves on the corn had to be husked, or taken off. Everyone tried to husk the most ears of corn. When the work was done, it was time for a big meal. Someone played a fiddle, and the others danced and sang.

Life on the frontier was hard, yet families kept coming. These people helped our country grow.

SKILLS FOR SUCCESS

GATHERING INFORMATION FOR A REPORT

Suppose you have to write a short report. The report must tell something about transportation. To write this report, you will need to gather facts. Even before gathering any information, however, you must choose a subject.

Reading for a Purpose

When choosing a subject, you should decide on something that interests you. An interesting subject will be easier to write about.

Perhaps you like airplanes. You might want to report on this subject. However, airplanes is too large a subject for a short report. You must pick a smaller part of this subject. Then you will be able to cover your subject in the space you have.

You might decide to write about the first airplanes. You may know that Orville and Wilbur Wright made the first successful airplane flight at a place near Kitty Hawk, North Carolina. Now you need to gather more facts about how they invented the airplane. To do this, you must visit a library and do some reading.

The library card catalog can help you find nonfiction books on a subject. You may also find facts about your subject in an encyclopedia.

When you begin reading about your subject, write a few questions down. They will help you remember the facts you need to find.

Here are some questions about the Wright brothers:

1. How did the Wright brothers learn about flying?
2. When did they start trying to invent an airplane?
3. What did their airplane look like?
4. Where did the Wright brothers build their airplane?
5. Who first flew their airplane?
6. How high did their airplane go on its first flight?

The answers to these questions could be the main parts of your report.

Taking Notes

As you read about your subject, you should take notes. Many students take notes on cards. They write one fact on each card. They also write where the fact came from. This helps them if they must check the fact later on.

Here is an example of a note card:

The Wright brothers built a small, light engine for the first airplane.

World Book Encyclopedia
vol. 21, p. 421

On this card is a fact about the Wright brothers' early flights. The fact came from an article in *The World Book Encyclopedia.* The article appeared on page 421 of volume 21.

Making an Outline

Once you have found the facts you need, you can **organize** your report. To organize is to put something in order. In this case you are writing about an important event in the past. You should put your notes in the order in which things happened.

Writing an **outline** is the next step. An outline lists the things you want to say in your report. It further organizes your information.

You will probably not use all of your notes in the outline or final report. You should choose the most important facts, ideas, and events to write about.

Here is part of an outline for a report on the Wright brothers:

TITLE: ORVILLE AND WILBUR WRIGHT

I. The Wright brothers wanted to learn about flying.
   A. Decided to build and test gliders.
   B. Made more than 1,000 test flights.
II. Orville and Wilbur Wright built the world's first successful airplane.
   A. First successful flight at Kitty Hawk, North Carolina, on December 17, 1903.

In this outline the first important idea follows the roman numeral I. It could be the main sentence in a paragraph. The facts marked *A* and *B* tell more about this main idea.

The sentence marked II could be the main sentence in another paragraph. Facts about this main idea would be labeled with capital letters, beginning with *A* again.

CHECKING YOUR SKILLS

Put these steps in order:

1. Choose a subject to write about.

2. Write down questions about the subject.

3. Read and take notes on cards.

4. Write an outline.

5. Use the outline to help you write the report.

6. Put the note cards in order.

164

3. THE SOUTHEAST TODAY

To Guide Your Reading

Look for these important words:

Key Words
- sugar cane
- soybeans
- textiles
- crude oil
- refineries
- pulp
- tourists
- tourism
- slough
- Mardi Gras

Places
- Birmingham, Alabama
- Everglades National Park
- Caribbean Sea

Look for answers to these questions:

1. Why is the Southeast growing so quickly?
2. What kinds of farming and factories are found in the Southeast?
3. Where did the ancestors of many of the people in the Southeast come from?

The Southeast is one of our country's fastest-growing regions. Many businesses move to the Southeast each year. They come because of the region's many resources. Many people move there, too. Some come for jobs. Others come for the mild climate.

Farming

The Southeast has almost anything a farmer might want. Good soil, warm weather, and lots of rain allow almost any warm-weather crop to grow here. Florida leads all other states in growing **sugar cane** and oranges. Sugar cane is a plant from which

Sugar is made from the juice of the sugar cane plant.

165

Fires in "smudge" pots set out among Florida orange tree groves
help save the crop from damaging frosts.

sugar is made. Oranges from central Florida go to orange juice factories in that state. The frozen juice is sold all over our country.

Soybeans and cotton are main crops of the Southeast. The soybean is a small bean used in many foods. Arkansas grows more rice than any other state. Georgia is our biggest peanut grower. North Carolina and Kentucky grow the most tobacco.

Farmers of the Southeast raise large numbers of beef cattle. They also raise dairy cows, hogs, and poultry. Almost half the chickens we eat come from Arkansas, Georgia, and Alabama. Florida is a leading state for beef cattle.

Manufacturing

At one time most people in the Southeast were farmers. Now most people work in manufacturing. The number of factories has grown fast in the last 20 years.

Two important industries in the Southeast are food processing and **textiles,** or cloth. Many factories process the fruits and vegetables grown in the Southeast. Other factories turn cotton and other materials into wide

Machines pick the cotton and remove its seeds. Workers lay out a pattern to cut the finished textile and turn it into clothing.

Cotton is first made into thread and wound around spools or bobbins. Then a weaving machine blends many bobbins of thread into cloth.

sheets of cloth. This cloth is turned into clothing at still other factories. The Southeast, in fact, leads the nation in the textile industry.

Minerals and Fuels

Though ships bring oil from other countries to the Southeast's ports, some oil comes from the Southeast itself. Factories in the region turn oil into many products. When oil is pumped from the earth, it is called **crude** **oil.** Factories called **refineries** change crude oil into gasoline and heating oil. Other factories make things such as plastics, paints, and textiles from oil.

Mining is another important industry in the Southeast. Millions of dollars' worth of coal, iron ore, and limestone are mined here each year. The Appalachian Mountains near **Birmingham, Alabama,** contain large amounts of these minerals. These resources have made Birmingham a steel-making center.

Lumbering

Large forests cover much of the Southeast. From these forests come lumber for building homes and oils for making paint. In the Southeast an important wood product is **pulp.** This ground-up wood mixed with water is used in making paper. More paper comes from these forests than from anywhere else in America.

The Tourist Industry

Sunny weather and interesting places draw millions of **tourists** (TUHR•uhsts), or visitors, here each year. Favorite ocean resorts are Florida's Miami Beach, South Carolina's Myrtle Beach, and Virginia Beach in Virginia. Florida's Everglades and Kentucky's Mammoth Cave are national parks of special natural beauty. Visitors explore history in places like Jamestown and Williamsburg, in Virginia. Williamsburg looks the way it did in the 1700s. The John F. Kennedy Space Center and Walt Disney World in Florida are also popular for tourists.

Tourism is the selling of goods and services to tourists. Many people in the Southeast work to provide food, shelter, information, and entertainment for visitors. You are going to read about one of these workers.

Places like Miami Beach attract tourists to Florida, the "Sunshine State."

Debby Turner, Everglades Park Guide

Debby Turner welcomes a group of students to **Everglades National Park.** Today she will lead the class on a trip in the park. Ranger Turner is a park guide. She answers questions and tells visitors about things to see and do in the park.

Ranger Turner tells the students about some of these exciting things. If they are lucky, they may see a tiny tree frog. The tree frog has suction cups on its feet. The cups let the frog hang upside down from leaves!

This playful green tree frog is right at home in an Everglades forest.

Willow and bay trees grow on "tree islands" in Everglades swamps.

The ranger leads the group along a trail. The trail is next to a freshwater **slough** (SLOO). In winter the slough is a marshy field of tall, dry grass. After lots of rain the slough becomes a wide river that flows slowly through the grass, moving south. Finally it empties into Florida Bay and the Gulf of Mexico.

Ranger Turner tells how trees fight for space to grow in the Everglades. One tree, the strangler fig, will wrap itself tightly around another tree. In time the fig will strangle the other tree. Another tree, the stopper, smells like a skunk. The unpleasant smell stops rats and mice from chewing it.

When it is time to return, the group walks slowly back along the trail. Ranger Turner stops suddenly. She points to a log by a water hole. The log starts to move. It's a live alligator!

Alligators use their feet and tails to dig water holes in the sloughs, the ranger explains. (Another name for the water holes is gator holes.) In dry times these holes are the only places with water. Fish cannot live out of water, and animals and birds need water to drink. The gator holes help all these animals and birds

169

stay alive. Of course, alligators eat everything they can get in their jaws. Many of the fish become dinner for the alligators.

Ranger Turner enjoys being a guide in the Everglades. She wants people to know how special it is. Even with its mosquitoes, she thinks there is no better place to work!

People of the Southeast Today

Many families and their ancestors have lived in the Southeast for hundreds of years. Some ancestors may have come from England, Scotland, Ireland, France, or Spain.

Many French-speaking people live in Louisiana. They, along with all the other people of New Orleans, celebrate a French holiday called **Mardi Gras** (MAHR.dee GRAH). Every year at Mardi Gras time New Orleans holds a giant carnival.

Many black people make their homes in the Southeast. Their ancestors came from Africa. These ancestors also added many things to our heritage. Their foods, music, ways of farming, and new words such as *yam, banana,* and *banjo* have made our heritage broader and richer.

Many Spanish-speaking people have settled in the Southeast

As their French-Canadian ancestors did, Cajun trappers still hunt along the Mississippi bayous, slow-moving streams near the river's mouth.

in recent years. Some are from Mexico. Most are from Cuba and other islands in the **Caribbean** (kair.uh.BEE.uhn) **Sea.** This sea is southeast of Florida.

Reading Check

1. What are some of the Southeast's most important crops?
2. What are textiles?
3. How is oil used in the Southeast's industries?
4. What unusual things might you see in the Everglades National Park?

170

CHAPTER 8 REVIEW

WORDS TO USE

Copy the sentences below. Fill in the blanks with the right words from the list.

independence   **textiles**
pulp   **tourism**
refineries

1. Americans wanted ＿＿ from England.

2. Another word for cloth is ＿＿.

3. Crude oil is changed into gasoline and heating oil in ＿＿.

4. Paper is made from wood ＿＿.

5. Selling goods and services to visitors is called ＿＿.

FACTS TO REVIEW

1. Why is the Mississippi River important to the Southeast?

2. What was the Declaration of Independence?

3. What are some products made from oil?

4. Name three products from the Southeast that use wood.

5. In what ways do people in the Southeast make a living?

IDEAS TO DISCUSS

1. Why is the Southeast important to people all over the United States?

2. Have you ever been a tourist? What are some of the things you did on your visit? Why was your visit important to the people who lived there?

3. George Washington and Thomas Jefferson were important American leaders. What do you think makes someone a leader? Who do you think are important leaders today?

⬤ SKILLS PRACTICE

Gathering Information for a Report Suppose you are asked to write a report on the Everglades National Park.

1. What are some questions you might ask about the Everglades?

2. Where could you look for answers to your questions? Where will you write the answers to your questions?

3. What should you do after putting your notes in order?

CLOSE-UP

UNITED STATES TERRITORIES AND PUERTO RICO

Did you know that you can go nearly halfway around the world and still be in the United States? Besides our 50 states, the United States has 2,300 islands. These islands are United States **territories.** They are governed by the United States. You can find these places on the map on pages 422–423. Some Pacific territories are **American Samoa** (sam•OH•uh), **Guam** (GWAHM), **Wake Island,** and the **Midway Islands.** In the Caribbean are the **U.S. Virgin Islands** and **Puerto Rico** (PWAIR•toh REE•koh). Puerto Rico is a kind of territory called a **commonwealth.** As a commonwealth, Puerto Rico governs itself.

American Samoa

Guam

Puerto Rico

U.S. Virgin Islands

Puerto Rico

Puerto Rico is an island about 1,000 miles (about 1,610 km) southeast of Florida. It has more than two-thirds of all the land in the territories. It also has about nine-tenths of all the people in the territories. All Puerto Ricans are American **citizens** (SIT•uh•zuhnz). A citizen is a member of a nation.

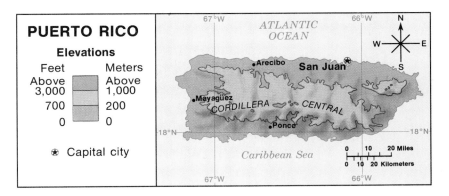

The Land and Climate

Puerto Rico is a beautiful, warm, and sunny island. Along the shore are miles of sandy beaches. All around the island's coast is a plain that measures from 5 to 12 miles (about 8 to 19 km) wide. A mountain range runs through the center of the island.

From time to time the mild weather of Puerto Rico gives way to fierce, driving storms called **hurricanes.** These storms bring strong winds and heavy rains. A hurricane can destroy trees, houses, and bridges. Long ago, Indians living in Puerto Rico named these storms Huracan (hoor•uh•KAHN). Huracan was one of their gods, the evil god of storms. Our English word *hurricane* comes from this Indian name.

173

An early Spanish settlement on Puerto Rico

Puerto Rico Long Ago

Christopher Columbus landed on Puerto Rico in 1493. Spanish settlers soon followed him. The island became the last stop for ships returning to Spain with gold from other colonies.

During its 400-year rule, Spain brought many changes to Puerto Rico. The Spanish built large sugar-cane plantations. They brought the language, religion, and laws of Spain to the island. The Spanish laid out each new town around a **plaza** (PLAH•suh), or central square, like towns in Spain.

Spain gave up Puerto Rico to the United States after a war in 1898. Yet Puerto Rico kept many parts of its Spanish heritage. It became more like the United States as well. Today Puerto Rico is a mix of Spanish and American customs.

Puerto Rico Today

What is it like to live in Puerto Rico today? In some ways it is like living in one of the 50 states. In other ways it is like being in a different country.

Like the people in the 50 states, most Puerto Ricans live in or near cities. The largest city is the capital, **San Juan** (SAN WAHN). It is on Puerto Rico's northern coast. In San Juan you will find modern apartment buildings, large stores, factories, and rush-hour traffic jams. These are things you would find in any other city in our country.

In the heart of the city is "Old San Juan." Here the buildings have been fixed up to look as they did when the Spanish built them long ago. The houses and shops have tiled roofs and floors,

174

A plaza scene in old San Juan

balconies, and shutters on the windows. Palm trees and flowers line the streets.

All over the island are signs of the new and old Puerto Rico. **Ponce** (PON•say) is a city on the southern coast. Ponce has the feeling of the old Spanish days. Yet Ponce also has some of Puerto Rico's newest and most important industries, including oil refineries and chemical plants.

More than a million people visit Puerto Rico each year. Tourism is one of the most important ways that people make a living on the island. Visitors come to Puerto Rico for its warm climate, sunny beaches, and clear, blue water.

Arecibo (ah•ray•SEE•boh) is one of the most unusual places to visit. It is the home of a large telescope. Scientists use this telescope to learn the secrets of faraway stars and planets.

For early explorers, Puerto Rico was a far frontier of the earth. Today people in Puerto Rico are exploring the vast frontier of space.

An ancient Spanish fort looks out over modern San Juan.

175

CHAPTER 9

The Great Lakes States

Start with freshwater lakes. Add rivers that run in every direction. Mix in rich farmland and lots of minerals. Add thousands of factories. What do you have? You have the Great Lakes region.

The Great Lakes region is a place where more than 45 million Americans live. Everything from cornflakes to cars is made there. In this chapter you will find out how the Great Lakes states developed into such an important region.

1. THE LAND AND ITS RESOURCES

To Guide Your Reading

Look for these important words:

Key Places
- Ohio River
- Illinois Waterway

Look for answers to these questions:

1. What landforms and bodies of water are found in the Great Lakes region?
2. How do the rivers and lakes here link the Great Lakes states with the rest of our country?
3. What are the important natural resources of this region?

Thousands of years ago, giant glaciers pushed south over the middle of our country. They flattened hills and filled in valleys with rich soil. They dug five large holes in the soft rock of the region. As the ice melted, water filled the holes, forming the five Great Lakes. These five lakes are the world's largest group of freshwater lakes.

The states lying next to the lakes are called the Great Lakes states. No mountains are in these states. Some hills are found in the north and the south, but most of the land is a plain formed by the glaciers. The flat land and good soil make this a valuable farm region. It is one of the best places

Acres and acres of fertile farmland help make Iowa our country's leading producer of corn.

in the world for growing corn, soybeans, and other crops.

Bodies of Water

Few places have the water resources equal to the Great Lakes region. Besides the Great Lakes themselves, many smaller lakes are scattered throughout the region. The northern states in the region—Minnesota, Wisconsin, and Michigan—have hundreds of these small lakes.

Small and large rivers run through all of the states. The **Ohio River** forms the boundary of three southern states in the region. They are Ohio, Illinois, and Indiana. Look at the map on page 179. Find the rivers that form the western boundary of the region. Of the five Great Lakes, which ones form the northern boundary?

These rivers and lakes are more than just places on a map. They link the Great Lakes region with the rest of the United States. They also link the region with the world. Using the New York State Barge Canal or the St. Lawrence Seaway, ships can go from Minnesota to the Atlantic Ocean.

Still another group of waterways connects Lake Michigan to

The northern forests of Minnesota are dotted with lakes. "Minnesota" comes from Indian words meaning "sky-reflecting water." Why might this state be called "the land of 10,000 lakes"?

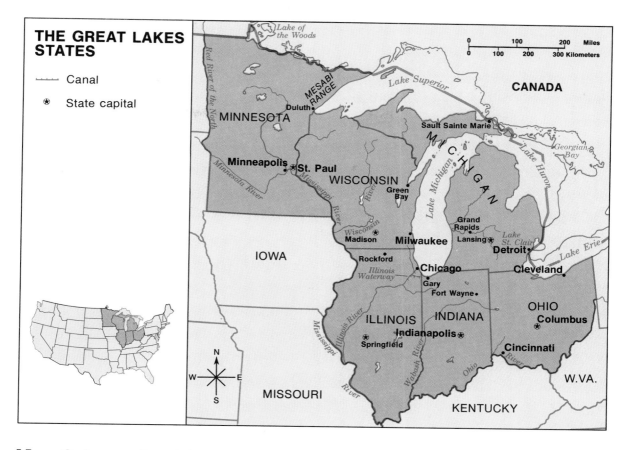

New Orleans, Louisiana. Beginning at the city of Chicago, Illinois, the **Illinois Waterway** flows along small rivers and canals to the Illinois River. This river runs into the Mississippi. Boats and barges travel the Illinois Waterway. They carry the raw materials and the finished goods of the Great Lakes states.

Climate

Summers in the Great Lakes states are mostly warm, sunny, and humid. These states have fairly high rainfall then. Much of their rain comes from the Gulf of Mexico. This rainfall helps farmers of the Great Lakes states grow many important crops.

Winters in the Great Lakes States are long, cold, and snowy. Harsh winter storms sweep down from the cold north. Cities and towns around the Great Lakes get more snow than those farther away. The Great Lakes themselves bring on this weather. The next paragraph explains why this happens.

Bodies of water always change temperature more slowly than land. In winter, the Great Lakes are not chilled as quickly as the surrounding land. The air over

179

People are drawn to Minnesota's clean air and crystal-clear lakes.
The state has wilderness areas for summer and winter recreation.

The city of Chicago is built up to the edge of Lake Michigan. Parts of
the beautiful lake front make a playground for the entire city.

the Lakes is also warm and holds much moisture. Clouds filled with this moisture blow toward the land from the Great Lakes. As the clouds hit the cooler air of the land, they give up their moisture as snow.

Natural Resources

Some people say that the Great Lakes are the region's most valuable resource. They provide water for homes and factories. They form transportation routes for goods. They also provide recreation for millions of people who enjoy boating, fishing, and swimming.

Rich soil makes the Great Lakes region one of the world's best places to farm. From this fine dark soil, Great Lakes farmers grow record amounts of corn, soybeans, and oats almost every year. Their dairy cattle graze on the thick green grass.

Large forests cover much of northern Minnesota, Wisconsin, and Michigan. They are part of a great pine forest that spreads across Canada. Farther south are scattered woodlands of oak and hickory. In the northern forests are many lakes left by the glaciers.

Many important minerals are found in the Great Lakes states. Wide layers of coal lie beneath the

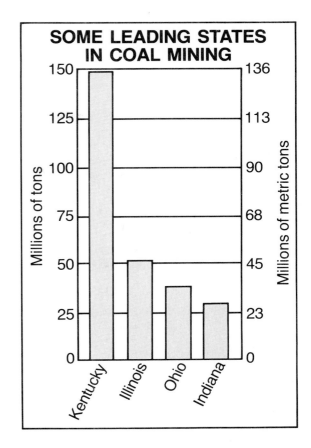

soil in Illinois and Indiana. Iron ore is mined in Minnesota, Michigan, and Wisconsin, making steel an important industry here.

Reading Check

1. How were the Great Lakes formed?
2. Name two ways a ship can get from the Great Lakes to the Atlantic Ocean.
3. Why do cities near the Great Lakes have more snow than those farther away?
4. Name three ways the Great Lakes are an important resource to their region.

2. THE GREAT LAKES STATES LONG AGO

To Guide Your Reading

Look for these important words:

Key Words	People	Places
• bartering	• Jean Du Sable	• New Salem, Illinois
• pioneers	• Abraham Lincoln	• Springfield, Illinois
• elected		
• Civil War		

Look for answers to these questions:

1. How did Chicago get its start as a major city on the Great Lakes?
2. What was the early life of Abraham Lincoln like?
3. What was the Civil War?

About 200 years ago, only a few brave people went west. They traveled along rivers in canoes, setting traps for beavers. These trappers also brought goods with them for **bartering,** or trading. They traded their goods with the Indians for beaver and other furs the Indians had. Beaver skins were valuable. People in Europe paid high prices for beaver hats.

Jean Du Sable

One of the best traders was a man named **Jean Du Sable** (ZHAHN doo SAH•bluh). Du Sable was born on the island of Haiti (HAY•tee) around 1745. Haiti was then a colony of France. Du Sable went to school in France and then went to New Orleans, Louisiana. He began traveling up the Mississippi River to work as a fur trader. He married an Indian woman and settled on a farm in Peoria, Illinois.

After settling in Illinois, Du Sable went back and forth from Canada trading furs. On his way he would stop at a certain place on Lake Michigan. It was at the mouth of a small river that ran into the lake. The Indians called it Eschikagon. Here Du Sable built a trading post and a cabin. He brought his family to live there soon after.

To gather the wild rice that grew well in the marshy areas along the Great Lakes, Indian women beat the rice into their canoes with wooden paddles.

Jean Du Sable was Chicago's first permanent citizen. When the American Revolution ended in 1781, he had already started a thriving settlement that would grow into America's second-largest city.

The trading post was in a good place. Du Sable could take his furs along the lake to be sold. He could also take his furs to rivers that ran south into the Mississippi. His fur trade grew quickly.

More trappers and traders came to this place, and a small settlement grew up. Today this place is the city of Chicago. It is now one of our country's most important centers of transportation and trade.

Young Abe Lincoln

Pioneers, or the first settlers, who came to the Great Lakes states came to farm its rich, deep soil. Some came by covered wagon or on foot. Other settlers traveled on river flatboats or rafts. From one such pioneer family came **Abraham Lincoln,** our sixteenth President.

Abe Lincoln was born in a small cabin in Kentucky. The family moved to Indiana when he was seven. For a time the Lincolns lived in a "half-faced camp." It was a shelter of just three walls facing a campfire.

Since his family was so poor, Abe worked all day in the fields. He often could not go to school, but Abe read all the books he could find. He would walk miles to get a book. At night he stayed up late to read. Sometimes he even plowed the fields with a book on the plow.

Young Abe Lincoln grew up strong and tall. He stood 6 foot 4 inches (193 cm). When Abe was in his twenties, he moved to **New Salem, Illinois.** New Salem was a tiny village near **Springfield,** soon to become the state's capital. Lincoln worked for several years in New Salem.

Today New Salem, Illinois, has a state park with the town built to look as it did in the days when Abraham Lincoln studied by firelight.

184

People liked the friendly, honest Lincoln. While in New Salem, Lincoln was **elected** to the state government. To be elected means to be chosen by vote. Lincoln also became interested in law. He studied on his own. He once walked 30 miles (about 48 km) to hear a court trial.

Abe moved to Springfield to work as a lawyer. Several years later he was elected to the U.S. Congress in Washington, D.C. Finally, he won the highest honor of all. In 1860 Abe Lincoln was elected President.

The Civil War

Lincoln became President at a dangerous time in our country's history. The country was divided about many things, including slavery. Abe Lincoln hated slavery. He often spoke against it.

Some Southern states voted to break off from the United States. They tried to form their own country. A terrible war broke out. It was called the **Civil War.**

During the Civil War battles were fought in many parts of our country. Many Americans on both sides were killed. During the war, Lincoln freed the slaves. After four long years, the war finally ended. Lincoln had kept the United States whole. It was now a free country for all.

A book-lover all his life, Abraham Lincoln reads to his youngest son, Tad. Lincoln always remembered a book he had read about another president, George Washington.

Just a few days after the war's end, Lincoln was shot and killed by a man who hated him. The entire country felt the loss of this tall, quiet, peace-loving President. Today we remember Lincoln as one of our greatest leaders.

Reading Check

1. Why did Jean Du Sable go to the Great Lakes?
2. What modern city grew up from Du Sable's trading post?
3. How did Lincoln learn enough to become a lawyer?
4. What happened during the Civil War?

JOHNNY APPLESEED

A United States stamp honoring Johnny Appleseed

Today we still get apples fresh off the tree from farms or from our own gardens.

In the early 1800s a young man left his home in Massachusetts. He headed west to Ohio, Illinois, and Indiana. His name was John Chapman.

John traveled alone. He followed Indian trails through the woods. He paddled along rivers in a canoe. At night he slept in the open. When he was hungry he picked nuts and berries. In his pack John carried apple seeds. When he saw a place he liked, he cleared the brush away and planted some apple seeds. Then he went on.

In a few years the seeds had grown into little apple trees. Sometimes John stayed a while and sold young trees. Often he left his trees for settlers to discover and enjoy. He planted 1,200 acres (about 485 ha) of his own land. It was not long before people called him Johnny Appleseed.

Sometimes Johnny wore a cooking pot for a hat and a coffee sack for a coat. He often went barefoot, even in the snow! Children loved to hear Johnny tell of his adventures. Their parents also liked Johnny and enjoyed hearing his tales.

Johnny enjoyed living in the wilderness. He did not believe in harming any living thing. Johnny once said that he was sorry he had killed a rattlesnake that had bitten him.

Johnny's apple trees are gone now, but he became an American legend. After Johnny died, many stories were told about his life. Some of them were tall tales. In fact, no one has ever proved the stories were true. Today people can visit a place set up to honor Johnny Appleseed in Fort Wayne, Indiana.

3. THE GREAT LAKES STATES TODAY

To Guide Your Reading

Look for these important words:

Key Words
- harvest
- open-pit mines
- coke
- ingots
- assembly plant
- assembly line

- metropolitan area
- location
- construction
- architects
- foundation

Places
- Central Plains

- Mesabi Range
- Detroit, Michigan
- Chicago, Illinois
- O'Hare International Airport
- Sears Tower

Look for answers to these questions:

1. What farming and manufacturing are done in the Great Lakes states?
2. How are corn and steel used in manufacturing?
3. Why is Chicago an important city?

Even though you may live far from the Great Lakes states, you have probably used something from this region in the past few hours. The farms, mines, and factories of these states provide many things you use each day.

Farming

The Great Lakes region is part of the **Central Plains.** Among the many crops grown in the rich soil here, one in particular stands out. It is corn.

The wide Corn Belt stretches from the Great Lakes states to the Plains region. You will read about this region in the next chapter. The Corn Belt grows more corn than anywhere else in the world. Most of the corn crop is used to feed farm animals. However, there is enough left for each American to eat 85 pounds (about 38 kg) of corn a year!

Corn on the cob, popcorn, and cornflakes all start out as corn seeds. Farmers plant corn in spring and **harvest,** or gather, it in late summer or autumn. Corn grows quickly. When it is ready to be picked, the plant may be 10 feet (about 3 m) tall.

187

Iowa is the leading corn grower. After Iowa, Illinois leads in corn. Grassy hills make Wisconsin the leading dairy state. Fruits and vegetables are grown in Wisconsin and Michigan and sold in cities of the Great Lakes region.

Minerals

The **Mesabi** (muh•SAHB•ee) **Range** has large mines of iron ore. These low hills are in northern Minnesota. Most of the ore lies close to the surface. Miners use giant machines to dig the ore from holes in the ground. These deep hole mines are known as **open-pit mines.**

Railroad cars or ships take the ore to steel mills. Many of the mills are near coal mines. This is why Illinois, a leading coal state, is also a leader in steel-making. Its neighbors, Ohio and Indiana, are also important in steel-making.

Manufacturing

Thousands of things are made in the Great Lakes states. To list everything would take a whole book! Just from steel come many products: tractors, cars, mattresses, and refrigerators. The list could go on and on.

The Great Lakes states are one of the world's centers of manu-

The Mesabi Range produces all of Minnesota's iron ore. About 95 percent of all iron ore used in the United States comes from Minnesota.

facturing. More than one-fourth of all our manufactured products come from these states. Here is how two raw materials—corn and steel—are made into finished products.

Making Cornflakes

To make cornflakes, dry corn kernels are first cut off the cob. Part of the kernel is ground into hominy (HOM•uh•nee). The hominy is cooked over steam for a few hours. Then vitamins are added, and the hominy is dried. A machine turns the hominy into flakes. Now the flakes are toasted in giant ovens. When cool, the cornflakes are packed into boxes and shipped to grocery stores.

Making Cars

Your family car may have begun as minerals from the Great Lakes states. The iron might have been mined in northern Minnesota. Then it might have been shipped by barge on Lake Michigan to a steel mill near Chicago.

At the mill the iron ore goes into a blast furnace with limestone and **coke.** Coke is a fuel made from coal. Limestone helps remove waste materials, and coke helps heat the ore. When these minerals get hot enough, the pure iron melts. It sinks to the bottom.

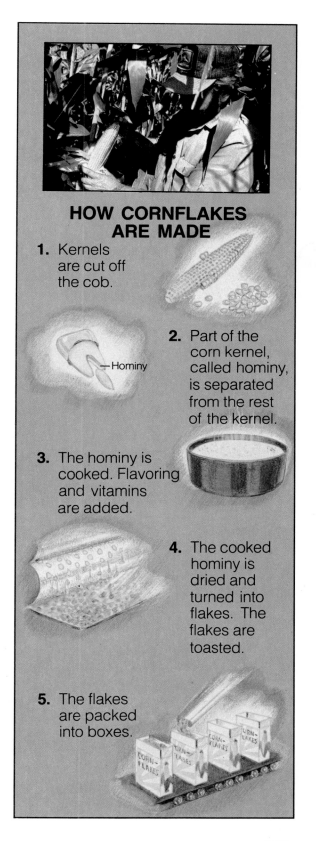

HOW CORNFLAKES ARE MADE

1. Kernels are cut off the cob.

2. Part of the corn kernel, called hominy, is separated from the rest of the kernel.

— Hominy

3. The hominy is cooked. Flavoring and vitamins are added.

4. The cooked hominy is dried and turned into flakes. The flakes are toasted.

5. The flakes are packed into boxes.

The waste materials rise to the top and are poured off.

Next, the melted, or molten, iron goes to another kind of furnace. Here it is mixed with other metals to make steel.

Molten steel is formed into blocks called **ingots.** Some ingots are squeezed through giant rollers to make sheets of steel.

These sheets of steel then go to an automobile factory. Here they are made into an automobile body. Thousands of other car parts are made in different factories. All the parts are put together, or assembled, in an **assembly plant.** Many assembly plants are in and around **Detroit, Michigan.** In fact, Detroit has been called the automobile capital of the world.

Automobiles are built on an **assembly line.** A moving belt carries the unfinished car past the workers. Each worker adds a different part. When the finished car comes off the assembly line, other workers test it. They make sure the car works properly.

Molten steel is made into sheets from which auto parts are cut. On an automobile assembly line, each worker adds a different auto part to keep the work running smoothly and quickly.

Chicago

About 45 million Americans live in the Great Lakes states. Most of these people live in the large cities on or near the Great Lakes. Some of them live in cities on large rivers. Find some of these cities on the map on page 179.

The largest city in the region is **Chicago** (shi•KAHG•oh), **Illinois.** Today almost 3 million people live in this busy city. This number of people makes Chicago the third-largest American city. Several smaller cities surround Chicago. A large city with other cities near it is a **metropolitan area.** The metropolitan area of Chicago has more than 8 million people. This is more than twice the number of people in Chicago itself.

Chicago lies near the center of our country at the southern tip of Lake Michigan. Its **location,** where it is, has made Chicago one of our busiest ports. This location has also made Chicago an important center of transportation. It is a perfect meeting place for railroads from the east and the west. Thousands of trucks travel in and out of the city each day. In Chicago **O'Hare International Airport** is the world's busiest airport.

When people drive to Chicago they can see the city long before they get there. That's because they see the city's skyscrapers. Chicago was one of the first cities to have skyscrapers. These tall buildings are sometimes 100 stories high. The **Sears Tower** in Chicago is 110 stories high. It is the tallest building in the world.

Many people are needed to plan and to build skyscrapers. One such person is Jack Kirkland, a construction worker.

The railway systems that meet in Chicago are especially important for transporting goods during the cold winter months, when many of the region's waterways freeze.

A rich heritage in city buildings and a huge steel industry made
Chicago the birthplace of the steel-framed skyscraper in the 1880s.
Some of the tallest skyscrapers can be seen here today.

Jack Kirkland, Construction Worker

Mr. Kirkland is in charge of a **construction** crew. *Construction* means building. His daughter, Patty Kirkland, asked him to explain his work to her class. When Mr. Kirkland came to class, the students had many questions to ask him.

Student: Mr. Kirkland, what does your crew do?

Mr. K.: My group welds, or joins together, the building's steel frame.

Student: How many people work on a skyscraper?

Mr. K.: We need hundreds of peo-ple. First, a group of people make a plan for the building. They are called **architects.**

Student: How long does the planning take?

Mr. K.: It often takes more than a year. The architects must be sure the building will be strong. It has to stand up against the strongest winds. Every part of the building must be just the right size.

The next step is to dig the building's **foundation.** The foundation is the base. For a skyscraper the workers may dig a very deep foundation. It may go down more than ten stories. When the foundation is dug, we can start building up. Workers use cranes to lift the parts into place. Other workers, like my

Construction workers follow hundreds of instructions to build a skyscraper.

group, weld the steel frame together. Electricians put in wires for electricity. Plumbers put in pipes. Carpenters, painters, and many other workers finish the building.

Student: Is it dangerous to work on a skyscraper?

Mr. K.: Working at a thousand feet above the ground can scare the bravest person. We have ways to protect ourselves. We wear safety belts and shoes with rubber soles. You will always see us with our hard hats on. If a hammer falls from above, it will bounce off the hat.

Student: Mr. Kirkland, what do you like most about your job?

Mr. K.: I like to see the building go up a little higher each day. When it is all done, though, I get a thrill just driving past our building.

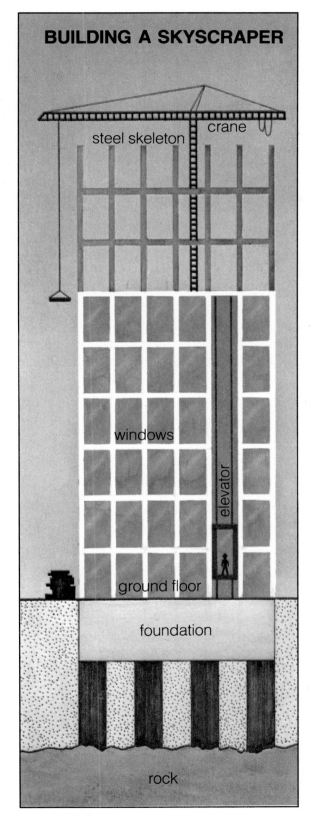

BUILDING A SKYSCRAPER

steel skeleton

crane

windows

elevator

ground floor

foundation

rock

193

Some cheeses in Wisconsin are made from recipes brought from Europe.

A museum in Blue Mound, Wisconsin, displays tools Norwegian immigrants used.

People of the Great Lakes States

As in other regions, the people of the Great Lakes states come from many different backgrounds. They have their family roots in countries all over the world. The ancestors of some families were Scottish and Irish pioneers who came through the Cumberland Gap.

Immigrants from other countries settled in the Great Lakes region a little later. These immigrants named their towns for the countries from which they came. Some even made the towns look like places in Europe. You can still find towns here with names like Germantown, Holland, Poland, and Russiaville. What countries do you think some of the immigrants to this region were from?

Reading Check

1. What is the main crop of the Great Lakes states?
2. What are two minerals that come from the Great Lakes states?
3. How are cars made on an assembly line?
4. What makes Chicago a major transportation center?

194

SKILLS FOR SUCCESS

READING FLOW CHARTS

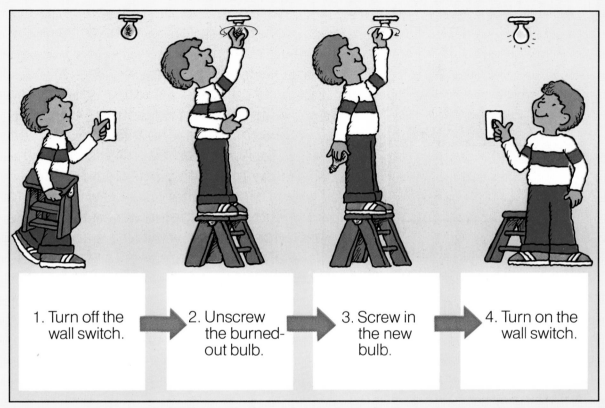

1. Turn off the wall switch. → 2. Unscrew the burned-out bulb. → 3. Screw in the new bulb. → 4. Turn on the wall switch.

Have you ever built a model or baked bread? If you have, you had to do the steps in the right order. You probably followed directions or a recipe.

Many tasks have a number of steps. Here is a step-by-step list for safely changing a light bulb.

1. Turn off the wall switch.
2. Unscrew the burned-out bulb.
3. Screw in the new bulb.
4. Turn on the wall switch.

The drawing at the top of the page is one way to show the order of these steps. You read the pictures from left to right. Another way to show how to do something is by drawing a **flow chart.** A flow chart is a drawing that shows the order in which a list of steps should be done. Above is a flow chart made from the list.

The arrows tell you to read the chart from left to right. The arrow on the left gives the first step. What is the last step?

STEPS IN BUILDING A SKYSCRAPER

1
Architects plan building.

2
Workers dig foundation.

3
Workers weld steel frame together.
Cranes are used to lift parts into place.

4
Electricians put in wires.
Plumbers put in pipes.

5
Carpenters, painters, and other workers finish the building.

Some flow charts have arrows that point down a page. You would then read the chart from top to bottom. Look at the flow chart on this page. It shows how a skyscraper is built. Do you read the chart from left to right or from top to bottom?

Besides following the arrows, you can also sometimes follow the numbers in a flow chart. The chart on this page has five numbered steps. How many steps does the flow chart on page 195 have?

Books often use flow charts to show the order in which things are done. When you read a flow chart, always remember to follow the arrows and the numbered steps.

CHECKING YOUR SKILLS

Use the flow chart on this page to answer these questions.

1. What is the first step in putting up a skyscraper? What is the last step?

2. When is the foundation dug, after step 1 or after step 3?

3. Which step comes first, putting in water pipes or building the outside of the skyscraper?

4. Make your own flow chart showing the steps in which you do some everyday job, such as washing dishes, cleaning your room, or mowing the lawn.

CHAPTER 9 REVIEW

WORDS TO USE

Write the numbers 1 to 5 on your paper. Use the words from the list to fill in the blanks. Write the words on your paper.

Civil War   **pioneers**
elected   **Springfield**
Abraham Lincoln

Our sixteenth President, (_____)(1), was born in a log cabin in Kentucky. He and his family later moved to Indiana with some of the first settlers, or (_____)(2). When in his twenties, Lincoln moved to a town near (_____)(3), the present state capital of Illinois. There the people of Illinois chose him by vote, which (_____)(4) him to the state government. Lincoln later became a member of the U.S. Congress and then President of the United States. During his term as President, Americans fought the (_____)(5).

FACTS TO REVIEW

1. Name two ways glaciers shaped the Great Lakes states.

2. How do products from the Great Lakes region reach other parts of the world?

3. Why are the Great Lakes states good for farming?

4. How did Chicago begin?

5. Why did the Civil War begin?

6. What state leads in growing corn? What state leads in dairy farms?

7. How is most corn used?

8. How do miners get iron ore from the Mesabi Range?

9. Why are many cars made in the Great Lakes states?

10. Why does Chicago's location make this city important?

IDEAS TO DISCUSS

The cities of the Great Lakes region have many large factories. What are some good things about having so many factories in one place? What do you think some problems might be?

○ SKILLS PRACTICE

Reading Flow Charts Make a flow chart showing how cornflakes are made. Write at least four steps. Look back to page 189 for help.

CHAPTER 10

The Plains States

About this chapter

What did you have for breakfast this morning? Did you have cereal? Did you have bread or sausages? The chances are good that some of your breakfast came from the Plains states. These six states make up one of the world's best farming and ranching areas.

Farming and ranching were not always in this area, however. In this chapter you will read how the Plains states changed when pioneers and the railroad moved in. You will discover what industries are important to the region now and why this region is important to the United States.

198

1. THE LAND AND ITS RESOURCES

To Guide Your Reading

Look for these important words:

Key Words
- monument
- gateway
- groundwater
- windmills
- tornadoes
- hailstorms

Places
- St. Louis, Missouri
- Interior Plains
- Central Plains
- Great Plains
- Black Hills
- Badlands
- Mississippi River
- Missouri River

Look for answers to these questions:

1. How does the land change from east to west in the Plains states?
2. What bodies of water are found here?
3. What is the climate of the Plains states?

Let's take a make-believe car trip across the Plains states. Our starting point will be **St. Louis, Missouri.** A huge arch stands along the Mississippi River in St. Louis, Missouri. The arch is the tallest **monument** in the United States. A monument is something that is built to remind people of the past. The arch in St. Louis is in the form of a **gateway,** or entrance. It reminds us that St. Louis was the "Gateway to the West." It was the city many pioneers passed through on their way west. Now as you head west from St. Louis, fields of corn, oats, and soybeans stretch out for as far as you can see.

Trappers, explorers, railroad workers, and settlers passed through St. Louis on their way west. The Gateway Arch is a symbol of their starting point.

As you travel farther west you see a new crop in the flat fields. It is wheat. You see miles and miles of it. There is wheat to the north, south, east, and west.

Now the land begins to become hilly. Not much rain or snow falls here. You see herds of beef cattle and sheep. Your car trip ends as you reach the foothills of the Rocky Mountains. You traveled about 700 miles (about 1,125 km), passing through one of the great farming and ranching areas of the United States.

The Plains states lie within the **Interior Plains.** The Interior Plains can be divided into the **Central Plains** and the **Great Plains.** On the Central Plains corn and tall grasses grow well. On the Great Plains, however, only short grasses and wheat can grow. Missouri and Iowa are two of the Plains states in the Central Plains. The rest of the Plains states—Kansas, Nebraska, South Dakota, and North Dakota—lie mostly on the Great Plains. The land here is quite dry. Much of this land is used for raising beef cattle and sheep.

The Plains states are not perfectly flat. Most of the land has

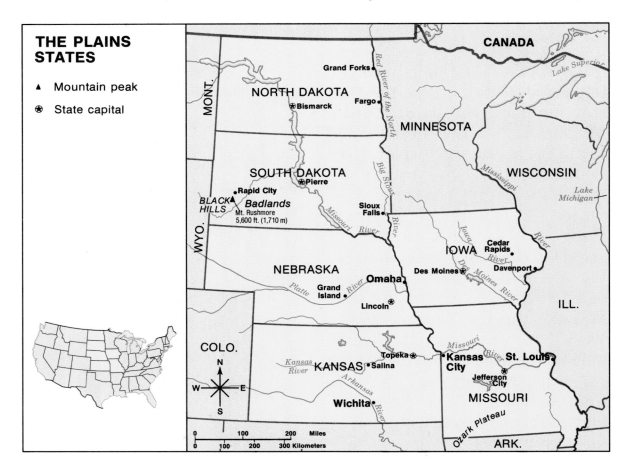

THE PLAINS STATES

▲ Mountain peak

✹ State capital

Forbidding but beautiful, the Badlands got their name by being difficult barriers to travel and impossible lands to farm.

a gentle roll. In South Dakota the **Black Hills** rise to more than 7,000 feet (about 2,130 m). These pine-covered hills are the highest place in the Plains states.

East of the Black Hills is a stretch of dry land called the **Badlands.** The country is rugged and wild here. Few plants grow. Millions of years of erosion and strong winds carved strange shapes in the hills. No pioneers settled here as they moved west. Why might you suppose they would call this the Badlands?

Bodies of Water

Rivers great and small cross the Plains. The **Mississippi** and the **Missouri** rivers are the two largest.

The Mississippi forms the eastern boundary of the Plains states. The Missouri River joins the Mississippi near St. Louis, Missouri. The Missouri begins more than 2,000 miles (about 3,220 km) away in the Rocky Mountains. It crosses the Great Plains on its way to the Mississippi. Look at the map on page

200. Through which states does the Missouri River flow?

Besides using water from their rivers, people of the Plains states use **groundwater** also. Groundwater is the water beneath the Earth's surface. Farmers and ranchers use pumps to bring the water from wells. Some of the pumps are driven by **windmills.** Windmills have wide blades set in the shape of a wheel. When a wind strikes the blades, the wheel turns. The turning wheel makes a pump work. The pump pulls up the groundwater. With windmills farmers make use of the

Early windmills were used to grind grain. In America they are used to pump water.

strong winds that often blow across the Plains.

Climate

Because the Plains states cover such a large area, the northern and southern states of this region have different climates. In the north winters are long and cold. Wild storms sometimes roar down from Canada, bringing snow and freezing temperatures. In the southern states winters are not so cold. The summers are longer and can be very hot.

The farther east you live in the Plains states, the more precipitation there is. In the Central Plains there is enough precipitation for crops and forests.

The Great Plains are drier. The Rocky Mountains are so high they block a great deal of rain coming from the Pacific Ocean. For most crops except wheat, not enough rain falls in the Great Plains.

The weather in the Plains states can change quickly. In this region cold winds from the North Pole meet warm, moist air from the Gulf of Mexico. When cold and warm air meet, huge storms can develop.

Every spring and summer **tornadoes** (tawr•NAY•dohz), or "twisters," form over the Plains region. A tornado is a tall, dry funnel of whirling wind. This

When a tornado threatens, many people in the Plains states go into their basements or cellars for protection.

funnel travels with the narrowest part near the ground. The bottom of the funnel can be as wide as a house. When the funnel touches the ground, it can blow apart houses and overturn cars and trucks. When a tornado goes through a town, some houses will be ruined while others across the street might remain unharmed.

Hailstorms also threaten the region. These storms drop pieces of ice that can ruin crops. The pieces of ice beat the crops to the ground, breaking the stalks or crushing the grain. Some of these pieces can be as large as marbles or even golf balls. Believe it or not, hailstorms often happen in warm spring weather!

Reading Check

1. What crop grows best on the Central Plains? On the Great Plains?
2. What is the highest place in the Plains states? In what state is it?
3. In what ways do the people of the Plains states get water?
4. How is the climate different in the Central Plains and the Great Plains?

203

SKILLS FOR SUCCESS

USING ROAD MAPS

A **road map** shows drivers how to get from one place to another. This road map shows a part of Iowa. The map key helps you read the map. It lists different kinds of highways that are on the map.

Interstate highways go through more than one state. The symbol shows these routes. The number of the highway is inside the symbol. No stop signs or stoplights are on interstate highways.

United States highways also go from state to state. The number of the highway is inside the ⑥ symbol.

State highways connect places inside one state. The highway number is inside the ⑤ symbol.

How do you find your way from one place to another? First, you must find both places on the map. Then run your finger along the highways that connect them. Look for the highway numbers.

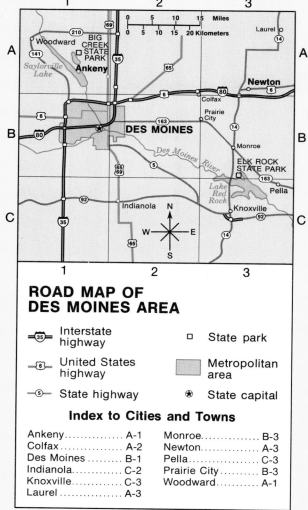

ROAD MAP OF DES MOINES AREA

- ⧼35⧽ Interstate highway
- ◦⑥ United States highway
- ◦⑤ State highway
- ▢ State park
- ▨ Metropolitan area
- ✸ State capital

Index to Cities and Towns

Ankeny	A-1	Monroe	B-3
Colfax	A-2	Newton	A-3
Des Moines	B-1	Pella	C-3
Indianola	C-2	Prairie City	B-3
Knoxville	C-3	Woodward	A-1
Laurel	A-3		

CHECKING YOUR SKILLS

Use the map to answer these questions.

1. What kind of highway is Highway 35?

2. Use the map grid. What cities are in box C–3?

3. You are traveling from Knoxville to Laurel. Will you go north or south on ⑭ ?

4. What is one way to travel from Indianola to Prairie City?

2. THE PLAINS STATES LONG AGO

To Guide Your Reading

Look for these important words:

Key Words
- bison
- treaties

People
- Buffalo Bill
- Sitting Bull
- George Custer

Look for answers to these questions:

1. What were some of the problems between the Indians and the pioneers?
2. In what ways did the settlers and the railroads change the Plains states?
3. Why did many Indians leave the Great Plains?

Farms and ranches cover the Great Plains today, but it was not always this way. About 130 years ago few farms or ranches were here. Roads were mere wagon tracks across wide, open grasslands. Millions of **bison** (BYS•uhn), or buffalo, lived on the Great Plains.

In those days most of the people who lived here were American Indians. The Sioux (SOO) were a large group. The Dakota, Kansa, Iowa, and Missouri Indians were part of the Sioux family. The places where they lived are now the states that were named after them.

The Indians of the Great Plains depended on the buffalo. They used almost every part of the

Indians painted picture signs on buffalo skins. The Indian chief in this painting wears such a painted buffalo robe.

animal. They ate buffalo meat. They made bedding and tepees from buffalo hides. They used buffalo bones to make tools.

The buffalo gave the Plains Indians almost everything they needed. What would happen if the buffalo disappeared?

The Railroads and the Hunters

When Lincoln was President, Americans were building a railroad from the Atlantic to the Pacific. One railroad company began building from the Pacific coast. The other started in Omaha, Nebraska.

Thousands of workers helped build the railroad. They all had to be fed. The railroad companies decided to feed them with buffalo meat. The railroads hired hunters to shoot enough buffalo to feed the railroad workers.

The most famous buffalo hunter was a man named William Cody. A railroad company hired him at $500 a month to kill 12 buffalo a day. Few people called Bill Cody by his real name. Everyone called him by his nickname. It was **Buffalo Bill.**

Buffalo were so numerous that trains were often stopped for hours while a herd rumbled across the tracks. Sometimes a million or more would be on the move across the Great Plains.

Sitting Bull

Later many more hunters killed almost all the buffalo. Indians had a hard time finding food. They also became angry at losing their land to the settlers who were coming to the Great Plains. Hundreds of settlers were killed. The U.S. army moved to stop the Indians. Little by little, many Indians were pushed farther into the Black Hills of South Dakota.

To try to bring peace to the Plains, the United States government signed **treaties** with the Indians. A treaty is a written agreement. One of these treaties promised the Black Hills to the Sioux Indians. No settlers were to move onto this land. This treaty was broken when miners discovered gold in the Black Hills. The Indians prepared for war.

One of the Indian leaders was Chief **Sitting Bull.** With him were about 2,500 Indian fighters. They made a camp by the Little Bighorn River in Montana. This river is near the western edge of the Great Plains.

The U.S. government ordered the Indians to move onto reservations. The Indians refused. Several groups of soldiers started to move against the Sioux. The leader of one group of soldiers was General **George Custer.** He and his soldiers marched to the Little Bighorn River to fight the Indians there. The Indians were prepared for the attack. Custer and all of his men were killed. Today this battle is sometimes called "Custer's Last Stand."

The Indians had few victories after Custer's Last Stand. More soldiers were sent to the plains. The Indians were soon defeated. The government moved them to reservations.

As the Indians left the Great Plains, more settlers moved westward. They were not only from the eastern United States. The pioneers also came from Europe. Many came from Russia, Czechoslovakia (chek•uh•sloh•VAH•kee•uh), Norway, Sweden, and Denmark. The pioneers plowed the prairie of the Great Plains. Corn and wheat replaced the grass. Cattle replaced the buffalo. The railroads brought the cattle and the crops of the plains to market.

Reading Check

1. What did the buffalo provide the Plains Indians?
2. Who was William Cody and why is he well known?
3. Why did the building of the railroad hurt the Plains Indians?
4. Why were treaties with the Plains Indians broken?

SETTLERS ON THE PLAINS

Nebraska pioneers
and the family cow

Crunch! Clomp! Crunch!

Something was walking on top of the house. The children looked up from their lessons. Pieces of dirt were falling from the ceiling.

"The cow's on the roof again," cried their mother. "Run outside and chase her off!"

This was an everyday event among pioneer families on the plains. When settlers moved to the plains, many had to build **dugouts.** A dugout was a house dug into a hillside. The roof was built of **sod,** a layer of grass-covered earth. Sometimes the family cow wandered from the hillside onto the grassy roof!

The settlers had to face many dangers. During the hot summers fires often swept across the plains. In some years, great clouds of grasshoppers came. They could eat up a wide field of wheat in a few hours.

The nearest store might be 100 miles (about 160 km) away. Pioneer women and girls had to know how to make soap, candles, and clothing. They learned to **preserve,** or keep, foods in the Indian way, such as by drying thin strips of meat in the sun.

The pioneer woman had to take care of the farm and the whole family. Without doctors nearby, a woman on the plains learned to treat snakebites, broken bones, and illnesses. If no schools were near, she taught her children.

Life on the Great Plains could be lonely. Neighbors lived miles apart. Everyone in a family worked hard all day long. After dinner, they might entertain each other with songs or stories.

3. THE PLAINS STATES TODAY

To Guide Your Reading

Look for these important words:

Key Words
- grain elevators
- thresh
- chaff
- combines
- winter wheat
- spring wheat
- meat-packing plants
- county seat
- county

Places
- Goodland, Kansas

Look for answers to these questions:

1. How has farming changed in the Plains states?
2. What kinds of manufacturing have developed in the Plains region?
3. What natural resources are here?
4. Why are there more small towns than large cities in the Plains region?

Like tall skyscrapers, **grain elevators** tower above the plains. These elevators store the tons of grain harvested in the Plains states. From here the grain is shipped to factories to be turned into cereals and other foods.

Why can the Plains states grow so much food? One reason is that the soil is rich. Another is that the land is level. The fields are big and flat enough to grow large amounts of crops. Still another reason is the climate. In the eastern plains the climate is just right for corn. In the western plains it is right for wheat. Finally, farm machines and new ways of farming have changed farm work.

From grain elevators, grain may be sold to flour mills or to overseas markets.

Combined harvester-threshers, or combines, allow today's farmers to do more work in much less time than it took 100 years ago.

Wheat Farming

Wheat farming has changed greatly over the years. Farmers used to plow their fields with horses and mules. They planted seeds by hand. When the plants were ripe, farmers had to cut and **thresh** the wheat. To thresh is to separate the wheat from the **chaff.** The chaff is the outside cover of the grain. Even with horse-drawn machines, it took farmers many hours to plow, plant, cut, and thresh a field of wheat.

Farmers today use machines to prepare the soil and to plant seeds. To harvest the wheat, farmers use huge machines called **combines.** A combine cuts and threshes the wheat all at once.

Today's wheat farmers use better seeds and fertilizers than in the past. They have learned to grow two kinds of wheat also, **winter wheat** and **spring wheat.** Winter wheat grows in the southern Great Plains. It is planted in the fall. The plants grow until winter comes. When spring comes, they start to grow again. In summer, the crop is harvested. Spring wheat grows in the northern Great Plains. It

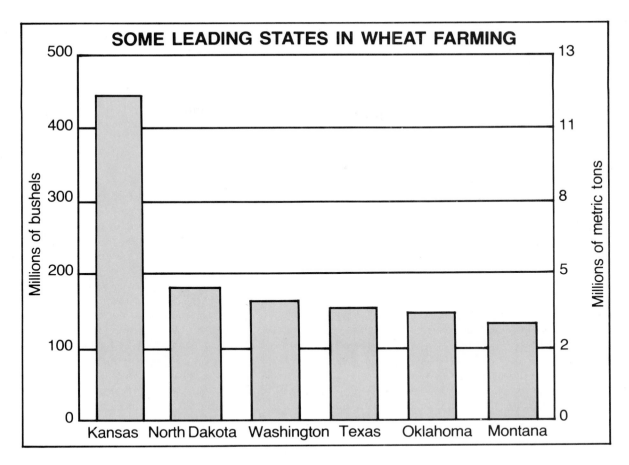

SOME LEADING STATES IN WHEAT FARMING

Millions of bushels — Kansas, North Dakota, Washington, Texas, Oklahoma, Montana — Millions of metric tons

cannot live through cold winters. Spring wheat is planted in spring and harvested in summer.

Not only does wheat from the Great Plains feed Americans, but it also feeds many other people around the world. Kansas and North Dakota grow more wheat than any other states.

Beef Cattle and Sheep

Cattle and sheep ranches spread out over Nebraska, Kansas, North Dakota, and South Dakota. In some parts of these states the land is too hilly for growing wheat. Cattle and sheep graze on the short grass there.

One kind of grass that grows on the prairie is buffalo grass. It is one of the best kinds of grasses to feed a herd. In summer the cattle and sheep eat the green grass. In winter they eat the dry brown grass that is left. When snow covers the ground, ranchers put out hay for the animals.

Manufacturing

You have read that wheat, corn, and cattle are important products of the Plains states.

211

These tractors and farm machinery are for sale in a Plains state.
Why would it be useful to have farm machine factories in this region?

What kind of manufacturing do you think is important here?

Since so much grain and meat come from the Plains states, food processing is an important industry. Factories in these states turn grain into breakfast cereals. Wheat is also ground into flour in large flour mills. Much of the flour is shipped to bakeries where it is made into bread.

Meat-packing plants turn meat into hot dogs and cold cuts. Sides of beef go from the plants to supermarkets. Kansas City, Missouri, and Omaha, Nebraska, are meat-packing centers.

The Plains states make more than food products. They also make farm machines. Such machines as tractors and combines are used on farms all over the Plains states. Factories in Des Moines (dih•MOYN), Iowa, make many of them.

You might not think of this, but small airplanes are also useful in the Plains region. Some doctors and lawyers use planes to cover the many miles between small towns. Wichita (WICH•uh•taw), Kansas, makes more small airplanes than any other city in our country.

212

Minerals and Fuels

The rich soil of the Plains region provides several minerals and fuels. South Dakota has the largest gold mine in the country. North Dakota has large amounts of coal and oil. Many of the Plains states produce cement, sand, and gravel, as well as oil.

People of the Plains States

Most of the land in the Plains states is used for farming or ranching. Yet most of the people in this region are not farmers or ranchers. They live and work in cities and towns.

There are fewer large cities on the Plains than in most regions. Instead there are many small towns. **Goodland, Kansas,** is one of these towns.

Goodland is a small town of about 6,000 people. It is an important center for the people who live around it. It has an airport and a modern hospital. It also has three large parks and a new library.

Goodland is also the **county seat** of Sherman County. A county seat is a town or city that

The school bell of the first schoolhouse in Goodland sits in front of the county seat building.

Raising a calf is hard work, but winning first prize makes it all worthwhile.

Furniture of a pioneer is displayed at the county's historical museum.

is the center of government for a **county.** A county is part of a state. It includes towns and other communities. Each county has its own government, which builds roads and makes sure laws are obeyed.

Like many towns in the Plains states, Goodland holds a county fair each summer. Large crowds enjoy games, animal shows, and calf-roping matches. Some people come to see new farm machines.

Sometimes when people come to Goodland, they go to the county's historical museum. On display at the museum are costumes worn by the early settlers of the state. Tools, furniture, and all the other things people used long ago are also displayed. Visitors can see pictures of farmers living in sod houses, and the railroad that people rode on their way to Goodland. Many of the early settlers were the ancestors of people still living in Goodland.

Reading Check

1. Where is grain stored?
2. What does a combine do?
3. What do cattle graze on?
4. Why is Goodland, Kansas, important to the county?

214

SKILLS FOR SUCCESS

READING NEWSPAPERS

The newspaper's city room is buzzing with activity. As they do every day, people are rushing about. Reporters sit at their desks, writing their stories on computers. The editor calls a reporter over. "I heard about a woman who has started a construction company. Why don't you go see her and get the story?"

In a few hours you can read the story in the newspaper.

ST. LOUIS MOTHER TURNS TO BUILDING HOMES

By Robert Nicholas

ST. LOUIS——For the past five years a St. Louis woman has been running her own construction company. Susan Malcolm has repaired 15 homes in that time. All of the buildings are in the Soulard part of the city. Mrs. Malcolm has also continued to raise her five children during those five years.

First comes the **headline.** Headlines are in large letters to catch your eye. Next is the **byline,** in smaller letters. The byline tells who wrote the story. At the begin-

Reporters work quickly to gather the latest information for news stories.

ning of the story is the **dateline.** It tells where the story was written. What is the headline of this story? What name is in the byline? What is the dateline?

Reporters write their stories so people can get the news quickly. The first part of a news story has the most important information. Each paragraph that follows tells more about what happened.

The first paragraph usually tells *who, what, when,* and *where.* In

215

Mrs. Malcolm said she talked to people and did research before going into business. "My family gave me a lot of help, too," she said. "They understood how much I really wanted to do it."

Soulard is one of the oldest parts of St. Louis. Many people from Germany settled there about 150 years ago. They built many large brick houses. Mrs. Malcolm said she has always cared about the neighborhood. She wanted to fix up the charming old buildings.

this story, the *who* is Susan Malcolm. The *what* is that she runs her own construction company and has repaired 15 houses. *When* is during the past five years. *Where* is Soulard, a part of St. Louis.

The second and third paragraphs tell more about Mrs. Malcolm. They help answer the questions *how* and *why.*

Most news stories are written in this way. They have the same parts as the article you just read.

CHECKING YOUR SKILLS

1. Here are the parts of a news story from a school newspaper. The parts are not in the right order. Read the parts carefully. Think about how the story should be set up. Write the letters of the parts in the order you decide is best.

a. Jean Levi and Wally Rogers were elected to the Drew School student council yesterday. The two fourth-grade students are the youngest members of the student council.

b. FOURTH GRADERS WIN ELECTION

c. Drew School

d. The results of the election surprised many of us. Few students expected the fourth graders to win.

e. By Marsha Ferrin

f. Jean said they won "because we worked hard on school projects." They plan to start other projects at Drew School.

2. Now identify the *who, what, when,* and *where* in the first paragraph of the above news story you put in order.

CHAPTER 10 REVIEW

WORDS TO USE

Copy the paragraph below. Fill in the blanks with the right words from the list.

chaff
combine
grain elevators
thresh
windmills

Plains farmers sometimes use (_____)(1) to pump groundwater to their crops. After wheat is grown, farmers must cut and (_____)(2) it. The farmers separate the wheat from the (_____)(3). Today wheat farmers use a large machine called a (_____)(4). They store wheat in (_____)(5).

FACTS TO REVIEW

1. Why is corn grown on the Central Plains? Why is wheat grown on the Great Plains?

2. Why was the buffalo important to the Plains Indians?

3. How did the coming of the railroad change life in the Plains states?

4. Why are cattle raised in the western Great Plains?

5. Why was St. Louis, Missouri, called the "Gateway to the West"?

IDEAS TO DISCUSS

1. Only 1 out of 30 Americans is a farmer or a rancher. Yet American farmers and ranchers raise more food than our country uses. How can a rather small number of people grow so much food?

2. Which would you expect to find in a Plains city, a meat-packing plant or a steel mill? Why?

◯ SKILLS PRACTICE

1. **Using Road Maps** Look back at the map on page 204. You are going from Des Moines to Elk Rock State Park.

   a. What is the shortest way?
   b. On what kind of highway will you travel?

2. **Reading Newspapers** Find a short newspaper article and paste it on a sheet of paper. Label the headline, the byline, and the dateline. Then find and label the *who, what, when, where, why,* and *how* parts.

217

CHAPTER 11

The Southwest

About
this
chapter

"The wide, open spaces," "black gold," long-horn cattle, mysterious Indian ruins. All these things are important parts of the Southwest. Yet the Southwest is also a region of modern cities and industries.

You will come to know the Southwest's colorful past as well as its busy present as you read this chapter. You will also begin to understand how the Southwest is different from the other regions you have read about.

1. THE LAND AND ITS RESOURCES

To Guide Your Reading

Look for these important words:

Key Words
- mesas
- saguaro cactus
- yucca
- cloudburst

Places
- Colorado Plateau
- Sonoran Desert
- Chihuahuan Desert
- Rio Grande
- Sun Belt

Look for answers to these questions:

1. What landforms are in the Southwest?
2. How did rivers shape the land?
3. Why is the Southwest a good ranching and farming area?
4. What is unusual about the climate in the Southwest?

Some people think that the Southwest is mostly a desert. Though it is true that big deserts are here, the Southwest has many other kinds of land. Under the sunny Southwest skies lie towering, snow-capped mountains and lush pine forests. There are rainy plains, fertile river valleys, and rocky canyons in brilliant colors! All over the world, people still think of this land as "the wide, open spaces."

The Southwest is a larger region than the Northeast and the Great Lakes states put together. Yet it has only four states. They are Arizona, New Mexico, Oklahoma, and Texas.

The Rocky Mountains and the Colorado Plateau

The highest parts of the region are the Rocky Mountains and the **Colorado Plateau.** The Colorado Plateau begins at the western edge of the Rocky Mountains. This huge plateau covers much of northern New Mexico and Arizona. The Colorado Plateau gets its name from the Colorado River, which runs through it. Very little rain falls on this rough land.

Rivers like the Colorado have cut deep canyons in the plateau. At one time the Colorado River was wider. Over many years it wore away the rock to form the Grand Canyon.

The rivers have also helped make flat-topped hills called **mesas** (MAY•suhz). *Mesa* is the Spanish word for table. Spanish explorers were the first people from Europe to see these hills. As they looked across the open land, the mesas must have reminded them of tabletops!

The Great Plains

As the Great Plains stretch west to the Rockies, the land gets higher. The highest part of the plains is in the Southwest. Cattle and sheep graze on the short grass that grows here. In fact, this is some of the world's best cattle country.

The land gets lower south of the Great Plains. This flat land is part of the Coastal Plain that stretches from the Northeast across much of the Southeast. A warm climate and plenty of rain make this part of the Coastal Plain good for farming.

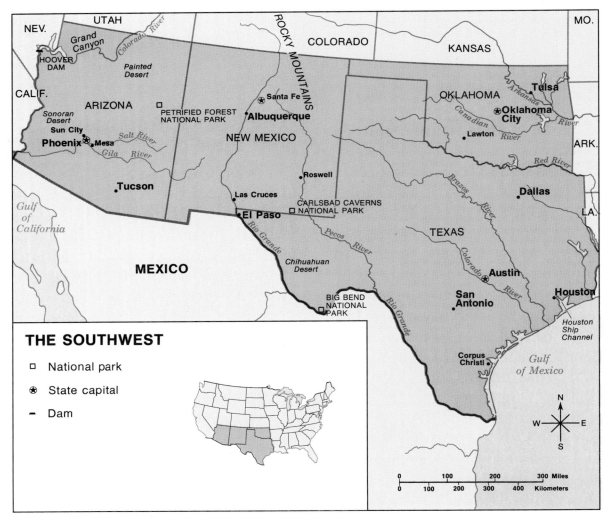

THE SOUTHWEST

□ National park

✴ State capital

- Dam

The Sonoran and Chihuahuan Deserts

The **Sonoran Desert** is one of the world's most beautiful deserts. In no other desert are there so many kinds of cactuses. The largest is the **saguaro** (sah•GWAH•roh) **cactus.** The saguaro is a giant plant. It may grow taller than 50 feet (about 15 m) high. Its secret is that it can store almost any rain that falls. About three-quarters of the plant is water.

Miles of white sand dunes cover the northern part of the **Chihuahuan Desert.** One plant that grows in this desert is the **yucca** (YUHK•uh). Some sand

Sometimes only the yucca's top shows above a sand dune. Yuccas can grow almost anywhere in the West.

The Sonoran Desert in southwest Arizona has several wilderness preserves that protect its rare animals and plants.

221

dunes are as high as a five-story building. As the sand dunes get higher, the yucca keeps growing.

Bodies of Water

High in the Rocky Mountains snow melts to form rivers. The Colorado River is the largest one that flows into the Southwest. The second largest is the **Rio Grande.** These two rivers flow in different directions. The Colorado flows southwest to the Gulf of California. The Rio Grande flows southeast and empties into the Gulf of Mexico.

Climate

The Southwest is a land of sun and warm temperatures. It is part of the **Sun Belt,** a wide area of sunny and mild weather. The Sun Belt stretches from Virginia through the Southwest and into southern California.

Not all of the Southwest is dry, however. Eastern Texas gets a lot of rain. Heavy snow falls on New Mexico's mountains in winter.

When it does rain in the dry places, sometimes it really pours! The sky may suddenly get dark. Then a **cloudburst,** or a sudden hard rain, may quickly flood the

Six million years ago the Colorado River's rippling waters began to carve through the colored rock to create the Grand Canyon.

With thunder, lightning, and sheets of rain, a cloudburst sweeps across a vast desert landscape in the Southwest.

canyons. Cloudbursts wear away the rock and earth. During a cloudburst half a year's rain may fall in a few moments.

Natural Resources

Beneath the sandy soil of the Coastal Plain are large pools of oil. Oil is also found underground beneath the Gulf of Mexico.

Other fuels are important in this region. Natural gas is produced in Texas, New Mexico, and Oklahoma. Coal is found in New Mexico and Oklahoma. New Mexico also supplies about half of our country's uranium.

Two valuable minerals, copper and potash, are mined in the desert areas of this region. Potash is used in fertilizers.

Reading Check

1. How did the Colorado Plateau get its name?
2. What makes the Sonoran Desert different from other deserts?
3. Why do crops grow well on the Coastal Plain in Texas?
4. Where is the Sun Belt?

SKILLS FOR SUCCESS

USING TRANSIT MAPS

Most cities have **transit systems.** These are buses or trains that people use in their community. **Transit maps** show where trains or buses travel and stop. Look at this map of downtown Phoenix, Arizona.

The green line shows the route of the Washington-Jefferson bus. Buses on Washington only go west. Buses on Jefferson only go east. What are the other bus routes?

Suppose you are starting at Washington Street and Central Avenue. You want to go to Seventh Avenue and Van Buren Street. You could ride the Washington-Jefferson bus west to Seventh Avenue. Then you would **transfer,** or change, to the Seventh Avenue bus. This bus would take you north to Van Buren Street.

CHECKING YOUR SKILLS

Use the map to answer these questions.

1. You are riding the Central Avenue bus from Van Buren Street to the public library. In which direction are you going?

2. To go from the State Capitol Building to Patriot's Park, what bus would you take?

3. To go from the public library to the State Capitol Building, what two buses would you take?

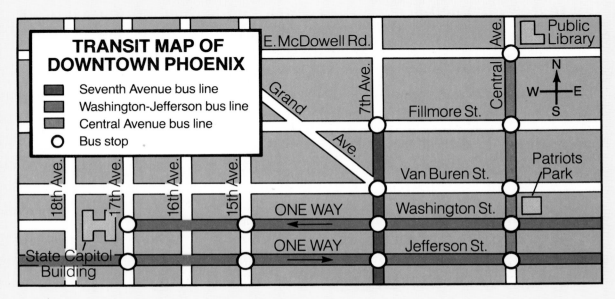

TRANSIT MAP OF DOWNTOWN PHOENIX
- Seventh Avenue bus line
- Washington-Jefferson bus line
- Central Avenue bus line
- O Bus stop

2. THE SOUTHWEST LONG AGO

=== To Guide Your Reading ===

Look for these important words:

Key Words
- missions
- Sooners

People
- Sam Houston

Places
- Santa Fe, New Mexico
- San Antonio, Texas
- The Alamo
- Indian Territory

Look for answers to these questions:

1. How did Santa Fe, New Mexico, begin?
2. How did Texas become a free country before it became a state?
3. How was Oklahoma settled?

The year was 1610. On the Atlantic coast, Jamestown, Virginia, was three years old. Far away from Jamestown a governor from Spain was building another settlement. It was called **Santa Fe** (SAN•tuh FAY).

Santa Fe

Santa Fe was built between the Pecos River and the Rio Grande. This area is now in the state of New Mexico. The settlement was built as a capital of Spanish New Mexico. It is the oldest capital city in the United States.

Santa Fe also was a center of **missions** (MISH•uhnz). Missions were churches and schools started by priests around Santa Fe. The priests came to New Mexico to teach the Catholic religion to the Indians.

Large farms and ranches soon grew up around the town. Mines were dug in the nearby mountains. Gold and silver were brought to Santa Fe. From there they were sent on to Mexico.

In a few years Santa Fe was an important town. It had a large public square, or plaza, and many beautiful buildings. One was a building for the government. That building still stands today.

As Santa Fe grew, Spain built new settlements. In the 1700s missions and forts were built in Texas, New Mexico, and Arizona.

Famous heroes such as Davy Crockett and James Bowie were among the 130 Americans and Texans who fought 4,000 Mexican soldiers at the Alamo. The final struggle was within the old mission's walls.

Spain found it could not hold on to its land in North America. In 1821 Mexico fought a war with Spain and won its independence. Mexico took over all the Spanish lands in the Southwest.

New people were coming into the region. In the 1820s farmers from the American frontier started settling in Texas. So many people came to Texas that the Mexican government became worried. It tried to stop Americans from moving into Texas. It made the Americans that were there obey Mexico's laws. When a new leader came to rule Mexico, the laws became harsher.

"Remember the Alamo!"

The Americans in Texas did not like the laws of the Mexican government. They decided to start their own government in Texas and to break away from Mexico. When this happened, a Mexican army marched into Texas. A group of about 130 Americans and Texans went to an old mission in **San Antonio.** It was called **The Alamo.** This name would become well known in our history.

Thousands of Mexican soldiers attacked the Alamo. Both sides fought bravely. Finally, the Mexican soldiers broke into the building. When the battle was over, no fighter in the old mission remained alive.

Soon other Americans and Texans joined the fight against Mexico. Their leader was **Sam Houston** (HYOO•stuhn). Houston told his army, "Remember the Alamo!" The Texans remembered this message. In 1836 they defeated the Mexican army. Texas became a free country.

Sam Houston became president of Texas soon after. Then in 1845 Texas became a state of the United States.

Sam Houston led the movement to make Texas a state. He then became a United States Senator and was later elected governor of Texas.

The Sooners

It took many years to settle Santa Fe and Texas. One part of Oklahoma, however, was almost settled in a day!

Indians from the Southeast had been forced to move to Oklahoma. For many years the land had been called the **Indian Territory.** Then the government decided to let anyone buy some of the land and settle there. April 22, 1889, was set for the opening. At noon on that day a gun went off. People raced to get the land they wanted. Some people raced away on horses. Some rode in covered wagons. Some even ran. All that day people went off to find good land.

What these people did not know was that others had not waited. The night before, some people had slipped across the line. They wanted to get the best land.

The people who went too soon were known as **Sooners.** Today Oklahoma is known as the Sooner State.

Reading Check

1. What is the oldest capital city in the United States?
2. Why did Mexico fight a war with Texas?
3. What happened at the Alamo?
4. Why is Oklahoma known as the Sooner State?

COWBOYS

Cowboy riding a "bucking bronco"

Off on a cattle drive

It is nearly dawn. The cowboys are sleeping with their boots on. They are ready for any trouble. Their horses are close by. The cattle are restless. Looking over the herd from his horse, the cowboy on watch notices the gathering storm.

Suddenly lightning flashes. Thunder rumbles. The cattle are wild-eyed. They jump to their feet and start to run wildly across the plain.

"**Stampede!**" shouts the cowboy on watch.

All the other cowboys quickly saddle their horses. The cowboy on watch rides alone at the side of the racing herd. He looks for the leader of the herd. He is trying to turn it. Soon the other cowboys are riding around the frightened cattle. Working together, they push the cattle into a circle and calm them. Soon the stampede ends.

About 100 years ago stampedes could happen on cattle drives. Cowboys had to drive large herds of longhorn cattle then from Texas to Kansas and Nebraska. From there the cattle would go by railroad to market.

On these long drives, cowboys had to work together. It was the only way a few cowboys could control thousands of cattle. Two cowboys rode up front to keep the herd pointed in the right direction. Riders on the sides kept the herd from spreading out. The cowboys at the back kept the slowpokes moving.

A ranch hand may still ride a horse to round up cattle for market, but life on the range is different today. Ranchers ship cattle to market by truck or train. The day of the cattle drive is over.

3. THE SOUTHWEST TODAY

To Guide Your Reading

Look for these important words:

Key Words
- reservoirs
- offshore wells
- pueblos
- adobe

Places
- Hoover Dam
- Lake Mead
- Houston, Texas
- Houston Ship Channel
- Carlsbad Caverns
- Petrified Forest National Park

Look for answers to these questions:

1. Why do many people come to the Southwest?
2. Why are dams and reservoirs important to the people in the Southwest?
3. What industries are found here?
4. What have various groups of people contributed to the heritage of the Southwest?

The Southwest is growing fast. Its warm, sunny climate and many new jobs attract more people each year. More people now live here than ever before.

Having more people means that more water is needed. To meet these needs, people here dig wells and build **reservoirs** (reh•suhv•WAHRS). Wells help people reach groundwater. A reservoir is a lake that stores water held back by a dam.

The **Hoover Dam** spans the Colorado River on the Nevada-Arizona border. **Lake Mead** is the reservoir formed by the dam. It stores the Colorado's water. This

The Hoover Dam on the Colorado River formed Lake Mead, one of the world's largest reservoirs.

229

lake is one of the world's largest reservoirs. Communities use the water of the reservoir during dry times of the year.

The Hoover Dam provides water and electricity to many parts of the Southwest. It irrigates a million acres of farmland that used to be desert. It has helped new and old industries grow in the Southwest.

Farming and Ranching

If you have seen cowboy movies, you may know that ranching is important in the Southwest. Texas ranchers raise more cattle and sheep than ranchers in any other state. However, you may not know that wheat is also grown in the Southwest. Farmers grow wheat in Oklahoma, eastern New Mexico, and northern Texas. These areas are at the southern end of the Great Plains.

Cotton is the largest crop of the Southwest. It is grown in each of the Southwest states. Oranges grow near the Rio Grande, and rice grows on the moist Coastal Plain of Texas.

Crops can grow all year long in the Southwest. Many areas do not get too cold for plants to grow. The farming regions have rich, red soil, too. In most places, however, the Southwest's farmland needs irrigation.

Minerals and Fuels

Valuable minerals and fuels lie underground in the Southwest. Metals such as silver and copper are also here. Mines in Arizona produce about half of the copper mined in the United States. The region has fuels such as coal, uranium, natural gas, and oil.

In Oklahoma and Texas are huge amounts of oil and natural gas. Oil is also found off the coast of Texas. **Offshore wells** drill and pump the oil found under the ocean floor.

Valuable "Texas crude" is produced by these offshore oil drilling rigs located in the Gulf of Mexico.

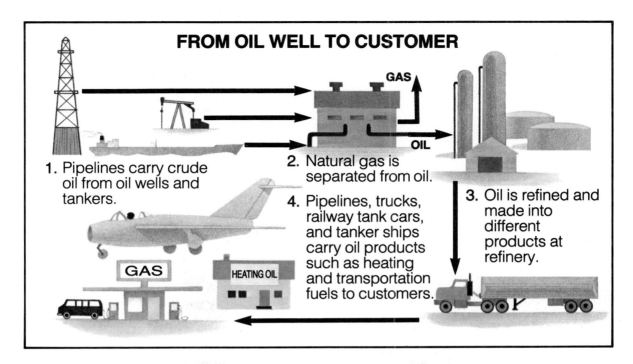

FROM OIL WELL TO CUSTOMER

1. Pipelines carry crude oil from oil wells and tankers.

2. Natural gas is separated from oil.

3. Oil is refined and made into different products at refinery.

4. Pipelines, trucks, railway tank cars, and tanker ships carry oil products such as heating and transportation fuels to customers.

GAS

OIL

GAS

HEATING OIL

Manufacturing

One reason for the Southwest's growth is its modern industries. Computers are made in cities such as Austin and Dallas, Texas, and Albuquerque (AL•buh•kur•kee), New Mexico. Factories in several large Southwest cities build airplanes and rockets.

Products made from oil also come from the Southwest. Some people call oil "black gold." Oil is a very valuable fuel. It's surprising how many things are made from oil. Phonograph records, lipstick, paint, and bug spray are just a few of them. These and thousands of other products make manufacturing important to the Southwest. Tulsa, Oklahoma, and Houston, Texas, are centers where these products are made.

Houston

Like New Orleans, Louisiana, Houston is a port that lies inland, yet it is our country's third-largest port. A wide waterway connects Houston with the Gulf of Mexico. It is called the **Houston Ship Channel.** A channel is a narrow, deep waterway that ships can use.

Houston is an important center of the oil industry. Oil tankers use the channel to bring crude oil to Houston's many oil refineries. Pipelines from Texas oil fields also bring oil to the refineries.

Each refinery has a dock where oil tankers deliver their oil. A large hose brings the oil from the ship right into the refinery. The crude oil is then changed into gasoline and heating oil.

Tourism

The Southwest's great beauty brings millions of visitors to the region each year. The mountains, deserts, and canyons are popular sights to see. Many people visit Indian towns and cities built by the Spanish.

People who like adventure can hike or ride donkeys down trails into the Grand Canyon. Another place adventurers enjoy is **Carlsbad Caverns** in New Mexico. These caverns are the largest caves ever discovered. No one really knows how long they are. The explored part is 23 miles (about 37 km) long. The caverns were discovered in 1901.

Petrified Forest National Park in Arizona is another amazing sight in the Southwest. Petrified wood is a fossil formed when minerals replace the natural wood of a tree. The tree is stone but still looks like a tree. Over many years the woods of this ancient forest turned to stone.

The strange, hanging rock "icicles" of Carlsbad Caverns formed when water and minerals dripped from the ceilings of the caves to the cave floor below.

People of the Southwest

One of the most interesting things about the Southwest is its mix of people. Spanish-speaking people, people from other parts of the country, and different groups of American Indians call the Southwest home.

Mexico, our neighbor to the south, has added much to the heritage of the Southwest. All the Southwest states have many Spanish-speaking people. Most cities have radio and television programs in Spanish. Throughout the Southwest are buildings built by settlers from Mexico.

Indian sheepherders learned to raise sheep from the Spanish settlers.

This radio announcer broadcasts music, news, and other programs in Spanish.

People of other backgrounds have come to live here. Some of the earliest farmers and ranchers were from the Southeast. People from Germany settled in east Texas about 140 years ago.

More American Indians live in the Southwest than in any other region. Some Indians live and work in Southwestern cities and towns. This is especially true in Oklahoma, where many Cherokee, Creek, and Choctaw Indians live. Other Indians live on reservations. The Navaho reservation lies in both Arizona and New Mexico. It is the largest reservation in our country.

233

Ancient Southwest peoples such as the Hopi had settled and farmed here centuries before the Spanish named these dwellings *pueblos.*

Many Indians live on the mesas of the Colorado Plateau. More than 800 years ago they built **pueblos** (PWEB•lohz) on the sides of cliffs. *Pueblo* is the Spanish word for village. Pueblo houses were built on top of one another. They were made with sun-dried clay bricks, called **adobe** (uh•DOH•bee). Some Indians still live in the pueblos.

Indians of the Southwest try to keep ancient arts and customs alive. Many still make their own weavings, silver and turquoise jewelry, and pottery. Children learn Indian languages in schools on their reservations.

The mix of people in our country is always changing. In the Southwest it has changed a great deal in the past 25 years. It's a place where you can meet new people all the time.

Reading Check

1. How do people in the Southwest meet their needs for water?
2. What makes the Southwest good for farming?
3. What are some products made from oil?
4. What did Indians of the mesas use to build pueblos?

SKILLS FOR SUCCESS

SEPARATING FACTS AND OPINIONS

A good reader or listener learns to separate **facts** from **opinions.** A fact is a statement that can be checked and proved. An opinion tells what a person thinks or believes. Here is an example of a fact:

The Grand Canyon is in Arizona.

Here is an example of an opinion:

The Grand Canyon is the most beautiful place in the world.

What is the difference between the two sentences?

A newspaper is a good place to find many examples of facts and opinions. Newspapers may even have different pages for facts and opinions.

News Stories

Most newspaper articles are news stories. Their purpose is mostly to tell readers facts. Read the news story below.

The article tells readers about the new rule and what the rule says. The story tells who made the rule,

Teenagers Told to Stay Away from Shopping Center

Shady Lane Shopping Center has a new rule, store owners announced today. Teenagers are not allowed at the shopping center at lunchtime. Some adult shoppers thought they were not getting enough attention in the stores. They complained that too many teenagers were shopping at the same time. Store owners said the new rule will begin next week. The shopping center will be closed to teenagers from 11 A.M. to 1 P.M., Monday through Friday.

when the rule was made, and why. Those are the facts.

Notice that there are also opinions in the story. Adult shoppers *thought* they were not getting enough attention. They thought too many teenagers were there.

Editorials

Newspapers usually have a special section in which newswriters can give their opinions. The editor of a newspaper writes articles called **editorials.** Most editorials give the newspaper's opinions about the news. Read this editorial. As you read, look for opinion words like *think* and *believe.*

New Shopping Center Rule Is Unfair

Shady Lane Shopping Center will not allow teenagers to shop at lunchtime. We think the adults' complaints were unfair. The shopping center is open to the public. Teenagers are members of the public. We believe they have the right to shop there. In our opinion, this rule may be against the law.

This editorial gives facts as well as opinions. It is a fact that the shopping center is open to the public. It is also a fact that teenagers are members of the public. In the newspaper's opinion the new rule is not fair and may be against the law.

The editor uses facts to support the opinion of the newspaper. Using facts and opinions in this way when you write or speak can help you communicate better. Knowing the difference between facts and opinions can help you better understand what you are listening to or reading.

CHECKING YOUR SKILLS

Look at the statements below. Write *fact* if the statement can be proved. Write *opinion* if the statement is what someone thinks or believes.

1. Shady Lane Shopping Center has 25 stores.

2. "I feel funny about the new rule," said Mrs. Thomas.

3. Many teenagers bring their lunches to school.

4. "We believe the new rule is fair."

5. "I think the adults were wrong," said one teenager.

6. The editor used facts and opinions in the editorial.

7. Many teenagers shop at noon.

8. The editorial was better written than the news story.

Now write four sentences of your own that contain either a fact or an opinion. Label each sentence *fact* or *opinion.*

CHAPTER 11 REVIEW

WORDS TO USE

Copy the words numbered 1 to 5. Next to each word write its meaning from the list below.

1. **cloudburst**
2. **mesa**
3. **mission**
4. **pueblo**
5. **reservoir**

a. Flat-topped hill
b. Sudden hard rain
c. Settlement run by priests
d. Lake that stores water
e. Spanish word for village

FACTS TO REVIEW

1. What is the climate of most of the Southwest?

2. Why are the words "Remember the Alamo!" important in Texas history?

3. Name two natural resources of the Southwest. Name two products of the Southwest that use these resources.

4. Why is Houston an important center of the oil industry?

5. In what ways does Mexico add to the heritage of the Southwest?

IDEAS TO DISCUSS

1. The Hoover Dam has brought more people and industries to the Southwest. Why do you think this has happened?

2. What are some good things and some problems a fast-growing region may have?

○ SKILLS PRACTICE

1. **Using Transit Maps** Use the map on page 224 to answer these questions.

   a. You are at the corner of Grand Avenue and Van Buren Street. You want to go to the State Capitol. Will you take the Seventh Avenue bus to Washington Street or to Jefferson Street?
   b. To go from Fillmore Street to E. McDowell Road, what bus will you take?

2. **Separating Facts and Opinions** Read each sentence. Tell whether it states a fact or gives an opinion.

   a. The Grand Canyon is beautiful.
   b. Iron gives the sand of the Painted Desert its colors.

CHAPTER 12

The Mountain States

About
this
chapter

Go west on the Great Plains and a beautiful sight will greet you. It is the Rocky Mountains. These huge mountains rise up thousands of feet. They make the tallest buildings seem like toys.

In this chapter you will discover what it is like to live in a mountain region. You will read how the mountains and the climate caused problems for Americans moving west. You will also read how people make their living here today.

1. THE LAND AND ITS RESOURCES

To Guide Your Reading

Look for these important words:

Key Places
- Intermountain area
- Great Basin
- Colorado Plateau
- Continental Divide
- Aspen, Colorado
- Sun Valley, Idaho

Look for answers to these questions:

1. What landforms are in the Mountain states?
2. What is the Continental Divide?
3. What kind of climate is in the Mountain states?
4. What natural resources are found here?

The Mountain states are the highest part of our country. The mountains in this region are so high that snow covers many of their peaks all year. The highest peaks rise more than 14,000 feet (about 4,270 m).

Mountains are the largest landforms in this region, but the Mountain states have much more than mountains. Three main kinds of land are in these states. In the east are the Great Plains. In the center are the great Rocky Mountains. In the west are the high, dry plateaus known as the **Intermountain area.**

Let's start in the eastern part of the Mountain states. We will look at each of the three parts a little more closely.

The Great Plains

The Great Plains meet the Rocky Mountains in the Mountain states. As the plains stretch toward the mountains, they slope upward. In Colorado, Wyoming, and Montana the plains are almost a mile above sea level. Few trees grow on the plains. Though the land is dry, it is suitable for cattle, sheep, and wheat.

The Rocky Mountains

The Rocky Mountains are not a single mountain range. They are made up of dozens of smaller ranges. They stretch through Colorado, Wyoming, Montana, Idaho, and Utah. Between these ranges are plateaus.

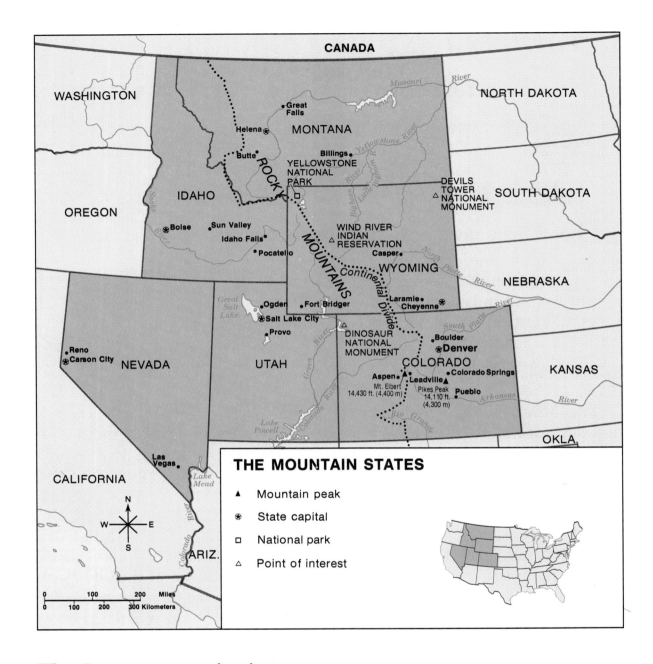

CANADA

WASHINGTON

MONTANA

Great
Falls

Helena ⊛

Billings

ROCKY

YELLOWSTONE
NATIONAL
PARK

Butte

IDAHO

OREGON

Boise ⊛   Sun Valley

Idaho Falls

Pocatello

NORTH DAKOTA

Missouri   River

Yellowstone River

DEVILS
TOWER
△ NATIONAL
MONUMENT

SOUTH DAKOTA

Bighorn River

Little Bighorn River

WIND RIVER
INDIAN △
RESERVATION

MOUNTAINS

Continental Divide

Casper

North Platte River

WYOMING

NEBRASKA

Great
Salt
Lake

Ogden ⦁ Fort Bridger

⊛ Salt Lake City

Provo

UTAH

Reno ⦁
⊛ Carson City

NEVADA

Laramie ⦁
Cheyenne ⊛

South Platte River

DINOSAUR
NATIONAL △
MONUMENT

Green River

Boulder
⦁ Denver

COLORADO

Colorado Springs

Aspen ⦁ ▲
Mt. Elbert
14,430 ft. (4,400 m)

Leadville ▲
Pikes Peak
14,110 ft.
(4,300 m)

Pueblo

Arkansas   River

KANSAS

Las
Vegas ⦁

CALIFORNIA

Lake
Mead

Colorado River

Lake
Powell

Colorado River

Rio Grande

OKLA.

ARIZ.

THE MOUNTAIN STATES

▲   Mountain peak

⊛   State capital

▢   National park

△   Point of interest

N
W   E
S

0   100   200   Miles
0   100   200   300 Kilometers

The Intermountain Area

West of the Rocky Mountains is a huge land that is high and dry. Some people call it the Intermountain area. *Inter* means between. The Intermountain area lies between the Rocky Mountains and the Sierra Nevada of California. It stretches from Canada to Mexico.

Part of the Intermountain area is made up of basins. You may recall that a basin is low, bowl-shaped land. Rivers inside a basin do not flow out. They either dry up or flow to a lake in the basin.

240

Bryce Canyon shows some of the unusual landforms found on the Colorado Plateau. The many shades of red, pink, copper, and brown on the canyon walls change in the sunlight.

The **Great Basin** is a large desert in this area. Nearly all the lakes in the Great Basin are salty. The Great Salt Lake in Utah is the largest lake in the basin.

High, flat plateaus cover other parts of the Intermountain area. One large plateau is known as the **Colorado Plateau.** Much of this land is high, dry, and hilly. The Colorado River crosses the plateau. It and other rivers have cut deep canyons and valleys into the land. With irrigation the valleys are useful for growing many kinds of crops. They also provide good grazing land for beef cattle and sheep.

Throughout the Intermountain area are small mountain ranges. Someone once wrote that these ranges look like caterpillars wriggling northward!

The Continental Divide

Many great rivers begin in the Rocky Mountains. Some, like the Snake, Columbia, and Colorado, flow west into the Pacific Ocean. Others, like the Arkansas, Missouri, and Platte, flow east. They join the Mississippi or flow into the Gulf of Mexico.

Look back at the map on page 240. A line runs down the Rocky Mountains. On one side are the rivers that flow east. On the other side are the rivers that flow west. This imaginary line is called the **Continental Divide.**

Climate

The Mountain states are the driest part of the United States. They get only about 15 inches (about 38 cm) of precipitation a year. Some areas are drier than others. Nevada gets only about 7 inches (about 18 cm) a year. It is the driest state in our country. About 30 inches (about 76 cm) fall in eastern Idaho in a year.

Most of the region's precipitation is snow. Melting snow from the mountains feeds the streams and rivers. Without these streams the Mountain states would not have enough water.

Temperatures change a lot from season to season in the Mountain states. In the northern states, such as Idaho and Montana, winters are mostly long and cold. Freezing blizzards howl down from Canada. Yet summers are warm and mild in these states. In the southern Mountain states the climate is quite different. Summers in Utah and Nevada can be very hot. Winters can be cold, but they are mostly mild.

Natural Resources

The Rocky Mountains themselves are the greatest natural resource of the Mountain states. The beauty of these mountains draws millions of visitors each year. National parks such as the

The deep winter snows that blanket some mountain areas make snowshoes, skis, or snowmobiles necessities.

This melting snow will soon be part of the valuable water supply of a Mountain state.

Mountain lions keep well hidden as they stalk the canyons and valleys.

Aspen trees grow among the pines in moister areas of the Rockies.

Grand Teton National Park in Wyoming and the Rocky Mountain National Park in Colorado preserve this wilderness for camping and hiking. Two popular places for skiing are **Aspen, Colorado,** and **Sun Valley, Idaho.** Besides recreation, the mountains provide minerals, fuels, and lumber.

The Rocky Mountains are rich in minerals. Early miners came to the mountains to find copper, silver, and gold. Today these metals are still mined in the Rocky Mountains. Other metals important to manufacturing, such as lead and zinc, are also mined here.

Oil, natural gas, and coal are three fuels that come from the Mountain states. Covering the Rocky Mountains' lower slopes are forests of pine trees.

Reading Check

1. What are the three main parts of the Mountain region?
2. Where is the Intermountain area? What kinds of landforms are in this area?
3. What are some rivers that form the Continental Divide?
4. Name two minerals and two fuels that come from the Mountain states.

SKILLS FOR SUCCESS

USING INTERVIEWING SKILLS

Sara Fox is a student in Leadville, Colorado. She wants to learn what this old mining town was like long ago. She decides to **interview,** or talk with someone to find out.

Preparing for the Interview

Sara makes a list of people to interview. Then she calls one of them, Mr. Harry Abnet, to ask if he will see her. When she speaks to Mr. Abnet, Sara tells him what she wants to talk about. They make an **appointment,** deciding on a time and place to meet.

Sara calls Mr. Abnet to make an appointment to interview him.

Sara takes a few notes when she interviews Mr. Abnet. She has a list of questions ready to ask.

The Interview

Sara's interview with Mr. Abnet begins like this:

> **Sara:** How did Leadville get its start, Mr. Abnet?
>
> **Mr. Abnet:** Well, some gold was discovered near here and then silver. The silver was found in lead, so that's how Leadville got its name. The town grew fast after the railroad was built.

Sara started with a question she had thought up before the interview. She has a list of questions to ask. Mr. Abnet's answers make her think of other questions, too.

As they talk, Sara does not argue or interrupt. She is there to get information. Mr. Abnet is happy to talk to someone who is interested in his story.

When the interview is over, Sara thanks Mr. Abnet. This thank-you makes Mr. Abnet feel that his time has been well spent.

After the Interview

Sara has taken a few short notes during the interview. She knows that she could not write every word. Later she will use her notes to help her write everything she can remember from the interview.

Using a Tape Recorder

Next week Sara will interview someone else. She wants to use a

After the interview, Sara fills in her notes with everything she remembers.

tape recorder during that interview. However, Sara knows that some people do not like to use a tape recorder. She will ask the person she is interviewing if it is all right to bring the machine.

CHECKING YOUR SKILLS

Look at the pairs of sentences below. They are rules to follow during an interview. Write down the sentence in each pair that is a good rule.

1. a. Start interviewing the person when you call on the telephone.
   b. Make an appointment to interview the person.

2. a. Make a list of questions to ask.
   b. Do not bring a list of questions.

3. a. Write down every word the person you are interviewing says.
   b. Take a few short notes during the interview.

4. a. Never use a tape recorder.
   b. Ask the person you are interviewing if you may use a tape recorder.

Pick a classmate or family member who has visited an interesting place. Interview that person according to the rules you have learned in this lesson.

2. THE MOUNTAIN STATES LONG AGO

To Guide Your Reading

Look for these important words:

Key Words
• Shoshone
• Mormons

• Meriwether Lewis
• William Clark

Places
• Pikes Peak

People
• Sacajawea

Look for answers to these questions:

1. How did Lewis and Clark help to open up the West to American pioneers?
2. What did Sacajawea do to help our country grow?
3. Why was crossing the Rocky Mountains so difficult?
4. What attracted pioneers to the Mountain states?

She was only 16 years old at the time of her greatest adventure. She was a **Shoshone** (shuh•SHOH•nee) Indian. At her death in 1812 only a few people knew her name. Today we know **Sacajawea** (sa•kuh•juh•WEE•uh) as an American hero who helped our country grow from coast to coast.

Why was Sacajawea important? Let's go back hundreds of years before she was born. People from Europe were exploring America then. They could travel only as far as the Rocky Mountains. The high, rugged mountains were a huge wall blocking the way. It would take many years before the region could be settled.

The Spanish came first. Spanish settlers pushed north from Mexico in the 1700s. Next came French fur traders from Canada. They found many Indian tribes living here. Yet Americans in the East knew very little about the Rocky Mountains in the early 1800s. Was it possible to take a wagon through the mountains?

Could a person go by river from the Atlantic to the Pacific? No one could say for sure.

Lewis and Clark

President Thomas Jefferson sent two men to find out. Their names were **Meriwether Lewis** and **William Clark.**

Lewis and Clark with a small group of men left St. Louis, Missouri, in May 1804. They spent the summer and fall going up the Missouri River. In November they stopped at an Indian village to spend the winter. The village lay at the edge of the Rocky Mountains. The hardest part of their journey was just ahead.

Sacajawea now enters our story. She was the wife of a trapper staying at the village. Lewis and Clark hired the trapper to help them find a way through the mountains. Sacajawea joined them because she could speak to the Indians.

Across the Rockies

In the spring the party started up the Missouri again. One day one of their boats tipped over. All

Sacajawea guided Lewis and Clark and a small group of men in six canoes up the Missouri. She courageously faced many dangers and stayed with the explorers throughout their journey to the Pacific.

their goods fell into the icy water. Sacajawea did not waste a moment. She jumped in and saved almost everything.

Now the party was in the mountains near Shoshone country. Lewis and Clark set up a meeting with the Shoshones to buy horses from the Indians. The Shoshones did not want to sell their horses. Sacajawea stepped forward. The Shoshone chief gasped in surprise. Sacajawea was his sister! He had not seen her in five years.

Sacajawea persuaded her brother to sell the horses. The Shoshones also helped guide the group through the mountains.

Lewis and Clark reached the Pacific after much suffering. Then they turned around and made the same trip back. They traveled 8,000 miles (about 12,900 km). The trip took them nearly three years! They had gone from the Mississippi River to the Pacific Ocean, opening up the land to Americans. Sacajawea had helped them do it.

Wagon Trains West

Wagon trains began crossing the mountains years later. The pioneers traveled some of the paths that Lewis and Clark had discovered.

When these pioneers were crossing the Rocky Mountains, they had no roads to travel. Their wagons broke down. Their oxen

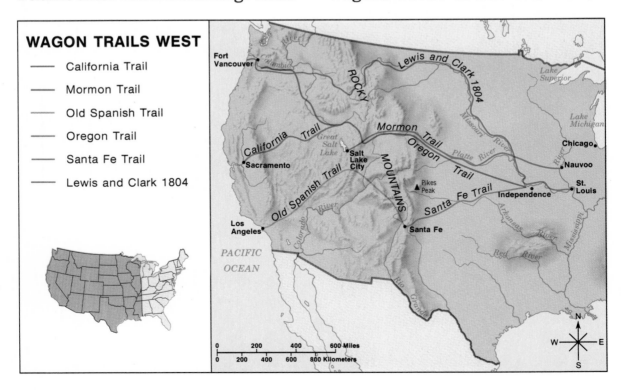

WAGON TRAILS WEST

—— California Trail
—— Mormon Trail
—— Old Spanish Trail
—— Oregon Trail
—— Santa Fe Trail
—— Lewis and Clark 1804

Though the land was dry, the soil was fertile near the Great Salt Lake. The Mormons built their city there and irrigated the land for their farms.

died. There was little water. The Rocky Mountains are steep and wide. Many settlers died before they finished crossing them.

The **Mormons** were the first large group to settle in the Mountain states. They came in search of religious freedom. The Mormons built Salt Lake City near the Great Salt Lake in Utah. Using irrigation, they turned the desert there into farmland.

Many pioneers came to the Rocky Mountains to search for gold and silver. Gold was discovered near **Pikes Peak,** Colorado, in 1858. Wagon trains set out for Colorado. The words "Pikes Peak or Bust!" were painted on their wagons. All too many people did not find the riches they were looking for. Even so, people kept coming west.

Finally the railroad reached the Rocky Mountains, bringing more people west. Towns, farms, and ranches began to spring up.

Reading Check

1. Why did it take so long for people to explore the Rocky Mountains?
2. Who sent Lewis and Clark west?
3. How did Sacajawea help Lewis and Clark?
4. What large group of pioneers settled in Utah? Why did they move there?

249

TRAILS IN THE WILDERNESS

Jim Bridger, Mountain Man and guide

Pioneers crossing the Rockies in wagons

Pioneers heading west bought supplies at Jim Bridger's trading post. It was just east of the Great Salt Lake. If the travelers stopped to rest, Jim would tell them stories about his early days as a fur trapper.

Jim Bridger lived alone in the Rocky Mountains for 20 years. He and other trappers were known as Mountain Men. They learned from the Shoshones and other Indians how to live off the land by gathering plants and hunting for food.

As the Mountain Men trapped beaver, they explored the wilderness. They found paths through canyons and passes over mountains. In spring and fall the men set traps along rivers. In winter the rivers froze so the trappers could not work. They lived in log cabins or tents until the ice melted in the spring.

The Mountain Men would gather for a meeting every summer. They would sell their furs then and buy supplies. At night they would talk about their adventures. Then each mountain man went back into the wilderness.

When the wagon trains started coming, the Mountain Men became guides. They led pioneers over the paths they had found years before. They showed them which streams were easy to cross. They led wagon trains across mountain passes and to water holes.

The Mountain Men helped many pioneers cross the Rocky Mountains. Just like Lewis and Clark, people such as Jim Bridger helped open up and settle the American West.

3. THE MOUNTAIN STATES TODAY

To Guide Your Reading

Look for these important words:

Key Words
- geysers
- sugar beets
- U.S. Mint

- Douglas fir
- volunteers

Places
- Yellowstone National Park
- Ouray, Colorado

Look for answers to these questions:

1. What kinds of farming and ranching are found in the Mountain states?
2. Why might the Mountain states be called a "treasure chest"?
3. What kinds of jobs might people have in the Mountain states?

Fewer people live in the Mountain states than in other regions of our country. Yet some of America's most beautiful places are in the Mountain states. Millions of visitors come here each year for vacations. They make tourism an important industry in this region. You can visit "dude" ranches, ski lodges, and almost a dozen national parks here.

Yellowstone National Park in Wyoming is our country's oldest national park. There visitors can see bubbling mud volcanoes and **geysers.** Geysers are springs of water that shoot jets of steam and hot water into the air. The most famous geyser here is Old Faithful.

Old Faithful erupts faithfully every 33 to 93 minutes. None of the other geysers at Yellowstone erupt as regularly.

Farming and Ranching

Many people in the Mountain states are farmers. Even more people are ranchers. Raising beef cattle, sheep, and dairy cows is important in the Mountain states. The cattle graze on land that is too dry or too steep for crops. The sheep graze on land that is too steep for cattle.

Wheat is the most important crop in the Mountain states. It grows well on the dry lands of the Great Plains. Most of the wheat grown in the Mountain states comes from Montana, Wyoming, and Colorado.

Farmers grow other crops by irrigating the land, but irrigation costs a lot of money. Therefore, farmers must often grow crops that sell for high prices. Some of these crops are peas, beans, and **sugar beets.** A sugar beet is a white beet from which sugar is made.

Irrigation has made a particularly dry part of southern Idaho bloom. The Snake River runs through this part of the state. Irrigation canals from the Snake bring water to the many large farms in this area. Potatoes are grown on many of them. In fact,

More than a few sweaters will come from the fleecy coats of these wool sheep. Western ranchers raise mostly wool sheep, either in fenced pastures or on large enclosed areas of the range.

These Idaho potatoes are well on their way to becoming hash browns or powdered mashed potatoes.

Idaho grows more potatoes than any other state.

Minerals and Fuels

The Mountain states could be called the "treasure chest" of our country. Almost 200 minerals and fuels are found here.

All the Mountain states except Wyoming have huge amounts of copper. Gold and silver are mined here, too. The Sunshine Mine in Idaho produces the most silver in the United States. In Denver, Colorado, a large **U.S. Mint** turns these metals into pennies, dimes, and other coins.

Just as valuable as these metals are the region's fuels. Wyoming has a lot of oil and natural gas. Large amounts of coal come from Colorado, Wyoming, Montana, and Utah.

Manufacturing

Food processing is one of the important industries in the Mountain states. Workers in Idaho turn their state's biggest crop into french fries, hash browns, and potato chips. Because of the surrounding ranches, Denver, Colorado, has become a major meat-packing center.

Most of the Mountain states' industries make products from minerals. Iron and steel are processed in Pueblo, Colorado, and other cities. Copper is refined in Salt Lake City, Utah. Wyoming has many oil refineries. Factories in Cheyenne (SHY•an), Wyoming, turn out fertilizers and other things made from oil.

The Mountain states do less manufacturing than some other regions for two reasons. First, fewer people live here. Second, it costs more money to move goods through the mountains.

Lumbering

The huge forests of the Rocky Mountains provide lumber and wood pulp for making paper. The most valuable tree here is the **Douglas fir.** This tree grows in many parts of the West. The Douglas fir provides much of our lumber. Small Douglas firs make great Christmas trees!

People of the Mountain States

Settlers from all over Europe helped build the Mountain states.

At rodeos, cowhands try not to "bite the dust" as they show off their skills in bull riding, calf roping, and wild "bronco" riding.

254

People from Canada and Mexico settled here, too. Some became ranchers or miners. Others became loggers or store owners. People from China came to help build railroads through the mountains.

Many Indians still live in the Mountain states. The huge Wind River Reservation is in west central Wyoming. It is home to thousands of Shoshone and Arapaho (uh•RAP•uh•hoh) Indians.

You can still get the feel of frontier times in the Mountain states today. Cowboy clothes are very popular. Many old buildings look as they did long ago.

The feeling of frontier times is shown in another way, too. It is shown in the way people lend a hand to a neighbor. The people in mountain towns depend on one another for help just as settlers in the Mountain states did years ago. **Ouray** (YOO•ray), a small town in Colorado, will show you how people help out.

Fire Fighters of Ouray

Most cities and towns have fire departments. Ouray is no different. However, Ouray, just like many small towns in our country, has no paid fire fighters. They

Small towns like Ouray, Colorado, are spread out miles apart across the Rocky Mountains.

Volunteer fire fighters learn to use all the equipment on a fire engine. They also practice working together.

With an oxygen mask, a fire fighter can enter a burning building to save a life.

At a moment's notice, this volunteer fire fighter can answer an alarm.

are **volunteers.** They get no money. Their only pay is the good feeling they get from helping out.

As volunteers, these fire fighters must know how to handle the fire hoses. They must also know how to run the pump that forces water through the hoses. They must learn how to use the air masks. The masks keep them from breathing deadly smoke.

When the volunteers are not practicing or putting out fires, they have other jobs. One owns a store. Another, Roy Franz, works for Ouray Public Works. The Fire Chief, Joe Mattivi, works at a gas station.

All the volunteers keep fire jackets, hats, and boots in their cars. If the alarm sounds, they stop what they are doing and answer it. Fire fighting has a special meaning to the volunteers of Ouray. The building they save may be the home or the store of a friend.

Reading Check

1. What is our country's largest national park? Where is it?
2. What minerals and fuels are found in this region?
3. What kind of manufacturing is done in the Mountain states?
4. How do the Mountain states still remind some people of the frontier days?

SKILLS FOR SUCCESS

USING YOUR TELEPHONE BOOK

People do not often think of the telephone book as a reference book. However, there is a lot of useful information in your community's telephone book.

The White Pages

The white pages list the names and telephone numbers of people. The list is alphabetical, by last name. Businesses are also listed in alphabetical order. The first word in a business's name is used. If a name begins with *the* or *a,* the second word is used. This means that "The Record King" appears in

the *R* list. It is listed as *Record King, The.* Look at the white page below. What is the telephone number of The Reader's Corner Bookstore?

The Yellow Pages

You will find the telephone numbers of most businesses in the yellow pages. They are listed by what they sell or do. A store called The Record King would be listed under *Records—Phonograph.* In the yellow pages types of businesses appear in alphabetical order. *Banks* comes after *Airlines* and before *Carpenters.*

Rainbow Records	
157 Montgomery	498-2768
Raintree Bakery	
693 Stevens St	234-0965
Rainwater, Michael 17 Davis Dr	234-9875
Ralston, Jeffrey 518 Jones St	987-5487
Ramirez, Robert	
1215 Washington Av	769-5439
Randolph, Peter 212 Bay Dr	654-7904
RAPID TRANSIT DISTRICT	
Transit Information	564-0965
Main Office 645 Market	564-0943
Ray, Mark 105 West Civic Dr	769-3045
Reader's Corner Bookstore, The	
1302 Lake Av	563-0982
Record King, The 111 Grant Av	987-2456
Recreation & Park Dept	
2396 Civic Dr	743-9872
Recycling Center, The	
212 Parkridge	987-6537
Red Hen Cafe, The 1720 Post	987-0532
Redding Hospital 850 Baker	489-6523

REAL ESTATE	
A & A Realty Co	
2497 Broadway	525-9843
Abbott Real Estate, Inc	
1515 Grant Av	987-2887
Action Real Estate	
698 South Portal Dr	587-6543
RECORDS—PHONOGRAPH	
A-1 Records 354 Westgate Av	474-8756
All About Music 2135 Lincoln Av	226-8767
American Music 5678 Jackson	987-4537
Arnold's Used Records	
2435 Garden Dr	234-0985
RESTAURANTS	
Abbie's Coffee Shop	
56 Parker St	862-9854
Alberto's Pizza 564 Glenn Dr	987-0465
Anchor Seafood Restaurant	
1517 Creekside Dr	286-7908

Fire

Fire _____

Areas	Police and Sheriff	Fire
Adams County Sheriff all emergencies	911 or 544-9898	
non-emergency	327-8655	
Boulder — all emergencies	911	911
non-emergency	763-9654	763-9654
Coal Creek Canyon	875-0965	875-0965
Denver — (within city limits) all emergencies	911	911
non-emergency	652-2265	623-7648

Police

Police _____
Sheriff _____
_____

Other Emergency Numbers

Ambulance & Hospital

Denver Emergency Ambulance	324-9865
Denver Emergency Hospital	567-0987

(For private Ambulance, see "Ambulance Service" in the Yellow Pages)

(For private Hospitals, see "Hospitals" in the Yellow Pages)

Rocky Mountain Poison Control Center	234-9863
Colorado State Patrol	658-7634

The Front of the Telephone Book

Have you ever looked at the front pages of your telephone book? These pages tell you what to do in an **emergency.** An emergency is something bad that happens all of a sudden. In an emergency, you often need to get help fast. The front pages of the telephone book have a list of emergency telephone numbers. You can find numbers for reporting fires, for calling the police, or for calling an **ambulance.** An ambulance is a truck that quickly takes people to the hospital. Use these telephone numbers only in true emergencies!

Look above at the page of emergency numbers for areas around Denver, Colorado. Some places use the emergency number 911. What places use 911?

CHECKING YOUR SKILLS

Answer these questions. Use the telephone-book pages in this section to help you.

1. What is the telephone number of The Red Hen Cafe?

2. What is the telephone number of Robert Ramirez?

3. What is the telephone number of a pizza restaurant?

4. What is the emergency telephone number for reporting fires?

258

CHAPTER 12 REVIEW

WORDS TO USE

Copy the sentences below. Fill in the blanks with the right words from the list.

U.S. Mint
sugar beets
Mormons
volunteers
Intermountain area

1. The land between the Rocky Mountains and the Sierra Nevada is called the ____.

2. Pioneers called ____ settled near the Great Salt Lake.

3. Sugar is made from sugar cane or from ____.

4. Many of our coins are made at the ____ in Denver, Colorado.

5. The fire fighters of Ouray are ____.

FACTS TO REVIEW

1. What are the three main parts of the Mountain states? Tell whether they are in the east, west, or center.

2. What is the Continental Divide? Name two rivers that flow east or west from here.

3. Name two ways Sacajawea helped Lewis and Clark.

4. What brings tourists to the Mountain states?

5. Why would a factory in Idaho be more likely to make french fries than cornflakes?

IDEAS TO DISCUSS

The Mountain states have fewer people living in them than other parts of our country. What are some good things about having fewer people living in a place? What things can you name that might cause some problems?

○ SKILLS PRACTICE

Using Your Telephone Book

Find and write down the telephone numbers of the following. Use the telephone-book pages on page 257.

1. Michael Rainwater

2. Redding Hospital

3. Recreation and Park Department

4. Rapid Transit Information

5. Abbot Real Estate

CHAPTER 13
The Pacific States

About
this
chapter

The Pacific Ocean borders all the Pacific states. One of them, Alaska, is the state that is farthest north in our country. Another Pacific state, Hawaii, is the farthest south. The other three Pacific states are Washington, Oregon, and California. In this chapter you will discover that each state's land and climate are different. You will also find out that the people in each state have jobs that depend on these differences.

260

1. ALASKA

To Guide Your Reading

Look for these important words:

Key Words
- fjords
- salmon
- tundra
- Japan Current
- Lower 48

- Inuit

Places
- Alaska Range
- Yukon River
- Brooks Range

- Arctic Coastal Plain
- Anchorage
- Juneau
- Fairbanks

Look for answers to these questions:

1. What is unusual about Alaska's land and climate?
2. Why can Alaska no longer be called a "wasteland"?
3. How do people make a living in Alaska?

Our forty-ninth state, Alaska, is our biggest state—and it is also our smallest state! It has more land than any other state. Alaska is more than twice as large as Texas. Yet Alaska has fewer people than any other state.

The Land

Because Alaska is so far north, many people think it is covered with ice and snow. This is true of many parts of Alaska. Thousands of glaciers can be found in mountain valleys and canyons in the state. It is also true that Alaska has vast forests, rich farmland, and modern cities.

To understand Alaska's land, think of it as four parts. In the south mountains come right down to the coast. These mountains are called the **Alaska Range.** The high cliffs jut out into the Pacific Ocean, forming long, narrow channels. These channels are called **fjords** (fee•YORDZ).

Two of Alaska's most important resources are found in the south. Thick pine forests cover the mountains. Billions of fish live in the coastal waters. **Salmon** (SAM•uhn) are the most important.

In the center of Alaska the land flattens out into low, rolling hills. Large rivers such as the **Yukon River** flow through this land.

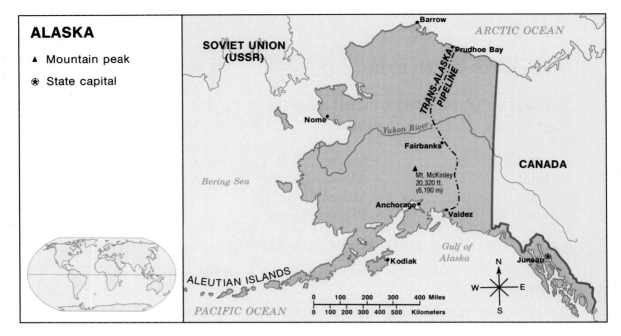

SOVIET UNION (USSR)

ARCTIC OCEAN

Barrow

Prudhoe Bay

TRANS-ALASKA PIPELINE

Nome

Yukon River

Fairbanks

CANADA

▲ Mt. McKinley 20,320 ft. (6,190 m)

Bering Sea

Anchorage

Valdez

ALEUTIAN ISLANDS

Kodiak

Gulf of Alaska

Juneau ✦

N W E S

PACIFIC OCEAN

0 100 200 300 400 Miles
0 100 200 300 400 500 Kilometers

North of the hill country is the **Brooks Range.** This huge range is part of the Rocky Mountains.

The most northern part of Alaska is the **Arctic Coastal Plain.** This plain lies next to the Arctic Ocean. Much of the Arctic Coastal Plain is **tundra.** Tundra is flat, treeless land that stays frozen most of the year. In summer a few inches at the top thaws and turns into grassy swamp. Beneath the tundra lies oil, Alaska's most valuable resource.

Like its land, Alaska's climate changes from south to north. On the southern coast, winter temperatures can be fairly mild. These mild temperatures are caused by the **Japan Current.** The Japan Current is a river of warmer water within the ocean. Winds that pass over the Japan Current warm up and then blow in over the coast. They bring warm temperatures and rain to southern Alaska.

Farther north the winters are long and bitterly cold. Northern Alaska is thousands of miles from the equator. It gets little of the sun's heat.

Alaska Long Ago and Today

Alaska was once a part of Russia. The United States bought Alaska in 1867. At that time many people thought it was foolish to own this frozen "wasteland." They changed their minds when gold was discovered in 1899. Since then even more valuable resources have been discovered. Alaska became a state in 1959.

The people of Alaska are not spread evenly over the state. Nearly half live in the city of **Anchorage** (ANG•kuhr•ij). This city is on the warm southern coast. Anchorage is a large, up-to-date city with tall buildings and new highways. It is also Alaska's main seaport. Near Anchorage farmers grow vegetables and raise dairy and beef cattle. Other major cities are **Juneau** (JOO•noh), Alaska's capital, and **Fairbanks.**

Life in Alaska's cities is much like that in any other American city. The big difference is that many goods cost a lot more money in Alaska. They must be shipped from the **Lower 48.** This is what Alaskans call the 48 states of our country that touch one another.

Life is very different outside of Alaska's large cities. People live in small villages. Many Alaskans hunt and fish for food.

Today Native Americans are the only people living in some parts of Alaska. One large group is the **Inuit** (IN•oo•it), or Eskimos. The ancestors of the Inuit were among the first people in Alaska. They learned how to live in Alaska's difficult climate.

The modern city of Anchorage is surrounded by Alaska's famed wilderness beauty.

Many of Alaska's people live in small seaside towns all along the coast. Fishing is one of Alaska's important industries.

263

Some of Alaska's oldest Inuit families live in Kotzbue, an Arctic Circle town.

Walruses and other Alaskan wildlife live happily in the icy Arctic waters.

Alaska's daring bush pilots fly people and goods to outlying areas too rugged for land travel. Canned foods and fresh oranges are some of the foods flown in.

The Inuit live along the coasts of Alaska. In the past they spent their winters in houses made of sod. Their summer houses were tents of skins. The Inuit hunted whales, walruses, seals, and other animals for food, clothing, shelters, weapons, and tools. For example the blubber, or fat, of whales was used as a fuel for lamps. These lamps provided both light and heat.

Though some of Alaska's Native Americans still follow the old ways, most now live in modern houses. Their lives have changed in other ways as well.

Crossing three mountain ranges and hundreds of rivers, the Trans-Alaska Pipeline carries about 1.5 million barrels of oil daily.

Airplanes now bring supplies to the villages. Snowmobiles allow people to travel more easily.

Important changes have also come since oil was discovered in northern Alaska. Many people of the villages as well as many people from other places now work for oil companies on the Alaska pipeline. This long pipe threads its way from the northern coast south through the wilderness. The Trans-Alaska Pipeline brings oil 800 miles (about 1,290 km) to the southern coast.

Many visitors now come to see the beauty of Alaska's great wilderness. Long ago the people of the Aleutian Islands called Alaska "The Great Land." Today we often call Alaska the "Last Frontier."

Reading Check

1. Why is Alaska both our largest state and our smallest state?
2. What is the tundra? Where in Alaska is it?
3. What country once owned Alaska?
4. How is life now changing in Alaska's villages?

2. HAWAII

To Guide Your Reading

Look for these important words:

Key Words
- Polynesians
- paniolos

Places
- Honolulu
- Oahu

Look for answers to these questions:

1. What landforms are in Hawaii?
2. Why does Hawaii have a warm, rainy climate?
3. What kinds of jobs might Hawaiians have?

Thousands of miles south and west of Alaska, a chain of beautiful islands rises out of the Pacific. This is Hawaii, our fiftieth state. It is made up of more than 130 islands.

The Land

The islands of Hawaii are really the tops of mountains rising from the ocean floor. Volcanoes formed these mountains millions of years ago. Though most of these volcanoes are inactive, a few, such as Mauna Loa (MOW•nuh•LOH•uh) and Kilauea (kee•low•AY•uh), still erupt from time to time.

The islands of Hawaii have high peaks as well as deep canyons. Lining the island coasts are miles of sandy beaches. In some places steep cliffs rise right out of the sea. Palm trees and bright flowers grow all over Hawaii.

"Pali" is the Hawaiian word for the steep cliffs, mostly of volcanic rock, that line the shores of the Hawaiian Islands.

266

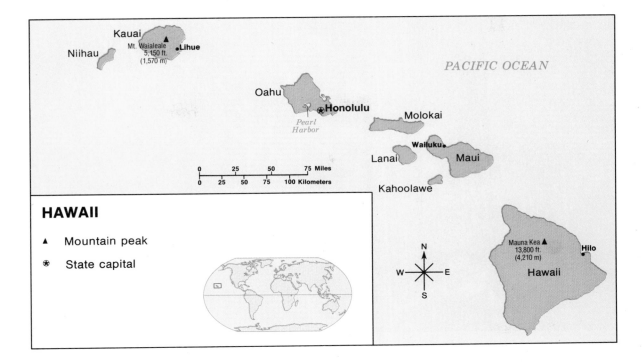

HAWAII

▲ Mountain peak

✦ State capital

The state of Hawaii has eight main islands. People live on seven of them. The other islands are too small for people to live on. The largest island is called Hawaii, the same as the state's name. The name means "Big Island."

Most of the time Hawaii's temperatures are warm, but not too hot. Winter and summer are much the same. In both seasons the temperatures are usually in the upper 70s F (20s C). Winds cool off the islands. They also bring heavy rains to parts of the islands. Mount Waialeale (wy•ahl•ee•AHL•ee), on the island of Kauai (KOW•eye), is the wettest spot in the world. This mountain gets at least 460 inches (about 1,170 cm) of rain every year.

Hawaii Long Ago and Today

Hawaii has a mix of people from many different backgrounds. The first Hawaiians have lived on the islands for about 2,000 years. These people are known today as **Polynesians** (pah•luh•NEE•zhuhnz). They came from other islands in the Pacific. Many different groups later came to Hawaii from Asia. Among them were people from China, Japan, and the Philippine Islands. Americans have been coming to Hawaii for more than a hundred years. The first of these American visitors came to build schools and churches. American planters came later to start sugar cane and pineapple plantations.

A harvester-conveyor speeds up the pineapple harvest. Workers pick the fruit by hand, and a moving belt carries it to a truck.

Cannery workers trim the pineapples before the fruit is sliced by machine.

Waikiki Beach attracts tourists to Honolulu all year.

"Hold on to your hat!" A junior cowboy gets a few tips and a riding lesson from his father, a paniolo on the Parker Ranch on the "Big Island" of Hawaii.

Hawaii's warm climate allows farmers to grow special crops. Among Hawaii's biggest crops are sugar cane, pineapples, and coffee. Some of these crops, such as coffee and pineapples, cannot grow in other parts of our country. Orchids (OR·kidz) and macadamia (mak·uh·DAY·mee·uh) nuts are other major crops. Trees that produce hardwoods are also important.

Many Hawaiians work in the fields where these crops grow. Other Hawaiians work in factories that make sugar and other food products. Hawaiians also raise beef cattle. **Paniolos** (pan·ee·OH·lohz) are the cowboys of Hawaii. They are some of the best riders and ropers in the world.

Honolulu (hon·uh·LOO·loo) is the largest city and capital of Hawaii. It is on the island of **Oahu** (oh·WAH·hoo). Four out of five Hawaiians live on this island. Honolulu began as a place where ships could get supplies. Today it is the center of trade and banking in Hawaii.

Honolulu is also the center of tourism, Hawaii's biggest industry. Waikiki (wy·kih·KEE) Beach is the most famous tourist spot. Facing this beach is Diamond Head, once an active volcano. Millions of visitors come each year to enjoy Hawaii's great beauty.

Reading Check

1. How were the islands of Hawaii formed?
2. What kind of climate does Hawaii have?
3. What groups of people live in Hawaii?
4. How do many people make a living in Honolulu?

3. THE PACIFIC NORTHWEST

To Guide Your Reading

Look for these important words:

Key Words
- spawn
- Chinook Indians
- aluminum

Places
- Coast Ranges
- Cascade Range
- Columbia Plateau

- Seattle, Washington
- Puget Sound
- Portland, Oregon

Look for answers to these questions:

1. How are Washington and Oregon alike?
2. What landforms are in the Pacific Northwest?
3. What kinds of industries are important here?

Washington and Oregon are sometimes called the Pacific Northwest. These two states are alike in many ways. They both have rocky coasts, high mountains, and heavy rainfall. Both have thick forests of pines. A total of 23 national forests are here.

The Land

Like two long fingers on the land, a pair of mountain ranges run from north to south through Washington and Oregon. In the west are the **Coast Ranges.** Farther east is the **Cascade Range,** the higher of the two ranges.

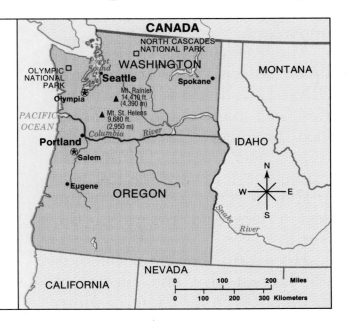

THE PACIFIC NORTHWEST

- ▲ Mountain peak
- ▢ National park
- ✳ State capital

Fertile farm valleys lie in the areas between both of these mountain ranges.

Winds from the Pacific Ocean bring heavy rains to the Coast Ranges. Some parts get as much as 140 inches (about 355 cm) of rain a year. These winds also drop rain on the Cascades, but by the time they cross the Cascades, the winds are dry. The land east of the Cascades gets little rain. This high, dry land east of the mountains is called the **Columbia Plateau.** This plateau gets only from 10 to 20 inches (about 25 to 50 cm) of rain a year.

Where it is rainy in the Pacific Northwest, the trees grow very tall. The mountain slopes are covered with towering Douglas firs and other kinds of pine trees. The forests of the Pacific Northwest give us much of our country's lumber. Most of it is used for building. However, as trees are cut down, new trees are planted to grow in their place.

The mountains of the Pacific Northwest have many rivers flowing toward the ocean. Many kinds of fish live in these streams. The salmon is the most valuable as well as the most unusual fish.

The Coast Ranges are near the Pacific Ocean. Why do they receive such heavy rainfalls?

We plant new forests so we will have lumber in the future. What are some of the ways people use wood?

Near the foot of Mount Rainier and along Puget Sound, Seattle developed in an area rich in water and timber resources.

Salmon are born in mountain streams. After a time they swim down to the Pacific. They live in the ocean from six months to five years. Then they swim back to lay their eggs in the streams where they were born. On the trip back, the salmon must leap over waterfalls and rapids. Some are caught in fishing nets. Those salmon that reach their goal **spawn,** or lay their eggs, in quiet pools of water. Then, weary from their trip, the salmon die. Soon their eggs hatch, though, and life begins again.

The Pacific Northwest Long Ago and Today

The **Chinook** (shih•NUHK) **Indians** live on the Northwest coast. Many Chinooks today work as farmers or ranchers. In the past these Indians fished and gathered food from the forest.

Farther north other Indian groups built villages along the rugged coast. They made large boats from logs to carry them in search of food. They caught fish and hunted seals and sea otters.

When American settlers came to the Northwest, they started farms. Today many crops grow in the mild climate and heavy rains of this region. Northwest farms grow fruits, nuts, berries, and vegetables. Washington is well known for its apples. Oregon grows many kinds of berries to be frozen or eaten fresh. Some are made into jams or jellies.

Most people of the Northwest live in big cities. **Seattle** is the largest city in Washington. It lies on **Puget** (PYOO•jit) **Sound.** Puget Sound is a body of water somewhat like a bay. It is almost 100 miles (about 160 km) long. From Seattle people can see Mount

Washington state is the nation's top manufacturer of the giant aircraft used by the world's large airlines.

Rainier, one of the highest mountains in North America.

Seattle began as a port for shipping lumber. Today Seattle still ships large amounts of wood products. Factories in Seattle build ships and airplanes. **Aluminum** (uh•LOO•muh•nuhm) is also manufactured in Washington. Aluminum is a lightweight metal used to make airplane parts.

Along the Columbia River lies **Portland,** Oregon's biggest city. Ocean ships go up the Columbia to Portland. There they load lumber from Oregon's forests. Some factories in Portland process foods and make paper. Other factories make machines such as chain saws for the lumber industry.

Reading Check

1. What two groups of mountains are in the Pacific Northwest?
2. Why is the Pacific Northwest rainy in the west and dry in the east?
3. Where is the Columbia Plateau?
4. Why is Seattle an important city?

PAUL BUNYAN AND THE LUMBERJACKS

Timber!

The people who cut down trees are called **lumberjacks.** In the early days lumberjacks led hard lives. They used long saws with a wooden handle on each end to cut down big trees. It often took two men all day to cut down a large tree.

Lumberjacks lived at camps far from town. They got up before dawn and worked until dark. At night, after a big meal, they sat up and talked.

Lumberjacks loved telling tall tales. Sometimes they held bragging matches. One man might say he could chop down a tree in a day. Another might say he could do it in half a day. Some of these tales were about a made-up hero. His name was **Paul Bunyan.**

As the lumberjacks made up stories about Paul Bunyan, he began to sound almost real. Soon Paul was a hero in the logging camps everywhere. He was supposed to be bigger, braver, and stronger than anyone else.

Each lumberjack tried to tell a better story about Paul Bunyan than the next person. One logger said that Paul Bunyan was so big that he pulled up pine trees by the roots to comb his beard. One might tell how Paul mowed down a forest with his three-mile-long saw. Another might tell how Paul dug a harbor in just one day and logged a state in one winter. That was nothing special for Paul Bunyan, still another logger would say. He could remember when Paul had to get some logs out of the forest and float them to the harbor. With just a sweep of his mighty hand, he scooped out a river!

4. CALIFORNIA

To Guide Your Reading

Look for these important words:

Key Words
- redwoods
- sequoias
- Gold Rush
- Forty-niners
- special-effects artist
- balsa

People
- Junipero Serra

Places
- Sierra Nevada
- Central Valley
- Sacramento
- San Joaquin
- San Diego
- San Jose
- San Francisco
- Los Angeles
- Hollywood

Look for answers to these questions:

1. What different kinds of climate are in California?
2. Who were the first settlers in California?
3. What was the Gold Rush?
4. How do people make a living in California?

California is the third-largest state in size, with more people than any other state. It has a treasure chest of natural resources on the land, under the ground, and in the nearby sea. Its mountains, ocean beaches, rich farmland, and large cities make it a land of variety and contrast.

The Land and the Climate

From Washington and Oregon the Coast Ranges stretch all along the coast of California. Higher mountains lie east of the Coast Ranges in California. They are the **Sierra Nevada.** Between the Coast Ranges and the Sierra Nevada is the huge **Central Valley.**

The Central Valley gets very little rain. Nevertheless, it is one of the best farmlands in the world. Hundreds of crops grow in the Central Valley. Among the main ones are lettuce, tomatoes, grapes, sugar beets, rice, and cotton.

Miles of irrigation canals provide water for this rich farmland. These canals connect the Central Valley to California's largest rivers, the **Sacramento** and the **San**

Joaquin (SAN wah•KEEN). Snow in northern California's mountains melts to feed these rivers.

Another important farming area, the Imperial Valley, is in southeast California in the Sonoran Desert. The Colorado River supplies water to this fertile but dry farming valley.

Different parts of California have different climates. The deserts in southeast California get fewer than 10 inches (about 25 cm) of rain a year. As many as 80 inches (about 200 cm) fall along the northern coast. In the damp, foggy northern region grow the **redwoods,** some of the world's tallest trees. Redwoods may grow to a height of 300 feet (about 91 m) or more.

Redwoods live to be hundreds of years old. They live so long because they are not bothered by insects or even fires.

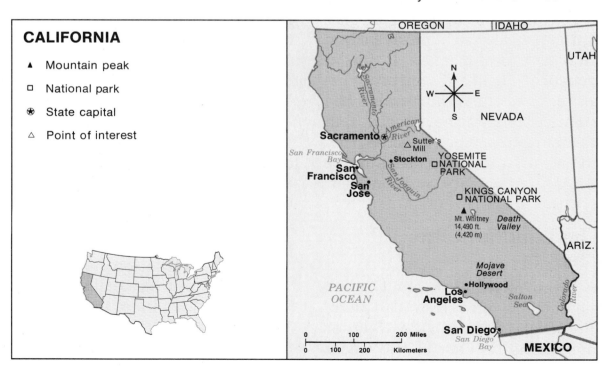

276

Along the coast and in the valleys of California, the climate is usually mild all year. Since the temperature rarely drops below freezing, farmers plant year-round in California.

Although some parts are wetter than others, most of California has two seasons. The wet season comes in the winter. The dry season runs from about April to November.

California has many beautiful places. High cliffs and rocks line much of its northern coast. In the north, the mountains are covered with forests. During the winter, much snow falls in the mountains.

At King's Canyon, in the southern Sierra Nevada, are the giant **sequoias** (si•KWOY•uhz). These huge trees are among the oldest living things in the world. Nearby is Mount Whitney, the second-highest peak in the United States. Farther south and east, in the Mojave Desert, is Death Valley. Death Valley is one of the hottest and driest places in the United States. At 282 feet (86 m) below sea level, this valley is the lowest point in the Western Hemisphere.

Death Valley is a 130-mile-long (209 km) desert of drifting sand in southern California. About 125 years ago borax was discovered here, and 20-mule teams were used to haul it out of the valley.

California Long Ago

Junipero Serra (hoo•NEE•puh•roh SER•uh), a Spanish priest, led the first settlers to California from Mexico. Father Serra built a chain of missions in California in order to teach the Indians here. Over the years large cities grew up around some of the missions. These cities include **San Diego** (SAN dee•YAY•goh), **San Jose** (hoh•ZAY), and **San Francisco.**

California became part of the United States after a war with Mexico in 1848. By that time, wagon trains of pioneers were pushing west. Then a discovery suddenly brought many more people west. The discovery was gold.

The Gold Rush

A man named John A. Sutter decided to build a sawmill on the American River in northern California. To build the mill, workers had to dig into the riverbed. As they dug, some shiny flakes of yellow metal appeared in the water. The yellow flakes turned out to be gold.

The word spread that gold had been discovered at Sutter's Mill. The **Gold Rush** was on! Many

Forty-niners could pan for gold or use a cradle. The heavy gold sinks to the bottom of the container as water washes out the dirt.

thousands of people crossed the Rocky Mountains to California. Others sailed from the Atlantic coast all the way around South America to California. The ocean trip often took six months.

The miners came to be called the **Forty-niners** because they arrived in California in 1849. A few Forty-niners became rich. Many more never found the gold they were seeking.

Along with the miners came other people who started hotels and stores. Suddenly towns were springing up all over. In 1850 California became a state.

California Today

Nine out of ten Californians now live in cities and towns. In the north San Francisco is the largest city. It is a city built on hills overlooking San Francisco Bay. Besides drawing thousands of visitors each year, San Francisco is also an important business center in the West. Many large companies have offices in San Francisco.

Farther south is California's largest city, **Los Angeles** (LOSS AN·juh·luhs). More than 12 million people live in the Los Angeles metropolitan area. The area

San Francisco started growing into a city during the Gold Rush. Today it is a city of skyscrapers and old homes.

Numerous expressways crisscross Los Angeles, the second-largest city in the United States.

Many of California's Spanish-speaking people are of Mexican-American heritage.

process food, build airplanes, and make clothing. Oil from southern California wells goes to refineries near Los Angeles.

Los Angeles is famous for one industry in particular—moviemaking. The part of Los Angeles called **Hollywood** is known as the movie capital of the world.

Judy Lee, Special-Effects Artist

Outside the sun is shining, but Judy Lee does not notice it. She is thinking of dark nights and monsters. Judy is a **special-effects artist** for a Hollywood movie company. Her job is to make what is not real seem real.

Special-effects artists make spaceships fly through outer space. They make planets explode. They can even make a monster that is no taller than your knee look taller than a skyscraper!

Judy is building a town for a monster movie. The town, complete with streets, houses, and stores, is on a big table in the middle of her workshop. The buildings, of course, are much smaller than real buildings. Judy makes some of her buildings from cardboard. She cuts out tiny holes for doors and windows. She uses glue to hold the roofs and walls together. For nighttime scenes tiny light bulbs in some of the

includes the city of Long Beach as well as many smaller communities. So many towns surround Los Angeles that it is hard to tell where one town ends and another begins!

Like San Francisco—and all of California—Los Angeles has a large mix of people. A great many Spanish-speaking people make their home in Los Angeles.

Why have so many people come to live in the Los Angeles area? Many have come for its pleasant, sunny climate. Others have come for jobs. Factories in the city

In the movies, a whole village or even outer space may fit on top of the work-table of a special-effects artist.

Every carefully crafted detail of this tiny village will be destroyed by one step of a movie monster's foot!

houses provide lights through windows.

A camera crew will film the town from far away. This will make the town seem bigger than it really is. It will look like a real mountain village. When the model of the monster stands in the streets, it will look real, too.

Judy uses **balsa** wood for a few buildings. Balsa is a soft wood that is easy to carve. Judy uses balsa because these buildings get crushed in the movie. She wants splintering wood to look real.

After several months the movie is finished. When Judy goes to see it with her friends, she wonders what the other people in the theater are thinking. Do they believe what is happening is real? Are they scared? She hopes so. She waits for the scene in which the monster stomps through the forest. It is going toward the village. Now the monster has reached the school. On the screen a huge foot comes closer to the roof of the school. At the last minute the children race to safety. Then a hairy foot smashes through the roof. The people watching the movie scream. Judy knows the huge foot is really only a few inches long. Yet for a moment, even Judy is a bit scared!

Reading Check

1. What are California's two main areas of mountains?
2. Name two dry places in California that have been turned into rich farmland.
3. Why did many settlers come to California in 1849?
4. For what industry is Los Angeles famous?

SKILLS FOR SUCCESS

USING POPULATION MAPS

A **population map** is a map that shows where people live. It also tells how many people live in different areas.

The map on the next page shows where people live in California. The map key tells what the colors stand for. The red areas show the centers of large cities. Many people live close together in these areas.

The red areas take up less space than all the other colors. Yet about half of California's people live in these places.

Yellow shows places that have fewer people than the red parts. Yet they still have many people. These places may be small cities or suburbs of large cities. Many people who live in suburbs work in nearby large cities.

In cities many people live in hotels or apartment houses. These buildings are usually close to other large buildings.

People who live in suburbs outside of large cities may live in houses for one or two families.

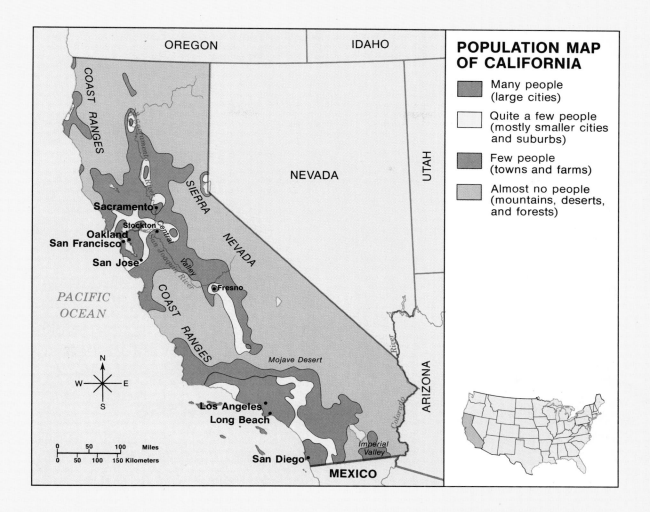

POPULATION MAP OF CALIFORNIA

Many people (large cities)

Quite a few people (mostly smaller cities and suburbs)

Few people (towns and farms)

Almost no people (mountains, deserts, and forests)

The purple color shows places that do not have many people. On this map of California you can see two large purple strips. One runs through the center of the state. The other is in the southern part of the state. The purple strip in the center of the state is the Central Valley. This valley has small cities and towns as well as mile after mile of farmland.

The green parts on the map stand for places that have very few people. This land is mostly forest, mountain, or desert.

CHECKING YOUR SKILLS

Use the map in this section to answer the questions.

1. Do more people live in eastern or western California? Are more large cities located along California's coast or inland?

2. Do more people live in the green or the red parts?

3. Is Stockton a small or large city?

4. Which is shown in purple on this map, the Mojave Desert or the Central Valley?

CHAPTER 13 REVIEW

WORDS TO USE

Copy the words numbered 1 to 5. Next to each word write the meaning from the list below.

1. **fjord**
2. **Inuit**
3. **lumberjacks**
4. **spawn**
5. **tundra**

a. Long, narrow channel going into the coast
b. Flat, frozen land
c. Eskimos of Alaska
d. People who cut down trees
e. Lay eggs

FACTS TO REVIEW

1. Why do most Alaskans live along the southern coast?

2. How has Alaska changed in recent years?

3. Why do many people go on winter vacations to Hawaii?

4. Why is farming in Hawaii important to people all over the United States?

5. Name two ways Alaska and Hawaii are alike.

6. Why does the Pacific Northwest have such a large lumber industry?

7. Name two ways Washington and Oregon are alike.

8. The Central Valley and the Imperial Valley have dry climates. Why is so much food grown there?

9. Why did people move to California long ago?

10. In what ways is the Pacific Ocean important to the people of the Pacific states?

IDEAS TO DISCUSS

Which part of the Pacific region would you most like to visit? What are you most interested in seeing? How is this place different from where you live? How is it like where you live?

◯ SKILLS PRACTICE

Using Population Maps Use the population map on page 283 to answer these questions.

1. Does most of the Central Valley have "quite a few people" or "few people"?

2. A metropolitan area is a large city with smaller cities around it. What metropolitan areas are there in California?

UNIT 3 REVIEW

WORDS TO REMEMBER

Copy the sentences below. Fill in the blanks with the right words from the list.

food processing   **refineries**
glaciers   **reservoir**
humid   **textiles**
metropolitan area   **trade**
needleleaf trees   **valley**

1. The Appalachian Mountains and the Great Lakes were formed by giant ____.

2. Floods once destroyed buildings and crops in the Tennessee River ____.

3. The Northeast and the Southeast have moist, or ____, summers.

4. Large forests of pine and other ____ ____ grow along the Pacific coast.

5. New York City is a center of ____; many goods are shipped to and from this city.

6. Meat-packing plants and bakeries are part of the ____ industry.

7. The Southeast leads in making cloth, or ____.

8. In ____, crude oil is changed into gasoline and heating oil.

9. The Los Angeles ____ ____ includes many towns and suburbs surrounding it.

10. Lake Mead, the ____ of the Hoover Dam, stores water from the Colorado River.

FOCUS ON MAIN IDEAS

1. Name two reasons the Northeast is an important place for manufacturing.

2. Why was the Declaration of Independence important to the people of the 13 colonies?

3. Why are the Great Lakes the most important resource of the Great Lakes states?

4. Name two regions in which tourism is very important. Explain why people visit these regions.

5. What foods come from the Interior Plains? From what parts of the plains do these products come?

6. What are some ways that people make their land better for farming?

7. How are the Atlantic and Pacific oceans important to the lives of Americans?

8. A good place for manufacturing needs several things. Name three of them.

9. For each product below, name a region in which it is important.

   a. corn
   b. wheat
   c. beef cattle
   d. oil

10. In what regions are these landforms?

    a. Coastal Plain
    b. Central Plains
    c. Coast Ranges
    d. Great Basin

ACTIVITIES

1. **Research/Using a Map** Use a large outline map of the United States. Cut out pictures from magazines of foods raised in each region of our country. Paste these pictures in the right places on the map.

2. **Research/Timeline** You have read about many important people in the Long Ago sections in this unit. Choose one of them and read more about him or her in an encyclopedia. Make a timeline of the important events in that person's life.

3. **Remembering the Close-Up** Spanish is the language of Puerto Rico. If you vacationed there, you might want to speak some Spanish. Find some basic words and sentences in a Spanish-language textbook or a traveler's Spanish phrase book. Practice saying some words you might need in Puerto Rico.

◯ SKILLS REVIEW

1. **Using a Road Map** Use the map on page 204 to answer these questions.

   a. What kind of highway is Highway 65?
   b. You are going from Newton to Big Creek State Park. What highways will you travel? In what direction will you be traveling?

2. **Separating Facts and Opinions** Which of the statements below are facts? Which are opinions? Explain your answers.

   a. In 1980 Alaska had about 400,500 people.
   b. He is the best pitcher in the United States.
   c. California grows more food than any other state.
   d. One of Hawaii's biggest crops is pineapples.

YOUR STATE

In this unit you have seen that your state and others make up a region of our country. The states of your region grow or make things that are needed in other parts of the United States.

A number of activities are explained below. As you do them, you will find out how people all over our country depend on your state. You will also see how your state depends on other states.

LEARNING ABOUT GEOGRAPHY

1. Pick one plant or animal that is raised for food or for use in other products in your state. Make a list of the things that are made from this plant or animal.

2. Use an almanac to find out at least four important products made in your state. Use the names of these products to make a word-search puzzle. First, write down the products' names. Then on a piece of graph paper, make a large square. Next, write the product names on the graph paper, one letter in each square within the large square. Write some names from left to right. Write other names from top to bottom. Fill in the empty spaces with other letters. Have your classmates find the words.

3. Make a table that shows how your state is important to the rest of our country. Use an encyclopedia or a book about your state to help you find the important resources and products.

LEARNING ABOUT PEOPLE

4. Find out about the people of your state at the library. Who were the first people to live in your state? Who came after them? Who lives there now?

5. Make a population map of your state. Use one color to show the largest cities. Use another color to show less-crowded areas. Label the large cities.

MAKING A TIMELINE

6. Make a timeline of your state's history. Have each mark cover 100 years of history. Be sure to show when your state joined the United States.

UNIT FOUR

AMERICA: A UNITED COUNTRY

Our country is made up of different regions, each with its own resources and kinds of land. Our country is also made up of different people. Yet the people and places of our country are **united,** or joined together, in many ways.

People in the United States share many things. We share our government. We are united by trade and transportation, too. Newspapers, radio, and television let us know what people in our country are doing. In America, we work together to meet our needs. We depend on one another to help us solve the problems we share.

CHAPTER 14

Americans Depend on One Another

About
this
chapter

You have read about the special resources and products of each region of the United States. In this chapter you will see how people from all these regions depend on one another. You will also see how people plan and work together to keep our country strong and free.

1. PEOPLE DEPEND ON ONE ANOTHER

To Guide Your Reading

Look for these important words:

Key Words
- self-sufficient
- specialization
- labor
- producers
- consumers
- wage
- profit
- interdependence

Look for answers to these questions:

1. Why must people buy what they need or want from other people?
2. What is the difference between producers and consumers?
3. What does interdependence mean?

Do you know the story of Robinson Crusoe? Long ago, Robinson Crusoe was stranded alone on a lonely island. He had to build his own house and get food for himself. He had to find water for cooking and for drinking. As his clothes wore out he had to make new ones. Robinson Crusoe was **self-sufficient.** That means he did everything for himself.

People in the United States today live very differently from Robinson Crusoe. We have the same needs for food, clothing, and shelter. Yet we do not make everything ourselves. We usu-ally buy the things we need. We depend on other people to help us meet these needs.

Specialization

Many people do many different jobs to provide you with food, clothing, and shelter. For example, it takes many people to build a house. Some people use machines to cut down trees in the forest. Other people work at saw-mills where the trees are cut into lumber. Other people use the lumber to build the house. These are just a few of the jobs people do before a house can be built.

When a person does only one special kind of job, it is called **specialization** (spesh•uh•luh•ZAY•shuhn). With specialization, people do not spend all their time making their own food, clothing, and shelter. They do certain jobs and are paid money for their **labor,** or work. Then they use this money to buy the things that they need and want from other people.

Producers and Consumers

When people make goods or provide services, they are **producers.** (Remember, a ser-vice is an activity a person does for another.) When people spend money to buy things that they need or want, they are **consumers.** People can be both producers and consumers.

Most of you have bought things, but have you ever been a producer? If you deliver newspapers or walk the neighbor's dog, you are a producer. You are providing a service. In return, you may receive a **wage.** A wage is money paid for the work you have done.

If you make a product like lemonade and sell it, you are a producer, too. You are making a good. You must buy lemons, sugar,

Producers provide services that help our society run smoothly.

Producers stay in business by supplying goods that fill consumer needs.

Producers often try to provide more than one choice for a type of product to meet different consumer needs in price, size, and quality.

and paper cups to make the lemonade. These are your costs of doing business. The money you make after you have bought these things is your **profit.** Profit is the money that is left over after you sell your product and pay your costs.

As a producer, you earn money. When you spend that money, you become a consumer. As a producer, you depend on other people to pay you for your goods or services. As a consumer, you also depend on other people. You depend on them to have stores and other businesses where you can buy things you need and want. You depend on other people and they depend on you. This is called **interdependence** (in·ter·dee·PEN·dens).

Reading Check

1. What is specialization?
2. What is a producer? What is a consumer?
3. What are three costs in making lemonade to sell?
4. How do you depend on other people to meet your needs?

SKILLS FOR SUCCESS

BEING A CAREFUL CONSUMER

Anyone who buys goods or services is a **consumer.** A careful consumer is someone who spends money wisely. Careful consumers get what they want without spending more than they need to.

Here are some ways you can be a careful consumer.

Compare Before You Buy

When you **compare** things, you see how they are alike and different. When you are shopping, you need to compare prices. You also need to compare **quality,** how good the products are. Comparing quality and prices is always a good idea. This kind of shopping is called **comparison shopping.**

Suppose you want to buy an electronic space game. What would you do first? The first step in comparison shopping is to find out what products are available. You can find this out by looking in stores and by reading advertisements. You might find that three space games are available— Cosmic Conflict, Galactic Clash, and Star Smash.

Next you must find out more about each product. Advertisements may tell you some impor-

How might comparison shopping help you stretch your money further?

tant things. For example, an ad for Cosmic Conflict might tell you that this game has four steps, or stages. The ads for the other games show that they have only three stages.

However, advertisements almost never tell you what is bad about a product. To find out about quality, you have to look further. One way to check on a product is to

294

look at it and touch it. Some products that look large and strong in advertisements turn out to be small and breakable.

Another way to check the quality of a product is to talk to someone who has the product. For example, a friend of yours might have Star Smash. Ask your friend how he or she likes the game. If your friend says that Star Smash is too hard or too easy, you might not want to buy it.

Once you have compared quality, it is time to compare prices. Perhaps Cosmic Conflict and Galactic Clash seem about equal in quality. You must now find out which game costs less, and where you can buy it.

You can check prices by visiting or telephoning stores. You can check newspaper ads, too. As you find out prices, you might make a list. Look at the list below. It is in the form of a table.

As you can see from the table, different stores sell the same game for different prices. Cosmic Conflict is more than four dollars cheaper at Big Toy Village ($16.88) than at Northeast Variety ($20.99). What is the lowest price in the table? Which game is offered for this price? Which store offers this price?

Now that you have compared quality and prices, you can decide which game to buy. Which would you choose? Where would you buy it?

Watch for Sales

Wise shoppers learn to wait for sales. Some items go on sale at a certain time of year. Usually this is after the time when they are most popular. Stores have these sales

Stores	Cosmic Conflict	Galactic Clash
Big Toy Village	$16.88	$15.77
Johnson's Toys	$17.97	$17.97
Northeast Variety	$20.99	$18.99

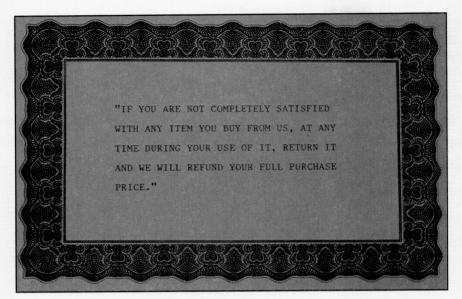

"IF YOU ARE NOT COMPLETELY SATISFIED WITH ANY ITEM YOU BUY FROM US, AT ANY TIME DURING YOUR USE OF IT, RETURN IT AND WE WILL REFUND YOUR FULL PURCHASE PRICE."

A product guarantee tells you that a manufacturer stands behind its product. For some products you may have to fill out a special form and send it to the manufacturer.

to clear their shelves. For example, ice skates often go on sale in spring. Store owners know that many people will not want ice skates until winter. To get people to buy ice skates, store owners sell them at a lower price.

Pay Attention to Guarantees

When you buy something, it should work the way it is supposed to. Many products come with a written **guarantee** (gair•uhn•TEE), a promise that the product will work. You have the right to return any product that does not work. National and state laws protect this right.

To make sure you can return a product, ask the person who sells it to you. Usually you will need to keep the sales slip. The store may limit the time in which you can bring back the product.

CHECKING YOUR SKILLS

Now answer the following questions.

1. What do advertisements tell you about a product? What *don't* they tell you?

2. Which cost less, 3 muffins for 90 cents, or the same muffins for 35 cents each?

3. How would you use comparison shopping to help you buy a bicycle pump?

4. You want to buy swim fins. You know that many people buy swim fins during the summer. You also know that few people buy them in September. Why might you buy swim fins at the end of summer?

5. Why is it better to buy a radio that has a guarantee?

2. REGIONS DEPEND ON ONE ANOTHER

To Guide Your Reading

Look for these important words:
Key Words
- communication
- technology
- industrialized

Look for answers to these questions:
1. Why do people in different regions of our country depend on one another?
2. How do transportation and communication link regions of our country?
3. How has technology helped the United States?

Just as people specialize in jobs, regions of our country specialize in different goods and services. Just as people have different talents and skills, regions have different natural resources.

No one region has everything it needs. Like people, regions trade what they have for what they need. People in one region depend on people in other regions for things they need and want.

Here are some examples. People of the Pacific states catch much more fish than they can eat. They freeze or can the extra fish. To do so, they use machines built in other parts of the country. They sell their fish to people all over the United States.

Canning is one way to preserve products for shipment to other regions.

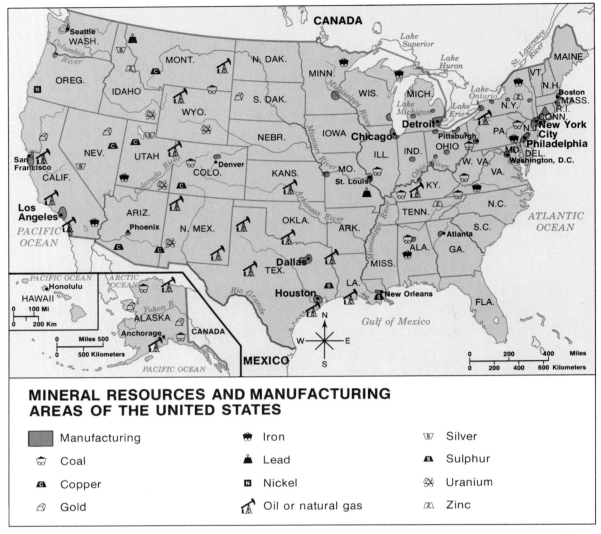

MINERAL RESOURCES AND MANUFACTURING AREAS OF THE UNITED STATES

▨ Manufacturing	🪙 Iron	⑤ Silver
⛏ Coal	▲ Lead	⬛ Sulphur
🅲 Copper	Ⓝ Nickel	✴ Uranium
▱ Gold	🛢 Oil or natural gas	ⓩ Zinc

People in coal-mining mountain regions sell their coal to people in manufacturing regions. The coal is used in factories. People in manufacturing regions make clothing and equipment to sell to people in mining regions.

Farmers in the Interior Plains grow wheat and corn. They sell their grain to factories that make flour for bread and enough breakfast cereal for the whole country. The farmers and the factory workers probably drink orange juice from Florida, Texas, or California.

Even a small business like a lemonade stand depends on several regions of the United States. The lemons might come from Florida, Texas, or California. The sugar might come from Hawaii. The paper cups are made from wood pulp that might come from the forests of Maine, Washington, Oregon, or Georgia.

Links Between Regions

You could not sell lemonade if you could not buy lemons, sugar, and paper cups. Some of these goods have to come from other regions. You depend on people from other regions to send you goods.

Interdependence is possible because the United States has an excellent system of transportation. In America, people can send goods by truck, train, ship, and airplane. Raw materials travel to factories from many different places. Factories send their finished products all over the country.

Before people send raw materials or products anywhere, however, they must know what to send and where to send it. People come to know these things through **communication** between the

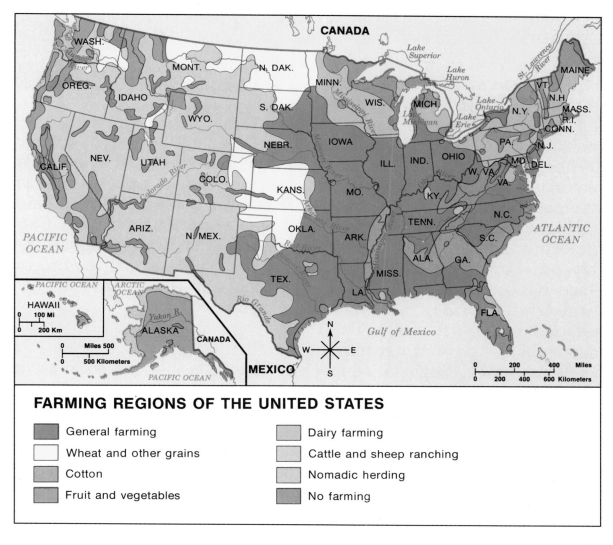

FARMING REGIONS OF THE UNITED STATES

- General farming
- Wheat and other grains
- Cotton
- Fruit and vegetables
- Dairy farming
- Cattle and sheep ranching
- Nomadic herding
- No farming

regions. Communication is the way we send and receive messages. Through communication, people know how much to charge for what they are sending also. Farmers, factory owners, shippers, storekeepers, and consumers need to communicate all the time. Telephones, telegrams, letters, and computers are some of the ways we communicate over long distances.

Technology in Our Country

We use modern machines to communicate and to move goods from one place to another. All of these machines are part of our **technology** (tek•NAHL•uh•gee). Technology is building, using, repairing, and improving modern machines.

It is hard to imagine our country without all the machines we rely on every day. The United States has become one of the most **industrialized** (in•DUS•tree•uhl•yzd) nations in the world. This means that we have a huge number of industries. People in industries use many kinds of machines to manufacture large amounts of goods.

Machines allow us to make more jeans, television sets, and toys faster than ever. Machines help us package and move goods

Today a message can be sent to the other side of the world in just seconds.

throughout the nation quickly. Machines like computers help us in our work. Machines also help people who provide services. Can you imagine fire fighters without fire trucks or police officers without two-way radios?

Reading Check

1. How do people from other parts of the country depend on farmers in the Interior Plains?
2. What are three kinds of communication?
3. Why do people depend on transportation systems?
4. What is technology?

300

MONEY

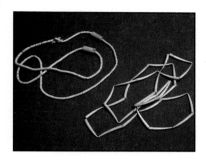

Some American Indians used shells as money.

Coins and paper bills of the United States

People use credit cards in stores, restaurants, and gas stations.

Nickels, dimes, quarters, and paper bills are all money. Money is what we use to pay for goods and services.

Coins and paper bills are not the only kinds of money people use. People often write checks. If you keep your money in a bank, the bank gives you checks to write. You write checks to the people to whom you owe money. These people then collect from the bank the amount of money written on your check.

People can also buy things with credit cards. A credit card is a piece of plastic with your name and account number on it. Stores use the card to fill out a form when you buy something. Each month you receive a bill that shows all your purchases. You can then send a check to the credit card company to pay this bill.

Money is not always coins, bills, checks, or cards, however. Money is whatever people decide to use to buy and sell goods and services. Long ago, American Indians in the Northwest used sea otter pelts, shells, and decorated copper as money. The Plains Indians used buffalo skins, corn, and horses.

Early settlers in North America used coins from Europe. When our country became a nation, the government began to make its own coins. Later it began to print paper money.

What people have used for money has changed a lot in the last 200 years. Do you think that money in the future will be different from what it is today?

SKILLS FOR SUCCESS

USING TIME ZONES

The sun does not shine on all the Earth at once. For this reason, people in different parts of the world set their clocks to different times. An area where people use the same clock time is called a **time zone.** A **time zone map** is a map that helps you figure out what time it is in different time zones.

This map shows the time zones in the United States. The time zone farthest to the east is the **Eastern Time Zone.** Just to the west of the Eastern Time Zone is the **Central**

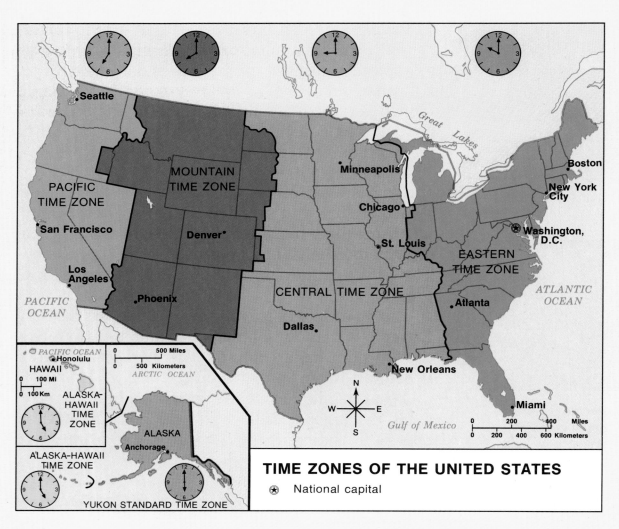

TIME ZONES OF THE UNITED STATES

⊛ National capital

Because different regions are in different time zones, it may still be broad daylight in Hawaii while the streetlights are lit in New York.

Time Zone. The time zone west of the Central Time Zone is the **Mountain Time Zone.** To the west of that is the **Pacific Time Zone.** Alaska and Hawaii have time zones, too. What are their time zones called?

Look at the clock face that shows 10:00. It is above the Eastern Time Zone. Now find the clock face that shows 9:00. It is above the Central Time Zone. When it is 10:00 in the Eastern Time Zone, it is 9:00 in the Central Time Zone. Find the clock face that shows 8:00. In which time zone is it 8:00? When it is 10:00 in New York City, what time is it in Denver?

If you know the time in one time zone, you can figure out the time in another zone. For each time zone to the west, subtract one hour. For each time zone to the east, add one hour. For example, when it is 6:00 in the Pacific Time Zone, it is 9:00 in the Eastern Time Zone. Since the Eastern Time Zone is three zones to the east, you add three hours.

CHECKING YOUR SKILLS

Use the time zone map to answer these questions.

1. In what time zone is Chicago?

2. Is Mountain Time one hour earlier or one hour later than Pacific Time?

3. If it is 8:00 in Chicago, what time is it in San Francisco?

4. If it is 2:00 in Phoenix, what time is it in Dallas?

3. FREE ENTERPRISE IN AMERICA

To Guide Your Reading

Look for these important words:

Key Words
- economy
- free enterprise
- competition
- standard of living

Look for answers to these questions:

1. What has free enterprise done for Americans?
2. How does competition help consumers?
3. Why might Americans have more choices than people in some other countries?

We Americans have plentiful natural resources and up-to-date technology. We produce the greatest variety of goods and services in the world.

The way a country provides and uses goods and services is called its **economy.** Not all economies are alike. In America, we have a **free enterprise** economy. Free enterprise means that people are free to own and run businesses and industries.

In a free enterprise economy, people have many choices about what they make, buy, and sell. The government does not make these choices for people. Free enterprise has helped the United States become one of the wealthiest nations in the world.

To understand how many choices our economy allows us to make, imagine you are shopping for a bicycle. In one store you find ten different kinds of bicycles. Why, you ask yourself, are there so many kinds of bicycles?

In our country, producers try to make bicycles that most people will want to buy. One producer may make the fastest bicycles. One may make the cheapest bicycles. Each producer wants the consumer to buy his or her product. Out of this **competition** (kahm•puh•TISH•uhn), or contest to get customers, comes a great variety of bicycles. Consumers in our country are then free to choose the bicycle they want and have enough money to buy.

304

Americans Have the Freedom to Make Choices

In the free enterprise economy, producers try to make and sell what consumers want. The government does not tell them what to make. The government does, however, set rules for health and safety that producers must follow.

In countries that do not have a free enterprise economy, people have less freedom of choice. In some countries, the government tells producers what they must make. The government may decide that factories must make tractors instead of bicycles. A few factories would be allowed to make bicycles, but people would have fewer kinds of bicycles to choose from.

Under free enterprise, producers of good products or services have more customers and make a good living. Free enterprise has helped many Americans have a high **standard of living**. *Standard of living* means how well people live in a country. It includes how much money a person has to spend on food, clothing, and shelter. It also includes the medical care and the education people can get in a country.

With free enterprise, consumers often have more choices for each product.

Countries without free enterprise may have few products for consumers.

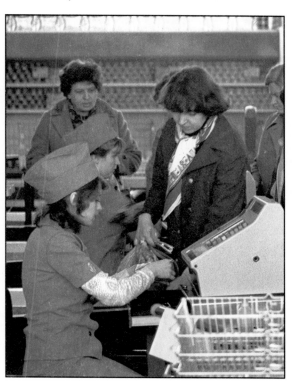

People who live in our "land of opportunity" have more freedom to choose the ways in which they might better their lives.

A Land of Opportunity

The United States has been called the "land of opportunity." For more than 200 years, people have been coming to our country to start new lives. They want to be able to meet their needs. They also want to be able to make their lives and their children's lives more pleasant.

Americans have the opportunities and the freedom to make their lives better. In our country, people can decide for themselves what jobs they want to do and where they want to work. With hard work, many people in our country are able to improve their standard of living.

Because so many people would like to live good lives here, we need to take care of our country. To keep America the "land of opportunity," we must use resources and technology wisely.

Reading Check

1. What does *free enterprise* mean?
2. What is competition? Why is competition among producers good for consumers?
3. What kinds of rules does our government make that producers must follow?
4. What things make up a standard of living?

306

CHAPTER 14 REVIEW

WORDS TO USE

Copy the words numbered 1 to 5. Next to each word write its meaning from the list below.

1. **communication**
2. **competition**
3. **labor**
4. **producers**
5. **standard of living**

a. Work
b. People who make goods or provide services
c. Sending and receiving messages
d. Contest to get customers
e. How well people live in a country

FACTS TO REVIEW

1. How was Robinson Crusoe self-sufficient?

2. How do people specialize?

3. How are people both producers and consumers?

4. What is interdependence?

5. How does specialization work in regions?

6. Why do we need a good communication system in the United States?

7. Give three examples of how regions are interdependent.

8. Name three ways machines help people.

9. What does it mean to live in a free enterprise economy?

10. Why is America called the "land of opportunity"?

IDEAS TO DISCUSS

1. Imagine that we did not have a free enterprise economy. How would your life and your standard of living be different?

2. You use a toothbrush every day. Think of five other things you use every day. How many of these things would you have if you were self-sufficient? What might you use instead?

◯ SKILLS PRACTICE

Using Time Zones Use the time zone map on page 302 to answer these questions.

1. What time is it in Los Angeles, California, when it is 4:00 in Anchorage, Alaska?

2. In what time zone is Washington, D.C.?

CHAPTER 15

Americans Make Decisions Together

About
this
chapter

The land, the people, the way people use the land—these make the United States a great nation. Another important reason for our country's greatness is its government. What does a government do? How can you as a citizen help your government? In this chapter you will read how Americans and the American government work together for our country.

1. MAKING CHOICES

To Guide Your Reading

Look for these important words:

Key Words

- majority rule
- represent
- republic
- local government
- state government
- federal government

Look for answers to these questions:

1. What do people in a democracy do to make choices?
2. Why do Americans elect leaders?
3. What kinds of problems do local, state, and the federal governments handle?

What do you do when you and your friends cannot decide what game to play? You might take a vote. You and your friends agree to play the game that gets the most votes. This way of deciding is called **majority rule.**

Majority rule is a way to make choices that are fair to the most people. Majority rule is the basis of democracy. In a democracy, people are free to make choices about their lives. They often make these choices by voting.

The United States has more than 200 million people. With so many people, countless choices must be made every day. Some choices have to do with only a few people. Only you and your friends must pick a game to play. Some choices have to do with many more people. All the people of your community, state, or country must choose what to do about shared problems. Should a new bridge be built in your community, or a new school? Should more money in America be spent on medicine or on transportation? These are examples of some of the choices that citizens must make.

Certainly, 200 million people cannot get together in one place to talk over every problem. Everyone cannot take part in every choice, and every choice does not concern every person. Instead, the leaders of our country work together to solve problems. Leaders make up our government. A government is the group of people who make and carry out laws for a community, state, or country.

In the United States we elect leaders who must speak for, or **represent,** us. When people elect their leaders, the government is called a **republic.**

Kinds of Government

In the United States there are three kinds of government. The first kind is the **local,** or community, **government.** Then there is the **state government.** Finally, there is the **federal,** or national, **government.**

These three kinds of government help people solve problems that they could not solve alone. Each kind of government handles problems of a different size.

Some problems belong only to the people of your community. These are problems like fixing streets and deciding whether to buy a fire truck. The people of your community are the best people to decide what to do. For this reason, local government takes care of problems like these.

Other choices belong to all the people in your state. Statewide problems include building highways, paying for schools and state parks, and setting rules for drivers. State governments take care of problems like these.

Local governments repair streets. State governments build highways.

Some problems concern everyone in our country. We must have an army, navy, and air force to protect us. We must make choices about trading with other countries. We must have fair rules that apply to all. These problems concern everyone, so the federal government deals with them.

Reading Check

1. How does majority rule work?
2. What is a government?
3. Name two examples of choices a local government might make.
4. What are two problems the federal government deals with?

SKILLS FOR SUCCESS

MAKING CHOICES

Personal Choices

Suppose you have five dollars to spend. You are trying to decide how you will spend it. Here are some steps to help you make up your mind.

First you need to think of the choices you have. You could spend the five dollars to see a movie and buy some popcorn. You could put the money in the bank and save it. Then, when you have more money, you could buy something like a special T-shirt or a bicycle.

Next you should think carefully about the **results** of each choice. Think of the good and bad things that could happen. For example, if you go to the movie, you will have fun. On the other hand, you will have spent all your money. If you put the money in the bank, you will miss some entertainment now. Later, however, if you add to that money in the bank, you might buy something that you could enjoy for a long time.

After you have thought about the results, you can make your choice wisely. You can then spend your money to get something that is most important to you.

Choices a Government Makes

Government leaders have choices to make, too. Suppose a state has $50 million to spend. This money could be used to build a new highway or a new state park.

People in government follow the same steps as you would to make a decision. They think about the possible results of each choice. For example, they might draw up a chart like this one.

Choices	Good Points	Bad Points
highway	quick travel brings in business and jobs	very expensive divides a neighborhood
park	recreation for people conservation, adds beauty to the state	less room for houses and businesses will not create many new jobs

311

People running for government often tell what they would do if elected. By listening to views of possible future government leaders, citizens can be sure to elect the person they want to represent them.

The government leaders must compare the two plans. Which is needed more, a park or a highway? Which would cause fewer problems for people? If you were a government leader, which would you choose? Why?

Voters Help Make Choices

The citizens of a state help to make choices. Suppose two people, Mr. Antolini and Mrs. Harrold, want to be elected to the state government. The state government must decide whether to build the highway or the park. Mr. Antolini thinks the park should be built. Mrs. Harrold thinks the highway should be.

The voters will choose the person they want to represent them. If they want the park, they may decide to vote for Mr. Antolini. If they want the highway, they may vote for Mrs. Harrold. The leader they choose will help the government make the choice most people want.

CHECKING YOUR SKILLS

Now answer the following questions.

1. Imagine you have ten dollars to spend. What choices will you have? How could you spend the money? Explain the reasons for the choice you make.

2. How do citizens help to make choices in government?

3. Your community has enough money to build a new library or a community swimming pool. What might be the good points and bad points of each choice? What choice would you make?

2. HOW GOVERNMENT WORKS

To Guide Your Reading

Look for these important words:

Key Words
- self-government
- Constitution
- branches

- Congress
- Senate
- House of
  Representatives

- executive
- President
- courts
- Supreme Court

Look for answers to these questions:

1. How did our early leaders set up our government?
2. What are the three branches of the federal government?
3. What are the duties of each branch of the federal government?

In a small group of people, each person can help solve a problem. In a large group, people need to tell representatives how they would like things done. Voters in our towns, states, and country elect representatives to speak for them in government.

Our nation's early leaders believed in **self-government.** They wanted the people of America to govern themselves. They did not want to be ruled by a queen or king in England.

After our country won its freedom from England, our leaders wrote the **Constitution** of the United States. The Constitution contains the most important laws of our country. It gives citizens the freedom to elect people to represent them. It gives the plan for our federal government.

Local and state governments used this plan as a model. They are set up in much the same way as our federal government. Each government has three parts, or **branches.** Each branch has a separate job to do. Each branch is just as important as the other two. Here is what each branch of our federal government does and how each works with the others.

Congress

One branch of government makes the laws. In the federal government, the lawmaking

313

The Senate and the House of Representatives usually meet in separate groups. Sometimes, however, they come together in what is called a joint session of Congress.

branch is called **Congress.** Voters in each of the 50 states elect people to Congress.

Two groups of people make up our Congress. One group is called the **Senate.** Each of the 50 states elects two senators to the Senate.

The other group that makes up our Congress is the **House of Representatives.** Members of this group are also elected from each state. However, different states have different numbers of representatives. The number of representatives elected depends on the population of a state. States with larger populations have more representatives in the House.

Members of Congress meet together in Washington, D.C., to make laws for the whole country. They give their opinions about each suggested law. Then they vote for the laws they think will be good for the most people.

Congress makes different kinds of laws. Some laws deal with spending money to protect our country, to build highways, and to help schools. Other kinds of laws protect our health and safety. Some laws make sure that all people are treated equally in schools, jobs, and housing. The Congress also makes laws that protect our country's natural resources.

BRANCHES OF OUR FEDERAL GOVERNMENT

Congress   President   Courts

The Executive Branch

To see that all of these laws are carried out, there is another branch of government. This branch is called the **executive** (ig•ZEK•yuh•tiv) branch. Besides seeing that laws are carried out, the executive branch often suggests laws to Congress.

In the federal government, the head of the executive branch is the **President.** The President and the Vice President are elected by all the voters of the country.

The President of the United States has one of the most important and difficult jobs in the world. The President is in charge of dealing with other countries for the United States. In addition, the President is the leader of the army, navy, and air force.

To help the President see that our nation's laws are carried out, many departments have been set up under the executive branch. The executive branch has more people than either of the other branches of our government.

The Courts

The third branch of government is the **courts.** Judges in courts make sure that people are obeying the law. They decide how people who break laws should be punished.

The most important court in the federal government is the **Supreme Court.** The Supreme Court has nine judges. Their main job is to make sure that the Constitution of the United States is followed. Supreme Court judges, or justices, decide whether laws passed by Congress agree with the Constitution. They make sure that state laws and court decisions follow the Constitution.

Reading Check

1. Why did our nation's early leaders want self-government?
2. What is the Constitution?
3. How is the Senate different from the House of Representatives?
4. What is the Supreme Court?

315

SKILLS FOR SUCCESS

SOLVING PROBLEMS

The Flint family has just received its October gas and electric bill. It is much higher than the Flints expected. The family cannot pay such high bills every month.

The Flints have a problem that they must work to solve. The first step in solving a problem is to say exactly what the problem is. The problem for the Flints is that they are spending too much money on **energy.** Energy is the power that makes things work. Gas and electricity are two kinds of energy.

The second step in solving a problem is to break it into smaller parts. The Flints decide to look at the parts of their gas and electric bill.

Look at this bill. It tells the *TOTAL DUE,* or the amount the Flints owe. It shows how much of the total is the cost of gas and how much is the cost of electricity. The high costs are the two parts of the Flints' problem. Which cost is higher?

The third step in problem-solving is to work on one part of

Statewide Power Company		
1758 N. Albatross Memphis, Tennessee 38101 (901) 555-8600	Thomas Flint 63 Weather Road Memphis, Tennessee 38106	Account Number NVT 18 23002-3 November 1, 1985
From October 1 to October 31:	This month last year:	
Gas $ 23.86 Electricity 89.72	Gas $14.86 Electricity $50.24	
TOTAL DUE $113.58	TOTAL $65.10	

316

the problem at a time. The Flints, for example, need to save money on their gas and electric bill. They must first decide whether to lower their gas or their electric costs.

The Flints want to know which kind of energy use became greater in the past year. Find the part of the bill that says "This month last year." Notice that the costs are lower. In October 1984, electricity cost almost $40 less than it did in October 1985. How much less did gas cost? Should the Flint family try to save gas or electricity?

During the next few months, the Flints work hard to use less electricity. They turn off lights when they leave a room. They open the

What are some ways to solve the problem of rising energy costs?

refrigerator as little as possible. They turn off the television and radio when no one is watching or listening. When the bill comes each month, the Flints compare it with the bill for October 1985.

The fourth step in solving a problem is to check whether you have really solved the problem. Next month, the Flints look at their bill. It is lower! They see that their electricity costs less.

The Flints have solved the problem of their electric bill. They are happy about the amount of money they have saved. Now they decide to lower their gas costs. They keep the heat lower in their house and wear sweaters when it is cold. On sunny days, they open the shades to let warmth into the house. They are glad to see that they have saved energy and lowered their bill.

CHECKING YOUR SKILLS

Now answer the following questions.

1. What are the four steps in solving a problem?

2. What problem did the Flints have to solve?

3. How did the Flints use less electricity?

4. How did the Flints know their efforts worked?

317

3. STATE AND LOCAL GOVERNMENTS

To Guide Your Reading

Look for these important words:

Key Words
- legislature
- governor
- council

- mayor
- city manager
- municipal court
- taxes

Look for answers to these questions:

1. What are the differences between state and local governments?
2. Why must people pay taxes?
3. What responsibilities do Americans owe to the American government?

Like the federal government, state governments have three branches. The lawmaking branch of state government is the state **legislature** (LEJ•uh•slay•chuhr). The voters in a state elect their representatives to the state legislature.

Representatives in the legislature meet in the state capital. There, they make laws for all the people of the state. These laws govern highways, colleges and schools, state parks, and many other things.

State government has an executive branch to see that all laws are carried out. The head of the state executive branch is given the title of **governor.**

Laws made by state legislatures may differ from state to state.

Some state court cases require a jury, a group of ordinary citizens who listens to two points of view and makes a decision about the case.

The third branch of state government is the courts. State courts judge people accused of breaking state laws. Many state laws have to do with crime. The laws about crime are usually a bit different in every state. Judges in state courts make sure state laws are obeyed. If they are not obeyed, judges and courts decide how the lawbreaker must be punished.

Local Government

As you might expect, many local governments also have three parts. The lawmakers of a community are members of the town or city **council.** The council passes laws for police and fire protection. It makes laws about schools and libraries, parks and playgrounds.

The head of the local executive branch of government is the **mayor** or **city manager.** Sometimes a community has both a mayor and a city manager. These people make sure the laws passed are carried out. They make sure the community departments, like the fire department, are running smoothly.

If your community is big enough, it will have a **municipal court.** This kind of court judges people accused of breaking laws in the city. These laws often have to do with traffic, parking, and other things important to the smooth working of a community.

Paying for Government

Our local, state, and federal governments provide many services that people could not provide for themselves. All of these government services, from bridges to libraries, cost money. Police, fire fighters, teachers, and other public workers must be paid.

People pay for government services with **taxes.** Taxes are the money that government collects from people who work or own property. When you buy certain things, you pay a sales tax. That money also goes to the government.

A city's police department makes sure that all laws are obeyed.

Protecting Our Rights and Freedom

One of the most important jobs of our government is to protect the rights and freedom of Americans. The Constitution tells about our many rights and freedoms. For example, Americans are free to express their opinions about their government. Americans have the right to vote for their leaders. All Americans have the right to a fair trial. These are rights that people in some other countries do not have. These rights make the United States the "land of the free."

Our government provides many services and protects our rights and freedoms. In return, we Americans have certain responsibilities that we owe to our government. We should be loyal to our country. We must obey local, state, and federal laws. As adults, we must pay our fair share of taxes. We must vote for the people we think will work hardest to keep our country strong and free.

Reading Check

1. What is the lawmaking branch of state government?
2. Who is the head of the state executive branch?
3. How do city councils help a community?
4. What are taxes?

CHAPTER 15 REVIEW

WORDS TO USE

Use one of the words in parentheses to complete each sentence.

1. The _____ contains the most important laws of our country. (President, Constitution)

2. The Congress is part of the _____. (federal government, state government)

3. The _____ is one group in Congress. (court, Senate)

4. Judges work in _____. (courts, councils)

5. A _____ is the leader of a state. (governor, mayor)

FACTS TO REVIEW

1. What are the three kinds of government in our country?

2. Why is it useful to have three kinds of government in our country?

3. Name three problems state governments take care of.

4. What is the lawmaking branch of our federal government?

5. What jobs does the President of the United States do?

6. What jobs do judges in the Supreme Court do?

7. What jobs does the mayor of a community do?

8. How do people pay for government services?

9. Name three rights all Americans have.

10. How can we as Americans be responsible citizens of our country?

IDEAS TO DISCUSS

How are local, state, and federal governments alike? How are they different from one another?

◯ SKILLS PRACTICE

Making Choices Your community has some money to spend on schools. The money can be used to buy computers for classrooms or instruments for music classes.

1. What steps should be taken to make the choice?

2. What are some good and bad points for each choice?

3. What choice would you make? Why would you make it?

CLOSE-UP

SYMBOLS OF AMERICA

The United States of America is more than a place. It is an idea. You cannot see or hear or touch an idea. However, you can see, hear, and touch things that show you what America means. These things stand for the idea of America.

Something that stands for something else is called a **symbol.** Our flag is a symbol of our country that people know around the world. Our national anthem, "The Star-Spangled Banner," and the Statue of Liberty are two other symbols of America. On the next few pages you will read about five symbols of America.

The Liberty Bell is a symbol of our country's basic idea of freedom.

The Liberty Bell

When England still ruled our land, Pennsylvania's lawmakers built a capitol building in Philadelphia. They ordered a bell from England for their capitol. The first time the new bell was tested in Philadelphia, it cracked. Bellmakers repaired it. It was rung for the first time in 1753.

In 1776 Americans wanted to be free from England. The bell was rung then to call people to listen to the Declaration of Independence. The Declaration of Independence said that the United States of America was now a free country. After that, Americans fought a war to gain and keep this freedom.

The bell in the capitol building became known as the Liberty Bell. During most of the war, the Liberty Bell was hidden in the basement of a church. After the Americans won the war, the bell was returned to Philadelphia. The capitol building there was called Independence Hall. For the next 60 years, the Liberty Bell was rung on important days, like the Fourth of July.

About 150 years ago, the bell cracked again. This time the crack could not be mended. The bell has not been rung since then. Yet the words upon the Liberty Bell still ring out: "PROCLAIM LIBERTY THROUGHOUT ALL THE LAND UNTO ALL THE INHABITANTS THEREOF."

Our flag is a symbol that links each state of our country.

The American Flag

The American flag was probably designed while our country was fighting for freedom from England. At that time there were 13 American states. The first American flag had 13 red and white stripes, each standing for one state. In the upper left corner were 13 white stars on a square blue background.

As more states joined the new United States, the flag changed. Congress decided to keep the 13 stripes to stand for the 13 original states but to add a star for each new state.

The flag flies over every school and public building in America. A flag stands in front of each place where people vote on Election Day. Many people fly flags on national holidays.

The flag must always be treated with respect. It should never touch the ground. As a symbol of our freedom, our flag should always fly free.

The Star-Spangled Banner

Oh, say, can you see, by the dawn's
  early light,
What so proudly we hailed at the
  twilight's last gleaming,
Whose broad stripes and bright stars,
  through the perilous fight,
O'er the ramparts we watched were so
  gallantly streaming?
And the rockets' red glare,
  the bombs bursting in air,
Gave proof through the night that our
  flag was still there.
Oh, say, does that star-spangled
  banner yet wave
O'er the land of the free and the home
  of the brave?

About 170 years ago, during a war with England, Francis Scott Key wrote these words. He wrote them on the back of an envelope as he stood on the deck of an English ship. The English were holding him prisoner while they attacked Fort McHenry, near Baltimore, Maryland.

Key spent a long, anxious night. He watched the rockets and bombs that English ships fired at Fort McHenry. At dawn he saw the American flag still waving over the fort. That meant the English had not taken the fort. When Key was set free the next day, he finished his poem. Copies of the poem were passed around Baltimore that day. Then a Baltimore newspaper printed the poem. People began to sing the poem to a popular English tune. Soon the song was being sung all over the country.

In 1931, Congress made "The Star-Spangled Banner" our **national anthem,** or national song. Today it is sung on important occasions. It is also

Francis Scott Key wrote our national anthem during a battle with England.

sung when people gather to enjoy themselves, as at sports events. It speaks of the fear we feel when our country is in danger. It reminds us of our pride when America's strength carries it through.

The Statue of Liberty

The beautiful copper Statue of Liberty was given to America by the people of France. It was a gift given to honor 100 years of American independence. The statue was built in France, then taken apart and shipped to New York City. It was completed in 1886.

Americans saw one part of the statue before the rest was finished. The right arm was shown at a great fair in Philadelphia in 1876. People stared in amazement at Liberty's huge arm and torch. Twelve people can stand on the rim of the torch. Liberty's index finger is 8 feet (about 2½ m) long. Even her fingernail is 10 inches (about 25 cm) across.

The top of Liberty's torch towers 305 feet (about 93 m), high above the waters of New York Harbor. Americans built the base, or **pedestal,** on which the statue stands. The words of an American poet, **Emma Lazarus,** appear on the pedestal. Those words have welcomed immigrants for almost 100 years. They help explain what the Statue of Liberty means to people entering our country.

...Give me your tired, your poor,
Your huddled masses yearning to
 breathe free,...

The Statue of Liberty has been and always will be a symbol of freedom to millions of

The Statue of Liberty is a symbol of freedom to all the world's people.

325

immigrants entering America. Her torch of liberty is always lifted to welcome the peoples of the world to our shores.

The Pledge of Allegiance unites each of us with every other citizen of our country's past, present, and future.

The Pledge of Allegiance

In many states, young people begin each school day in the same way. They stand up straight, place their right hands over their hearts, and say

> I pledge allegiance to the flag of the United States of America and to the republic for which it stands, one nation under God, indivisible, with liberty and justice for all.

You, too, may say these words almost every day. Do you know what they mean?

I pledge allegiance to the flag of the United States of America.... A pledge is a promise. Allegiance is loyalty. We promise to be loyal and true to our country's flag because it is a symbol of America.

...and to the Republic for which it stands.... We owe loyalty to the United States, our country. We owe loyalty to the beliefs that make our country strong.

...one nation under God, indivisible.... An indivisible thing cannot be divided. America is made up of many groups of people with different views. Yet we stand together as a nation to support our country.

...with liberty and justice for all. Every American has a right to liberty, or freedom. All people deserve justice, the right to be treated fairly. When we respect our fellow citizens and treat them fairly, we show loyalty to our country.

UNIT 4 REVIEW

WORDS TO REMEMBER

Copy the sentences below. Fill in the blanks with the right words from the list.

executive
free enterprise
industrialized
interdependence
legislature
local government
represent
specialization
taxes
technology

1. When people do one kind of job, it is called _____.

2. When people and regions depend on one another, it is called _____.

3. The United States is one of the most _____ nations in the world.

4. Building, using, repairing, and improving modern machines is _____.

5. Under _____ _____, people are free to own and run their own businesses and industries.

6. In America, we elect leaders to _____ us.

7. A city council is part of a _____ _____.

8. Our President is the head of the _____ branch.

9. The lawmaking branch of state government is the _____.

10. People pay the government for its services with _____.

FOCUS ON MAIN IDEAS

1. Why do people specialize in jobs?

2. Give three examples in which people are producers.

3. Why are regions of the United States interdependent?

4. How do transportation and communication bring our country together?

5. How does technology make our country strong?

6. Name two advantages of the free enterprise economy.

7. What does each of the three branches of government do?

8. What are some of the problems that the federal government must take care of?

9. What are some of the kinds of laws Congress makes?

10. Why is America called the "land of the free"?

ACTIVITIES

1. **Research/Writing** Find grocery store advertisements in your local newspaper. Compare the prices of three food items in as many store ads as you can. Where can you get the best prices? Write a few sentences telling what you found out.

2. **Research/Art** Imagine you want to run for mayor of your community. What jobs would you do as mayor? Make a poster that tells people why you should be mayor.

3. **Time Zone Maps** Find out which time zone you are in by looking at the time zone map on page 302. When it is 5:00 in your time zone, what time is it in these places:

   a. New York City
   b. Denver
   c. Los Angeles
   d. Anchorage

○ SKILLS REVIEW

1. **Being a Careful Consumer** Use the chart to answer these questions.

Stores	Bikes and Prices		
	Speedy 1	Super Ride	Deluxe
Mike's Bikes	$70	$75	$90
Deals on Wheels	$75	$85	$95
Bike Mania	$65	$70	$85

   a. What are the three kinds of bikes for sale?
   b. Which bike is the least expensive? Which is the most expensive?
   c. Which store would be the cheapest place to buy your bike?

2. **Solving Problems** The Hosleys' phone bill is too high. Here is their bill:

Long distance: $75.00
Local calls: $4.50

   a. What steps should the Hosleys take to solve their problem?
   b. What part of the bill should they work to cut back? How can they do that?
   c. How will the Hosleys know if they have solved their problem?

YOUR STATE

In Unit 4, you read how people and regions in America depend on one another to meet their needs and wants. You also read how Americans solve problems together through a representative form of government. Here are some activities that will help you understand interdependence and government in your state.

LEARNING ABOUT GOVERNMENT

1. Find out the name of the governor of your state. Find out the names of the senators who represent you in the federal government. Look in some newspapers or news magazines to find out what people in government are doing. Share with the class the newspaper articles you find.

LEARNING ABOUT HISTORY

2. Find out when your state became part of the United States. Try to find a picture of your state capital. What special landmarks are there? What government groups meet there? If you can, take a trip to visit your state capital with a parent, a guardian, or your class.

LEARNING ABOUT INTERDEPENDENCE

3. As explained in Unit 4, interdependence means that people in one region depend on people in other regions to supply them with things they need and want. Use an encyclopedia to find out about the three resources and products your state is famous for.

   Can you think of three things your family uses that come from another region? Where do they come from? How did they get to your region?

LEARNING ABOUT SPECIALIZATION

4. What special jobs do people in your state have? For example, many people in your state might specialize in coal mining or computers. Tell about a few of these jobs. Then draw a picture of yourself doing a job you would like to specialize in. Write two sentences telling why you might like that job.

UNIT FIVE

OTHER LANDS, OTHER PEOPLE

There are more than 160 nations in the world. The people of these nations speak 3,000 languages. They have many different customs and kinds of government.

Although it is often different, life in some parts of the world is much the same as in the United States. In many large cities people have the same kinds of foods, clothing, and houses.

In this unit you will explore many regions of the world. As you explore them, you will see how they are the same as or different from places in the United States. You will see how other people's lives are different from—or like—your own.

CHAPTER 16

Rivers Around the World

About
this
chapter

Rivers have always been important to people.
Look at any map and you will see cities clustered
along almost all large rivers. In this chapter you
will read about some of the world's most important rivers. You will also find out about the people who live near them.

1. MAJOR RIVERS OF THE WORLD

To Guide Your Reading

Look for these important words:

Key Words
- barge trains
- rain forest

Places
- Lake Victoria
- Mediterranean Sea
- Sahara
- Aswan High Dam
- Alps
- Rotterdam, the Netherlands
- North Sea
- Andes Mountains

Look for answers to these questions:

1. Why is farming in the Nile valley easier today than long ago?
2. Why is the Rhine River important to the people of six countries?
3. How is the Amazon River different from the Nile and the Rhine?

Some of the world's great rivers flow through Africa, Europe, South America, and Asia. Many of the world's people live along these rivers. As you read about each river, find it on the map on pages 334–335.

The Nile River

The Nile, the longest river in the world, is in Africa. It is about 4,145 miles (about 6,670 km) long. The Nile gets its water from a number of different lakes and rivers. Much of the water comes from **Lake Victoria** in the center of Africa. From Lake Victoria the Nile cuts through the middle of the Sudan and Egypt. It ends its long run north at the **Mediterranean** (med•ih•tuh•RAY•nee•uhn) **Sea.**

In Egypt the Nile crosses the world's largest desert, the **Sahara** (suh•HAIR•uh). Yet the valley of the Nile is rich and fertile. Almost all of Egypt's people live on this strip of farmland. The most fertile part is the Nile delta, formed by the river at its mouth.

People have been living in cities on the Nile for thousands of years. Each summer, heavy rains made the river flow over its banks. The floods left tons of silt that made the land rich. Farmers in Egypt planted their crops after the water level dropped. Since the rains came once a year, Egyptian farmers planted once a year.

Today farmers can plant crops twice a year in the Nile valley of Egypt. Sometimes they can plant three crops. Dams built across the Nile have made this possible. The largest of these is the **Aswan** (a•SWAHN) **High Dam.** Now the Nile does not flood in Egypt. The dams hold back much of the water from the fall floods. During the dry season, the water is slowly let out into the Nile. Egyptian farmers can use it to water their crops. Water power from the dam provides electricity to the people of the Nile valley.

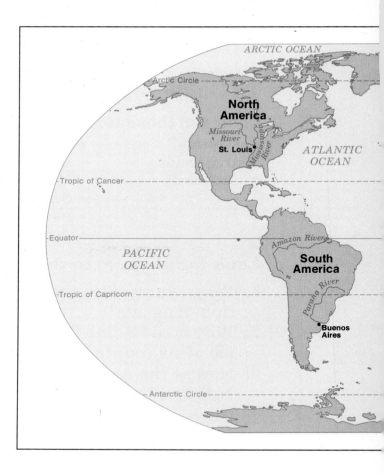

Some of the world's richest farmland is found along the banks of the Nile River.

Irrigation from the Aswan Dam has doubled crop production along the Nile.

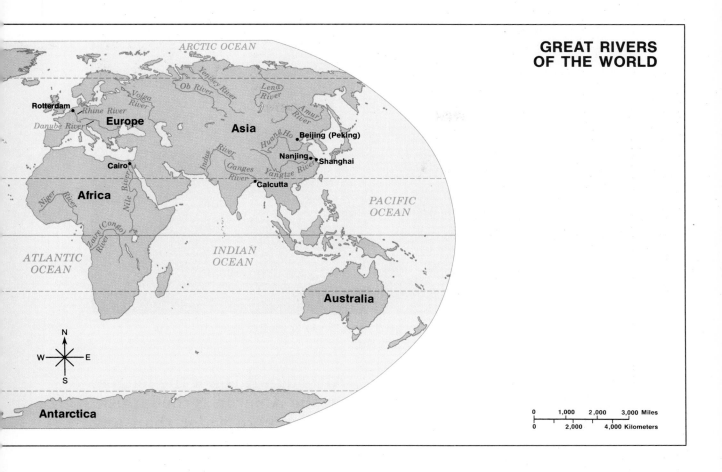

ARCTIC OCEAN

Yenisey River
Ob River
Lena River
Volga River
Amur River
Rotterdam
Rhine River
Europe
Danube River
Asia
Huang Ho
Beijing (Peking)
Nanjing
Shanghai
Cairo
Indus River
Ganges River
Yangtze River
Calcutta
Niger River
Africa
Nile River
Zaire (Congo) River
PACIFIC OCEAN
ATLANTIC OCEAN
INDIAN OCEAN
Australia

N
W E
S

Antarctica

| 0 | 1,000 | 2,000 | 3,000 Miles |
| 0 | 2,000 | | 4,000 Kilometers |

The Rhine River

The Rhine (RYN) River touches six countries in Europe. Three of these countries lie far from the sea. The Rhine links these countries to ocean ports. Along much of the river are some of Europe's largest factory areas. This makes the Rhine River the most important waterway in all of Europe.

The Rhine begins in Switzerland, high in the **Alps,** the large area of mountains that cross central Europe. From there it flows north to the tiny country of Liechtenstein (LIK•tuhn•styn) and crosses Austria. It passes by many large cities in West Germany and France. These cities have many factories. The Rhine then winds west through the Netherlands. More large factories are found here. The river ends its journey in **Rotterdam,** the world's busiest port. Here the Rhine empties into the **North Sea,** a part of the Atlantic Ocean.

The Rhine is filled with ships. Long lines of barges travel the river. These **barge trains** carry coal and iron ore to the factories.

335

A waterway deep enough for the world's large ocean ships links the Rhine River port city of Rotterdam to the North Sea.

They also carry to Rotterdam goods made in the factories of the many countries along the river. Large ocean-going ships arrive at and leave from Rotterdam. The ships carry their cargoes to places around the world.

The Amazon River

The Amazon (AM•uh•zahn) is a giant river, much larger than the Rhine. It is also the second-longest river in the world. Only the Nile River is longer.

The Amazon is on the continent of South America. Most of it lies in the country of Brazil. The Amazon begins high in the **Andes** (AN•deez) **Mountains** of Peru. Hundreds of branch rivers feed it along its route.

Although it is not the longest river, the Amazon *is* the largest. It carries more water than any other river. In fact, it carries more water than the Nile, the Rhine, and the Mississippi put together.

Because the Amazon is near the equator, its basin has a warm or hot climate. It is also very humid. Heavy rains fall almost every day. The rains water the **rain forest** covering most of the land along the river. A rain forest is a place where trees, vines, and other plants grow close together.

So many plants grow in the Amazon forest that few people live in it. It is hard to clear the rain forest for farms, roads, or cities. Soon after the plants are cut down, they grow back again.

Construction of Brazil's Trans-Amazon Highway has already begun. The highway will stretch 3,000 miles (about 4,830 km) along the Amazon.

Although few people live in the Amazon Basin, it is home to many animals. High in the trees live noisy monkeys and parrots. Down below on the river's banks are snakes and alligators. The ruler of the rain forest is the jaguar (JAG•wahr), the largest wild cat in the Americas.

For most of its route the Amazon flows east through Brazil. It travels about 4,000 miles (about 6,430 km) and empties into the Atlantic Ocean. Large ships can travel up the Amazon for 2,300 miles (about 3,700 km). That is almost as far as from New York City to San Francisco! These ships carry raw materials out of the Amazon rain forest. The most important raw materials are rubber and valuable woods, like mahogany and ebony.

Rubber comes from the bark of trees in the rain forest. It is used to make many things, from boots to machine parts.

Today the river is the only way to travel through the Amazon Basin. For this reason, little of the region has been explored. This may change in the years to come because the government of Brazil is now building highways there.

Reading Check

1. Why is the Nile River important to the people of Egypt?
2. What is the busiest port in the world? On what river is this city?
3. What is the longest river?
4. Why do few people live near the Amazon River?

SKILLS FOR SUCCESS

STUDYING THE EARTH AND THE SUN

At this moment you may think you are sitting still. Actually you are moving through space at thousands of miles an hour. The Earth is always moving. As the Earth moves it causes daylight and darkness. It also causes summer and winter. The movement of Earth helps explain why some places are warm and some are cold.

Night and Day

The Earth **rotates** (ROH•tayts), or spins, like a top. It takes 24 hours, or one day, for the Earth to make one whole turn. Look at the picture on this page. See how the Earth turns around an imaginary line. The line runs from the North Pole to the South Pole. This line is called the Earth's **axis** (AK•suhs).

Here is a simple way to show why we have day and night. The flashlight stands for the sun. It shines on the part of the globe that faces it. On this part of the globe it is day. The dark part of the globe is turned away from the light. On this part of the globe it is night. As it rotates, part of the Earth is always moving into light. Part of it is always moving into darkness.

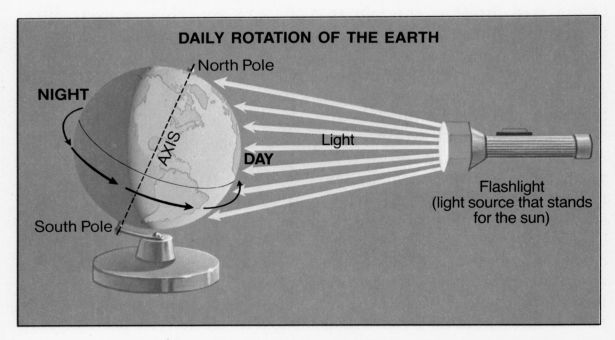

DAILY ROTATION OF THE EARTH

North Pole

NIGHT

AXIS

Light

DAY

South Pole

Flashlight
(light source that stands
for the sun)

The Changing Seasons

The Earth rotates all the time. It also **revolves** (rih•VAHLVZ) around, or circles, the sun. One trip all the way around the sun is called a **revolution** (rev•uh•LOO•shuhn). Each revolution of the Earth takes 365 days, or one year.

As the Earth revolves, our seasons change. This happens because the Earth's axis is not straight up and down. It is always tilted toward the North Star. Because of the tilt, a place gets different amounts of sunlight as the Earth revolves. A place gets more sun in summer and less in winter.

Look at the Earth on June 21. See how the Northern Hemisphere is tilted toward the sun. The Southern Hemisphere is tilted away from the sun. The tilt allows sunlight to shine more directly on the Northern Hemisphere. The sun's rays give more light and heat. It makes lands in the Northern Hemisphere warmer in June, July, and August. During these months there are more hours of light than darkness.

Now look at the Earth on December 21. It shows the Northern Hemisphere tilted away from the sun. The sunlight is less direct there. The days are shorter.

Seasons in the Southern Hemisphere are just the opposite. When the North has summer, the South has winter. When the North Pole tilts toward the sun, the South Pole tilts away. Then the Southern Hemisphere gets less direct sunlight.

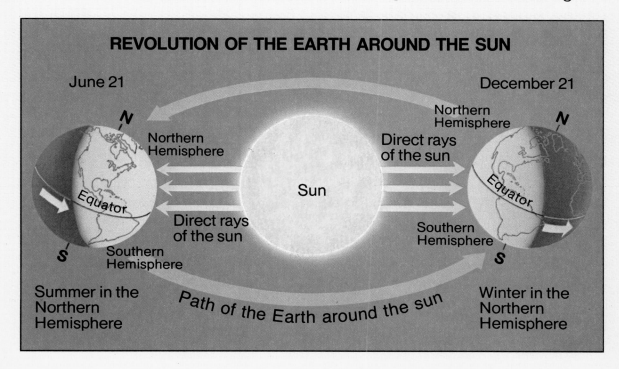

REVOLUTION OF THE EARTH AROUND THE SUN

June 21

N

Northern Hemisphere

Equator

Sun

Direct rays of the sun

S

Southern Hemisphere

Summer in the Northern Hemisphere

Path of the Earth around the sun

December 21

Northern Hemisphere

N

Direct rays of the sun

Equator

Southern Hemisphere

S

Winter in the Northern Hemisphere

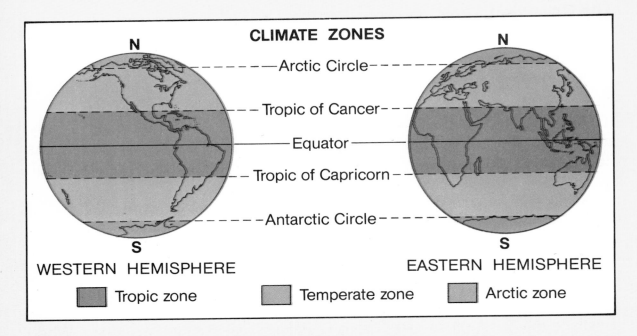

CLIMATE ZONES

- - - Arctic Circle - - -
- - Tropic of Cancer - -
Equator
- - Tropic of Capricorn - -
- - - Antarctic Circle - - -

WESTERN HEMISPHERE   EASTERN HEMISPHERE

Tropic zone   Temperate zone   Arctic zone

Climate Zones

The tilt of the Earth as it moves around the sun causes **climate zones** also. Climate zones are wide bands that circle the Earth. All the places in a climate zone have about the same climate.

The drawing above shows the Eastern and Western hemispheres. Find the equator, the Tropic of Cancer, and the Tropic of Capricorn. Look at the zones between the equator and the tropic lines. These zones are called the **tropics.** Places in the tropics have a warm climate. On Earth, these zones are the closest to the sun and receive the most heat and light. It is mostly hot all year. However, even near the equator, high mountains can be cool.

Now find the Arctic Circle and the Antarctic Circle. The zones between these circles and the tropic lines have a **temperate,** or mild, climate. It is usually warm in summer and cold in winter here.

Look now at the zones north of the Arctic Circle and south of the Antarctic Circle. Most areas in these zones have **arctic** climates. They are cold all year because they are the farthest from the sun.

CHECKING YOUR SKILLS

Use the pictures in this section to answer the questions.

1. Why do we have night and day?

2. Why do the seasons change?

3. Why is it colder at the Arctic Circle than at the equator?

4. What climate zone covers most of the United States?

2. THE YANGTZE RIVER

To Guide Your Reading

Look for these important words:

Key Words
- paddies
- flood plain
- bamboo
- shoots

- mulberry tree
- silkworm
- junks
- sampan
- giant paddlefish

Places
- East China Sea
- Grand Canal
- Yellow River
- Shanghai

Look for answers to these questions:

1. Why is the Yangtze an important link to China's interior?
2. How do the Yangtze's floods help people in China?
3. How do people make a living along the Yangtze River?
4. Why is the Grand Canal important?

More people live in China than in any other country. Most of them are farmers. Yet the land in much of China is either too dry or too mountainous for farming. Because of this, the Chinese live mostly along rivers or on the coast.

The Yangtze (YANG•see) River in China is the world's third-longest river. Half of China's people live near its banks. In fact, more people live along the Yangtze than live in the whole United States!

The Yangtze flows through China's history. One legend tells of an emperor who shot a dragon in these waters. Mao Zedong (MOW dze•DONG), a recent leader of China, once swam across the river to encourage his people to keep fit. Many other Chinese writers and leaders, as well as the families who live near its banks, have been touched by the great river.

The name *Yangtze* means "Child of the Ocean." Today the Chinese call the river by another name. It is Ch'ang Chiang (CHAHNG gee•AHNG). This means "The Long River."

The Yangtze is very long. It flows more than 3,400 miles (about 5,470 km) through the

341

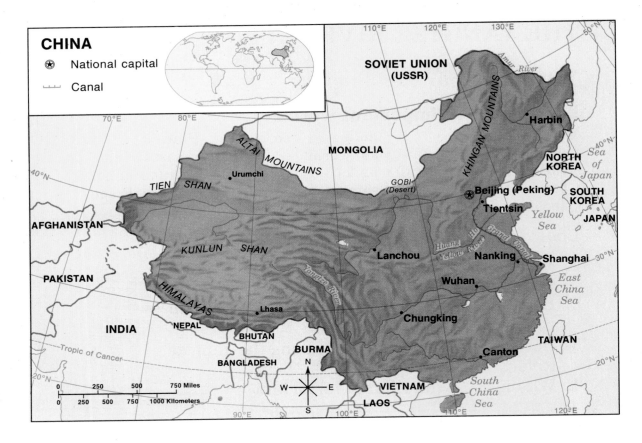

SOVIET UNION (USSR)

Amur River

KHINGAN MOUNTAINS

Harbin

MONGOLIA

ALTAI MOUNTAINS

Urumchi

TIEN SHAN

GOBI (Desert)

NORTH KOREA

⊛ Beijing (Peking)

Tientsin

SOUTH KOREA

JAPAN

AFGHANISTAN

KUNLUN SHAN

Yangtze River

Lanchou

Huang (Yellow)

Yellow River

Grand Canal

Sea of Japan

Yellow Sea

Nanking

Shanghai

PAKISTAN

Wuhan

East China Sea

HIMALAYAS

Lhasa

Chungking

INDIA

NEPAL

BHUTAN

BURMA

TAIWAN

Canton

BANGLADESH

Tropic of Cancer

0 250 500 750 Miles

0 250 500 750 1000 Kilometers

VIETNAM

LAOS

South China Sea

N W E S

Some parts of the Yangtze River flow through steep, misty mountain canyons.

center of China. The center is also China's busiest region. To the south of the river are China's richest farmlands. To the north are China's biggest factories.

Many cities and factories lie along the Yangtze because it is the only river in China that is wide enough and deep enough for large ships. In addition, it links China's interior to the sea. Its mouth is on the **East China Sea,** a part of the Pacific Ocean.

The Yangtze starts high up in the mountains of southern China. From there the river flows east. Much of the river's water is from melting snow in the mountains.

At first the Yangtze tumbles through miles of steep canyons. Some of these canyons are more than a mile (1.6 km) high. As it leaves this steep land, the river grows calmer and wider. It flows through a plateau of rich farmland. This is China's "rice bowl." Miles and miles of rice fields, or **paddies,** stretch out from the banks of the Yangtze.

Rice is an important food in this country of more than 1 billion people. In fact, the Chinese grow more rice than any other people in the world. The rice paddies along the Yangtze help feed China's people.

East of the plateau the river enters more canyons. Here the river drops to a **flood plain.** A flood plain is formed by river floods. The river carries silt with it as it floods the land. When the river drops back down into its bed, the silt remains on the land. After years of flooding, the silt builds up into a fertile plain.

Chinese farmers have grown crops on the Yangtze flood plain year after year. Yet the soil is still good for farming. Heavy rains flood the Yangtze every summer. Each time the river leaves behind a new layer of silt which keeps the soil rich. The plain also has mild winters and a long growing season. It is ideal for growing cotton, wheat, and many other crops. Cotton is one of China's most important crops. Most Chinese clothing is cotton.

Rice is a type of grass that grows well under water.

To grow rice, people flood the land with the river's water.

Plant Life Along the Yangtze

A tall plant grows all along the Yangtze. It looks like a tree, but it is really a giant grass. It is **bamboo.** Bamboo may grow as high as 100 feet (about 30 m). It is the world's fastest-growing plant. Some bamboo grows more than 3 feet (about 91 cm) a day!

Bamboo has many uses in China. It is as stiff and strong as wood. The Chinese make bowls and fences from bamboo. They also use it to make baskets, rope, and roofs. Bamboo pipes carry water from the river. The tender new **shoots** of bamboo are used in many Chinese meals. Shoots are the young branches of a plant.

What are some of the ways in which the Chinese use the sturdy bamboo plant?

From the cocoons of these silkworms will come some of China's prized silk.

China kept a great secret from the rest of the world for hundreds of years. Only the Chinese knew how to make silk. The **mulberry tree,** another plant of the Yangtze, was part of that secret.

Today we know that silk is made from the small cocoons of **silkworm** caterpillars. Silkworms are young moths. The Chinese collect the eggs from the adult insect. Silkworm caterpillars hatch from the eggs. The caterpillars love to munch on tasty mulberry leaves! When it is old enough, the silkworm spins a cocoon. Each cocoon provides a thousand threads of silk.

Living on the Yangtze

Millions of Chinese live in cities near the mouth of the Yangtze. Other Chinese live in small towns or settlements along the river. Some of these people are farmers or factory workers. Others make their living by fishing.

Two kinds of fishing boats are used on the Yangtze. **Junks** are light boats with tall square sails. These tall sails catch the slightest breeze moving over the river.

The other type of boat is a **sampan.** At one time sampans were homes for many fishing families. Some people who lived on sampans never set foot on land.

The Chinese government does not want people to live on these boats anymore. The government says this way of living is making the river unhealthy for others. Also, living on sampans makes it difficult for the government to keep track of people.

Some 500 kinds of fish are caught in the Yangtze. Many settlements along the river also have fish ponds. There people raise fish for food. Fish is one of the most important foods in China. Some of the fish are familiar to us. One such fish is the catfish. Then there is the **giant paddlefish.** This fish has a smaller cousin that lives

Wooden Chinese junks are used for fishing in harbors and on the open seas.

Today sampans are used mostly as cargo barges along rivers and canals.

Shanghai is a major Chinese port and industrial center. Everything from ocean-going ships and heavy machinery to textiles and carpets is made here.

in the Mississippi River. The Yangtze paddlefish is a strange-looking animal. It has a long nose. If you have a good imagination, the nose may look something like a paddle. The giant paddlefish is truly a giant. It can grow as long as 20 feet (about 6 m). It weighs more than 500 pounds (about 227 kg).

The **Grand Canal** joins the Yangtze River not far from the East China Sea. The Grand Canal is one of the world's great wonders built more than 2,000 years ago. It connects the Yangtze with the **Yellow River.** The Yellow River is China's second-largest river. Even today the Grand Canal is used for travel and trade. It is the oldest canal in the world that is still in use.

At the end of its long journey the Yangtze empties into the East China Sea. Near the river's mouth lies the great port of **Shanghai.** Shanghai has the largest population of any city in China. A city of skyscrapers and factories, it is China's business capital.

Reading Check

1. Where do half of China's people live?
2. Why is the Yangtze flood plain good for farming?
3. Name two important crops that grow along the Yangtze.
4. What is the Grand Canal?

346

3. NANKING, A CITY ON THE YANGTZE RIVER

To Guide Your Reading

Look for these important words:

Key Words
- luxuries
- farming commune
- wharves
- double-decker bridge

Places
- Nanking
- Yangtze River Bridge
- Beijing

Look for answers to these questions:

1. What is life like in a city on the Yangtze River?
2. What do students in China learn during their school years?
3. How do people live on farming and factory communes?
4. Why is Nanking a busy city?

About 200 miles (almost 320 km) from the mouth of the Yangtze is the city of **Nanking.** Nanking is a lovely old city with many parks and beautiful buildings. Graceful sycamore trees line its streets.

Most people in Nanking live in small apartments. When they leave for work in the morning, some people walk. Others may take a bus or ride a bicycle. Very few Chinese own cars. Cars and televisions are still **luxuries** (LUHKSH•uh•reez) in China. A luxury is something expensive that only a few people can afford.

The great port city of Nanking is also a center of Chinese learning and culture.

347

Rush hour in a Chinese city may bring fender-to-fender bicycle traffic. Farmers even use bicycles to bring their crops to market.

Almost everyone in Nanking has a bicycle. Chinese shoppers park their bicycles in front of stores. They do not lock them. They know that the bicycles will not be stolen.

School in Nanking starts at 7:30 A.M. It may still be dark when many young Chinese go to school. Both girls and boys wear long padded pants in winter. They also wear layers of padded cotton jackets. In China people sometimes measure cold weather by how many jackets they wear. Cold days are "one-jacket days." Colder days are "two-jacket days." Finally, there are very cold "three-jacket days." When the weather is hot, young people wear T-shirts and pants.

Chinese girls and boys like to play volleyball or Ping Pong at recess. Classes often exercise together. Everyone learns to sing in school. Many young people play musical instruments. Chinese children study reading, writing, and arithmetic.

Students all over China must work with their hands. In China, work is part of learning. Work starts in kindergarten. Students work in the school garden or in factories for a few hours every week.

When they are older, students spend one month a year working in a factory. They also spend one month on a **farming commune** (KAHM•yoon). A farming commune is a kind of village where people live and work together. On Chinese farming communes groups of men and women farm the land together.

Farm and Factory Communes

Farming communes outside Nanking grow rice, wheat, cotton, vegetables, and fruit. Almost every Chinese commune raises pigs and ducks.

Not all communes are on farms. There are also large factory communes. About 12,000 workers live on the Nanking Fertilizer Commune. The workers live in the commune with their families. They share the commune's doctors, library, and shops.

Commune members work six days a week. On days off they may fish, swim, or visit nearby parks. Workers often use free days to work in small gardens. They are allowed to keep what they grow in these gardens for themselves.

The government owns all the farms and factories in China. The Chinese are not allowed to choose which commune or job they want. They are told this by the Chinese government. People who live in the communes help make some decisions. For example, they may decide how to divide up the work. However, the government makes the most important decisions. It decides what the farms should grow and what the factories should make. The government also sets prices and decides how much workers should be paid.

Factories in Nanking manufacture trucks and other heavy farm machinery important for China's agriculture.

Over the years the farming communes have worked well. However, the Chinese government recently decided to try breaking up the communes into individual village farms. The farmers will work the land together in small groups. The government will still own the land. The farmers, though, will decide together what crops to plant, how to sell them, and what tools to buy. Six villages will form a town. These villages will elect leaders for a town government. These changes will be tried out during the next few years.

A Busy Port

The Yangtze River connects Nanking with the rest of the world. Huge ships travel up and down the Yangtze from Nanking to Shanghai. These ships stop at the **wharves** that line the Yangtze River at Nanking. A wharf is a platform built along the shore. Ships can load and unload their cargo here.

The ships carry many of the goods made in Nanking's factories. Some of these goods are fertilizer, cotton clothing, and steel. Mines near Nanking provide iron for the city's steel mills.

Ships loaded at the wharves of Nanking carry their cargoes along the Yangtze River. With all of its branches and canals, the Yangtze is a giant water transportation system of more than 18,000 miles (about 30,000 km).

The Yangtze River Bridge at Nanking completed the important railroad link between the cities of Shanghai and Beijing.

Nanking is one of the few places where a bridge crosses the Yangtze. It is called the **Yangtze River Bridge.** This new bridge stretches 3 miles (about 5 km) across the water. It is a **double-decker bridge.** A double-decker bridge has two levels. One level is above the other. On the upper level is a road for bicycles, cars, and people on foot. On the lower level a railroad crosses the river. This railroad connects Nanking with China's capital, **Beijing** (BAY•jing), farther north. China's capital used to be spelled Peking (PEE•king) in English.

The people of Nanking are proud of the Yangtze River Bridge. Now many more people can come to Nanking from other parts of China. They, too, can now enjoy the beauty of this city.

Reading Check

1. What do many people in Nanking use for travel in the city?
2. Why do students work in factories in Nanking?
3. What is a farming commune?
4. Who makes important decisions on a commune?

351

A FARMING COMMUNE ALONG THE YANGTZE

Mei Li's class

The commune
at work

A Yangtze River
duck farm

It is Saturday afternoon. Mei Li thinks, "When will this school day end?" There is one more class to go, but this class is Mei Li's favorite. She is learning Chinese **calligraphy** (kuh•LIG•gruh•fee), a beautiful way of writing Chinese.

Mei Li wishes she could become an artist when she grows up. She never tells anyone, though. When she grows up, the Chinese government will tell her what work she will do.

When school is over, Mei Li walks home. As she walks, she looks over the green fields that stretch out on all sides of her commune. In the distance she can see the Yangtze.

People are still working in the fields. They use heavy hoes to break up the soil. Some communes have tractors, but Mei Li's does not.

Mei Li visits the ducks. Some ducks swim up for the few grains of rice Mei Li tosses to them. These ducks are being raised for food in a stream that flows into the Yangtze.

When Mei Li arrives home, she goes to work in her family's garden. A few commune members have gardens given to them by the government. These members can use or sell what they grow.

After supper, Mei Li is ready for the evening movie. She carries a chair into the main street to find a good place to sit. A movie screen is stretched across the street at one end of the row of village buildings. The government provides the movies. The story is often about the history of China. Mei Li enjoys the movies anyway. She is also thinking about tomorrow, her day off.

CHAPTER 16 REVIEW

WORDS TO USE

Copy the sentences below. Fill in the blanks with the right words from the list.

flood plain **wharves**
luxury **sampan**
rain forest

1. A rainy place where trees and vines grow close together is a
____ ____ .

2. A ____ ____ is a flat place formed by silt left after floods.

3. A Chinese fishing boat is called a ____ .

4. Something expensive that many people cannot afford is a ____ .

5. Platforms where ships can load or unload cargo are ____ .

FACTS TO REVIEW

1. Why did the government of Egypt build dams across the Nile?

2. Name two reasons the Rhine is an important river.

3. Name two ways the Nile and the Yangtze are alike. Name two ways they are different from the Amazon.

4. How is the Yangtze important to the people of China?

5. What is life on a Chinese commune like?

IDEAS TO DISCUSS

1. Name three ways Nanking is like a city in our country. Name three ways it is different.

2. Name the things people need and some of the luxuries people want. Why do people want luxuries?

⃝ SKILLS PRACTICE

The Earth and the Sun   Answer these questions about the rotation of the Earth and its revolution around the sun.

1. How long is one rotation of the Earth? How long is one revolution?

2. It is summer in the Northern Hemisphere. Is the North Pole tilted toward the sun or away from it?

3. In what climate zone does Brazil lie? In what climate zone is most of China?

CHAPTER 17

Mountains Around the World

Fewer people live in mountain regions than in other places. The steep land and cold climate make it hard to build communities in many mountain regions. Farming and travel are also hard.

People meet these problems by finding special ways to live in mountain regions. You will explore some of these regions in this chapter. You will also find out the ways people around the world live in these high, faraway places.

1. MOUNTAIN REGIONS OF THE WORLD

─ To Guide Your Reading ═

Look for these important words:

Key Words
- imports
- export

- Sherpas
- yak

Places
- Mount Everest

Look for answers to these questions:

1. What do the Alps provide for people in Switzerland?
2. How do the Atlas Mountains change the climate in northern Africa?
3. How do people make a living in the Himalayas?

Wide bands of mountains cross all of the continents. Snow and glaciers cover their highest peaks, and powerful winds rush between them. The land is steep and rocky. Yet people have lived on mountains for thousands of years. They probably first moved to mountains for protection from warlike peoples. The mountains were land that no one else wanted.

In some mountain regions of the world, people live higher than 10,000 feet (about 3,050 m) above sea level. They must depend on themselves for food and for shelter. Almost everything they use comes from the natural resources around them.

In the following pages you will take a look at some of the world's mountain regions. As you read about each region, find it on the map on the next page.

The Alps

The Alps are the largest group of mountains in Europe. They cover most of the countries of Switzerland, Austria, and Liechtenstein (LIK•tuhn•styn). The Alps also reach into the nearby countries of France, Italy, Germany, and Yugoslavia.

For most of its history Switzerland was protected by the high, rugged Alps. Armies could not easily enter the country through the snowy mountain passes. The people in Switzerland lived in peace for hundreds of years.

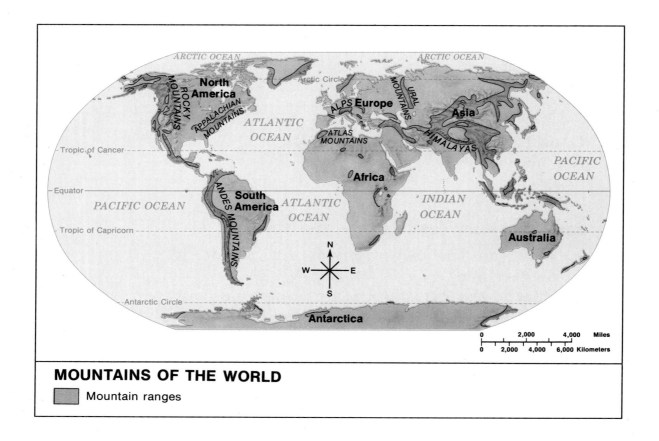

MOUNTAINS OF THE WORLD

☐ Mountain ranges

Glaciers long ago carved out the beautiful valleys that lie among the Alps.

The Alps protect Switzerland but provide few mineral resources. Farming is difficult on the steep sides of the mountains. In the valleys of the Alps, however, dairy cows graze on thick, green grass. From the milk of their herds, the Swiss make cheese. The United States **imports** much of their cheese. To *import* something is to bring it into a country for sale. What do you suppose we call one well-known cheese that comes from Switzerland?

Although Switzerland has little farmland and few mineral resources, it has several large cities. These cities have many factories. The Swiss manufacture watches, machines, chemicals, and textiles. They **export** these products to other countries. To *export* something is to send it to another country to be sold.

The beauty of the Swiss Alps attracts tourists. Many people climb the Alps or ski the snow-covered slopes. Rivers that begin in the Alps make electricity. The electricity provides power for a railway that passes through the mountains.

The Atlas Mountains

The Atlas Mountains stretch across northwestern Africa. North of the Atlas Mountains is a plain that gets plenty of water.

In which areas of the Atlas Mountains might you find fertile land?

To the south of the mountains is the Sahara, the world's largest desert.

Why is land north of the mountains so different from land to the south? The Atlas Mountains prevent rain-carrying winds from reaching the desert. Most of the rain falls north of the mountains. The remaining moisture falls as snow on the mountain peaks. Small rivers begin in the mountains and flow to the plain in the north. The other side of the mountains gets little or no moisture. The slopes are dry and rocky. Very little can grow there.

A few people live in the Atlas Mountains. Some of them have small farms in the valleys. Others graze animals in places where plants can grow.

On which side of the Atlas Mountains are deserts found?

The yak helps the Sherpas survive the bitter Himalayan climate.
People even saddle and ride these animals through the mountains.

The Himalayas

The Himalayas (him•uh•LAY•uhz) are the highest mountains in the world. **Mount Everest,** the world's highest mountain, is in the Himalayas. It is more than 29,000 feet (about 8,840 m) high. The Himalayas separate the countries of China and India. They are like a wall 5 miles (about 8 km) high. Many of these mountains are covered with ice and snow all year.

From three to five million people live in the high peaks of the Himalayas. Among them are the **Sherpas,** who grow crops such as potatoes, rice, and soybeans. They herd animals also. The animal the Sherpas depend on for just about everything is the **yak.** The yak is a cousin of the American bison. It has a long, thick coat that helps it live in the cold mountains. The yak provides meat, milk, butter, wool, and leather. It also carries goods.

Reading Check

1. In what countries are the Alps located?
2. What is the difference between the words *import* and *export*?
3. What kind of land is south of the Atlas Mountains? What kind of land is north of the mountains?
4. Why is the yak important to the people of the Himalayas?

358

VOLCANOES

Mount St. Helens, 1980

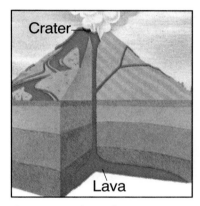

Cross section of a volcano

Molten lava

About a hundred years ago, a mountain exploded on the island of Krakatoa in the Indian Ocean. A dark cloud of ash covered the sky. Huge **tidal** (TYD•uhl) **waves** 100 feet (about 30 m) high swept over nearby islands. More than 30,000 people drowned. The mountain was a volcano.

A volcano begins as a crack in the Earth's surface. Lava flows out of the crack. Over the years and after many lava flows, the lava builds up around the crack to form a mountain.

Some volcanoes are quiet for many thousands of years. Others erupt, or throw out lava, every few years. These are called **active** volcanoes.

When Krakatoa erupted, the whole side of the mountain blew open. Mount St. Helens in the state of Washington erupted the same way in 1980. Volcanoes sometimes erupt from the top. Then the melted rock flows evenly over the mountain. This gives the mountain a shape like a cone. Japan's Fujiyama is a cone-shaped volcano. At the top is a **crater,** the opening.

About 500 active volcanoes are on land. There are thousands more in the sea. Underwater volcanoes often form islands. Volcanoes made many of the islands in the South Pacific.

Hot lava and ash from volcanoes can do great damage. A river of lava can move as fast as 35 miles (about 56 km) an hour. It destroys everything in its path before it finally cools and becomes rock. Volcanoes can be helpful, though, as well as harmful. Lava and ash mix with the soil and make it rich in minerals. Often trees and crops grow well in places once ruined by volcanoes.

2. THE ANDES MOUNTAINS OF SOUTH AMERICA

To Guide Your Reading

Look for these important words:

Key Words
- Incas
- Quechua Indians
- chuña

- terraces
- ponchos
- llama

People
- Francisco Pizarro

Places
- Cuzco, Peru

Look for answers to these questions:

1. How do the Andes Mountains compare to other mountains of the world?
2. In what ways did Francisco Pizarro change the Inca kingdom?
3. How are the Quechuas able to live in the Andes Mountains?
4. How do llamas help Quechuas?

Near the Pacific coast of South America are the Andes (AN•deez) Mountains. The Andes stretch the whole length of South America, more than 4,000 miles (about 6,440 km). They are the longest group of mountains in the world.

The Andes are also some of the world's youngest mountains. They are high, rugged, and steep. Wind and water have not yet worn down the peaks of the Andes. Some of the Andes Mountains are over 20,000 feet (about 6,100 m) high. Glaciers and snow cover their peaks all year. Only the Himalayas are higher than the Andes.

Among the high peaks and deep canyons of the Andes are many high plateaus. People have made these high lands their home for thousands of years. Between 15 and 20 million people now live in the Andes.

The Andes Long Ago

More than 400 years ago, an explorer from Spain landed on the western coast of South America. **Francisco Pizarro** (puh•ZAHR•oh) was searching for gold and silver. Pizarro and his soldiers climbed the Andes Mountains.

Irrigation water from mountain rivers has helped turn some of the dry lands among the Andes into farmland.

Incas made beautiful objects of gold, the metal sought by the Spanish.

There they found the huge, rich kingdom of the **Incas** (ING•kuhz). The Incas were a number of Indian groups ruled by a king. They lived in the region stretching from Ecuador to Argentina. The king of the Incas lived in the city of **Cuzco** (KOOS•koh). Today Cuzco is a city in the country of Peru.

The Incas had built beautiful cities, roads, and bridges high in the mountains. They farmed the mountain slopes. They mined gold, silver, and copper.

Pizarro wanted the gold and silver of the Incas. He and his soldiers killed the Inca king. Soon the Inca kingdom fell apart. The Indians of South America then came under the rule of Spain.

The Quechua Indians

The Incas were the ancestors of today's **Quechua** (KECH•uh•wuh) **Indians.** Most Quechuas live in the Andes Mountains of Peru and Bolivia.

The Quechuas live far from modern cities. It is cold high in the Andes where they live. The temperature is near or below freezing almost every day.

Farming is difficult in the Andes. Few crops can grow at the mountains' high altitudes. The potato is one crop that can grow here. The Indians of the Andes were the first people in the world to grow potatoes. It is still their most important food.

The Quechuas have learned how to keep potatoes from spoiling. They leave the potatoes on the ground to freeze at night. The potatoes dry in the sun the following day. After several days and nights, the dried potatoes are ground into a meal. The meal is called **chuña** (CHOON•ya). The *chuña* will keep for many months.

With few flat places to farm in the Andes, Quechua farmers must plant crops on the sides of the mountains. To do this, the Quechuas build **terraces** on the mountain slopes. A terrace is a flat shelf dug out of the mountainside. From far away these terraces look like steps.

Following Inca methods, the Quechuas build rock walls, sometimes 15 feet high, to prevent erosion of terraced farmlands.

362

Thin and Cold Air

If you are like most people, you are not used to the high altitudes of mountains. The higher you go in the mountains, the thinner the air will be. You do not have as much oxygen to breathe at these heights. You will get tired easily and feel dizzy. Yet the thin air of the mountains does not bother the Quechua Indians.

The people of the Andes have very large lungs. They can take in a lot of air with each breath. This helps them get enough oxygen. Because their arms and legs are shorter than ours, their blood does not have as far to travel. The people are strong from walking up and down mountains.

Quechuas often weave warm, colorful ponchos with ancient designs.

The thin air of the mountains cannot hold the sun's heat. The Quechuas wear many layers of clothing to protect them from the cold mountain temperatures. Men wear wool **ponchos** over shirts and pants. A poncho is a blanket with a hole in the middle. The wearer's head slips through the hole. Women wear several layers of warm skirts. The skirts are made of brightly colored wool.

The Llama

The Quechuas make their own clothing from wool. Children help gather the wool and make thread.

The Quechuas' wool comes from the **llama** (LAH•muh). The

Llamas are dependable pack animals along the old Inca trails still in use.

363

The Andes produce much of the world's copper. *Andes* is thought to come from a Quechuan word meaning "copper."

llama has a woolly coat and looks a little like a camel without a hump. It is the most important animal to the people of the Andes. From its wool a fine yarn is spun for clothing and blankets. The llama also carries loads up the steep mountain paths. The llama is very valuable to the Quechuas. They rarely kill the llama for meat.

Mining in the Andes

Many Quechuas work in mines. Some mines in the Andes have gold and silver. However, the Andes's tin and copper mines are more important today. Tin is used in making cans. The mines of the Andes meet much of the world's needs for these metals.

Long ago, llamas carried minerals from the mines to cities on the coast. Train tracks were later built over the mountains. One of the trains in Peru passes through a tunnel more than 15,000 feet (about 4,570 m) above sea level. It is the highest train ride in the world.

Reading Check

1. What did Pizarro want from the Incas?
2. What crop grows well at high altitudes?
3. Why are the Quechuas not bothered by the high altitude of the mountains?
4. What is a llama? How do the Quechuas depend on the llama?

3. CUZCO, A CITY IN THE ANDES

┌─ **To Guide Your Reading** ─────────────────

Look for these important words:

Key Words   **Places**
• ruins   • Lima
                         • Machu Picchu

Look for answers to these questions:

1. What sights might someone see in Cuzco?
2. How do people make a living in Cuzco?
3. Why do people from all over the world visit Cuzco and Machu Picchu?

Cuzco is a city high in the Andes of Peru. Once it was the capital of the Inca kingdom. Today Cuzco is still the center of Quechua Indian life.

Many people fly to Cuzco from all over the world to see the Inca **ruins.** Ruins are the remains of buildings, towns, and cities that have been destroyed. Several planes leave for Cuzco every day from **Lima** (LEE•muh). Lima is the capital of Peru.

Lima is a large and modern city. Signs everywhere are in Spanish. They remind people that Pizarro, the Spanish explorer, founded this city.

Imagine that you are flying from Lima to Cuzco. You will see many differences between living in the city and in the mountains. You leave Lima, which is at sea level. You reach Cuzco, more than 2 miles (about 3 km) above sea

PERU

⊛ National capital

△ Inca ruins

365

Skyscrapers and traditional Spanish architecture share Lima's skyline.

How is Cuzco (above) different from and similar to Lima?

The people of Cuzco still use these well-made stone streets built by Incas.

level. As you step from the plane, you begin to feel dizzy. The altitude makes it hard to breathe.

Some of Cuzco's streets do not look like streets at all. They are steep stairways. Cars and buses cannot drive up the stairs. Llamas, on the other hand, have no trouble with them. They travel in herds up and down the streets.

The Incas built Cuzco's stone streets almost a thousand years ago. Much of the Inca past remains in Cuzco today. Stone walls that once were large Inca buildings still stand. The Incas built the walls with huge stones. No cement holds the stones together. Still, they fit together so tightly that it is often impossible to push a knife between two of the stones.

The Marketplace

Near the Inca ruins in Cuzco are new hotels and restaurants that serve tourists. Tourism brings money into Cuzco. The people of Cuzco gather each day along the narrow streets to sell tourists handmade wool blankets, ponchos, sweaters, rugs, and caps.

The women spread blankets on the street to show their goods. Each one wears a different kind of hat. The shape, color, and decoration of a hat tells where the person wearing it was born.

On market day the people of Cuzco sell goods to one another. Most of them do not use money. They barter for goods. Someone might trade baskets for brightly woven cloth. Another person might trade a llama for food.

Children help their families at home. They also help them at the market. There are few schools for children. They and their families have no radios, televisions, or newspapers, either. The boys often watch over the family's small herd of llamas. The girls spin thread and weave the heavy, warm cloth.

At the market in Cuzco, people trade and sell crafts made according to traditions that go back at least 3,000 years.

Machu Picchu was an ancient Inca city only discovered in 1911.
Why would its high mountain location keep it well hidden?

Machu Picchu

There is much to see in Cuzco. However, there is even more to see about two hours by train from the city. There, high up in the Andes, are the ruins of **Machu Picchu** (MAH•choo PEE•choo). The Incas built this city on the top of a mountain. Machu Picchu is even higher in the Andes than Cuzco. From Machu Picchu you can see the peaks of the Andes for miles around. People who visit Machu Picchu never forget the sight.

Many people come to Cuzco and Machu Picchu each year. Yet even with all these visitors, life in the Andes has changed little over the years. The Quechuas must work hard. They are poor.

They live in tiny mud or stone houses that have no heat or electricity. The Quechuas manage to live on these cold, steep mountains for a reason. They want to follow the customs of their ancestors, the Incas. In this way the Inca heritage remains alive today. It is a heritage of which the Quechuas are proud.

Reading Check

1. What was the old capital of the Incas?
2. What is the capital of Peru today?
3. How do the Quechuas sell goods to one another?
4. What is Machu Picchu?

SKILLS FOR SUCCESS

USING DIFFERENT KINDS OF GRAPHS

A graph is a drawing that helps you compare facts or numbers. Different kinds of graphs show different kinds of information. Each kind of graph looks different from the others. Each kind of graph has a special purpose.

Reading Picture Graphs

Picture graphs are an interesting way to show numbers. This kind of graph uses pictures that stand for numbers. The key shows what each picture stands for.

The graph below shows how many very high mountains are in some South American countries. Each symbol (△) stands for one mountain. The graph tells you that there are 14 mountains over 20,000 feet (about 6,100 m) high in Chile. Now count the mountains in the box

for Peru. How many mountains over 20,000 feet high are in this country?

Sometimes picture graphs are used to compare large amounts. Look at the graph below. It shows how many people live in three large cities in South America.

POPULATION OF THREE CITIES IN SOUTH AMERICA	
City and Country	
Buenos Aires, Argentina	𝕏 𝕏 𝕏
Santiago, Chile	𝕏 𝕏 𝕏 𝕏
Bogotá, Colombia	𝕏 𝕏 𝕏 𝕏 𝕩
𝕏 = 1,000,000 people	

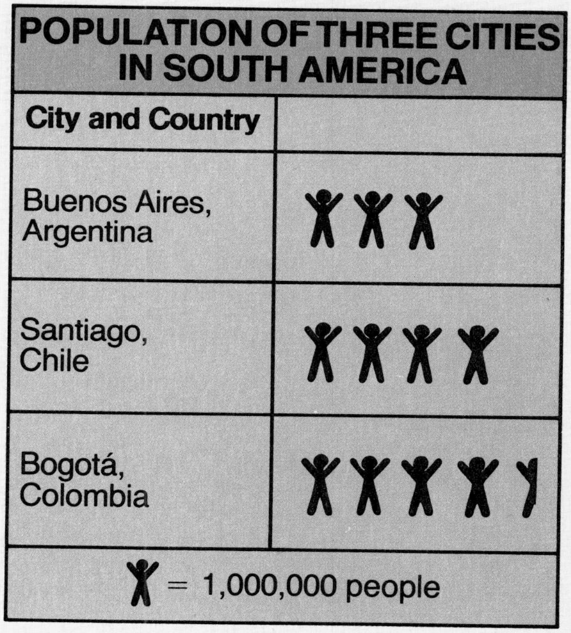

In this picture graph, each 𝕏 stands for 1 million people. Count the 𝕏 in the box for Bogotá (boh·guh·TAH). Four whole 𝕏 and a half of another are in this box. This means that Bogotá has about 4½ million people. Now look at the box for Buenos Aires (bway·nuh·SAR·eez). About how many people live in Buenos Aires?

HIGH MOUNTAINS IN THREE COUNTRIES	
Chile	△ △ △ △ △ △ △ △ △ △ △ △ △ △
Peru	△ △ △ △ △ △ △ △ △ △ △ △ △ △
Bolivia	△ △ △ △ △
△ = Mountain higher than 20,000 feet (about 6,100 m)	

Reading Line Graphs

Line graphs show changes over time. The line graph below shows how much gold was mined in Colombia from 1977 to 1981.

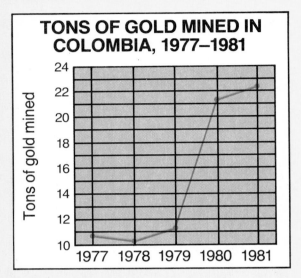

Along the bottom of the graph are the years. Along the left side of the graph are numbers. These numbers stand for the tons of gold that were mined.

Find the year 1977 at the bottom of the graph. Now go up until you come to the first dot. The line graph starts at this dot. It tells you that Colombia mined almost 11 tons of gold in 1977.

The next year listed is 1978. The dot for this year is above the 10. In 1978 Colombia mined more than 10 tons of gold, but this was still less than was mined in 1977. Look at the line that goes from the 1977 dot to the 1978 dot. It slopes down. This lets you see quickly that gold mining went down in 1978.

Reading Circle Graphs

A circle graph shows how a whole is divided into parts. This circle graph shows how many Peruvians are in different age groups.

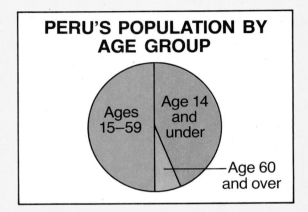

The green part of the circle graph stands for people between ages 15 and 59. This part is half of the circle. This means that half of the people in Peru are between the ages of 15 and 59. Does the blue part show more or fewer people than the green?

CHECKING YOUR SKILLS

Use the graphs on these pages to answer these questions.

1. Which country has more very tall mountains, Bolivia or Peru?

2. Which city has more people, Santiago or Bogotá?

3. Did Colombia mine more or less gold in 1981 than it did in 1980?

4. In Peru are more people age 14 and under or age 15 to 59?

CHAPTER 17 REVIEW

WORDS TO USE

Copy the sentences below. Fill in the blanks with the right words from the list.

exports   **terraces**
imports   **yak**
ponchos

1. The United States ____ cheese from Switzerland.

2. Switzerland ____ watches and other products to many countries.

3. The ____ is the most valuable animal for the people of the Himalayas.

4. The Quechuas grow potatoes on ____ dug on the sides of the mountains.

5. To keep warm, Quechua men wear wool ____ over their shirts.

FACTS TO REVIEW

1. Name two ways the Alps are a valuable resource to people.

2. Why is the land south of the Atlas Mountains drier than the land north of the mountains?

3. Why is the potato the main food of the Quechuas?

4. What is the highest mountain in the world? In what group of mountains is it?

5. Why might a llama be as valuable to a Quechua Indian as a car is to an American?

IDEAS TO DISCUSS

1. The Quechuas must depend on themselves to meet their needs. How is their life in the Andes different from life in a big city?

2. How is your way of life different from that of Quechua children?

◯ SKILLS PRACTICE

Using Different Kinds of Graphs Copy the items below. Decide which kind of graph would best show the information. Write *picture graph, line graph,* or *circle graph* for each item.

1. How much you have grown in each of the last three years.

2. What part of your class knows how to swim.

3. What part of the world is covered by water.

4. Numbers of students in each of five schools.

CHAPTER 18

Deserts Around the World

Every living thing needs water. For this reason, we think that deserts are lifeless places. Yet for thousands of years people, animals, and plants have found ways to live in deserts.

Deserts cover more than one-seventh of all the land on Earth. As the world becomes more crowded, desert lands and resources are becoming more important. In this chapter you will read how people are making these barren places useful.

1. DESERT REGIONS OF THE WORLD

To Guide Your Reading

Look for these important words:

Key Words
- oasis
- nomads
- stations
- Mongols

Places
- Arabian Peninsula
- Rub' al Khali

Look for answers to these questions:

1. What kinds of work do people do in the Sahara?
2. Why has life changed for the people of Saudi Arabia?
3. How do people make use of the Australian Desert?
4. What kind of life do people live on the Gobi Desert?

You read about deserts of the United States in other parts of this book. You found out that a desert gets less than 10 inches (about 25 cm) of precipitation a year. When you look at the world map on the next page, you will see that large deserts stretch across every continent. As you read about the deserts in this chapter, find them on the map.

The Sahara

The word *Sahara* means desert in Arabic. It is also the name of the world's largest desert. The Sahara lies across the northern third of the continent of Africa. The Sahara would cover almost all of the United States, including Alaska and Hawaii.

The Sahara is very hot and very dry. The Sahara desert town of Azizia, Libya, once had the hottest day ever measured—136°F (about 58°C). Most of the Sahara gets less than 1 inch (about 2.5 cm) of rain a year, though parts of this desert have gone more than ten years without a single drop!

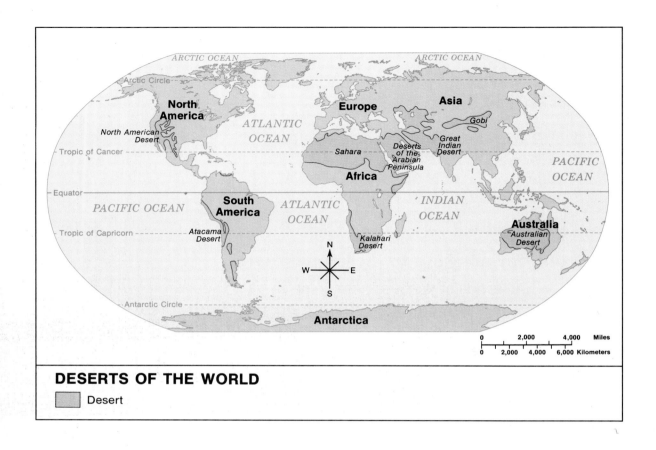

DESERTS OF THE WORLD

[ ] Desert

The Sahara has mountains, gravel-covered plains, and sand dunes.

Though some nomads own land on oases, other people farm the land for them. Most nomads move from one oasis to another, searching for grazing land for their animals.

Although the Sahara is hot by day, it can get very cold at night. The temperature may drop below freezing. In a single day the temperature can change as much as 80°F (about 27°C).

You may be surprised to learn that most of the Sahara is gravel. Sand dunes cover only about one-tenth of the desert.

About 2 million people live in the Sahara. Most of them live near an **oasis** (oh•AY•suhs). An oasis is a desert place with water. Most of it comes from springs that run under the ground. The people who live on oases (oh•a•SEEZ) grow grains such as wheat and barley. They may also grow olives, nuts, dates, and figs. Oranges are grown with the help of irrigation.

About 90 oases dot the Sahara. Groups of people wander from one oasis to another. They look for pasture for their sheep, goats, and camels. These people are **nomads.** They do not have one home. Instead they move from place to place.

The Deserts of the Arabian Peninsula

East of the Sahara is the Red Sea. If you crossed the Red Sea, you would come to the **Arabian Peninsula.** On this peninsula is the country of Saudi (SAWD•ee) Arabia.

Most of the land of Saudi Arabia is desert. In the desert in the center of the country, oases provide water for small farms and herding animals. One desert, however, supports no life. This desert is called the **Rub' al Khali.** Its name means "empty quarter." It covers most of the southern part of the Arabian Peninsula.

In the past, people could not have crossed this desert were it not for the camel. The camel is often called the ship of the desert. It carries people and supplies across the Rub' al Khali. The camel can travel several days on only a little water. The humps of a camel store fat that is used when food and water are scarce.

For many years people thought most of Saudi Arabia's deserts were useless. Since they are so hot and dry, it is almost impos-sible to grow anything there. The people in some areas were either poor farmers or nomads. In the 1930s the old way of life began to change. Oil was discovered beneath the sands of the Eastern Lowlands. This part of Saudi Arabia is on the Persian Gulf. These oil fields became some of the world's most valuable land!

Today our world depends on oil. Can you name some ways that oil is used? Without oil we could not have our modern life. Oil supplies nearly half of our needs for fuel in the United States. The supply of oil is limited, however. Oil cannot be remade by nature or by people. For this reason, it is expensive.

Oil has made some nations on the Arabian Peninsula very

The world's largest known oil deposits are found in the eastern part of Saudi Arabia.

Oil wealth has helped the rapid growth of Kuwait's cities.

wealthy. Besides Saudi Arabia, one of the wealthiest is Kuwait (kuh•WAYT). Both of these nations have used some of their new wealth to build homes and hospitals. They have also built many schools and roads, and even whole cities.

Life is changing quickly for the people of these nations. People who had been nomads now live in houses. People who used to herd goats and sheep now work in oil fields. They use trucks instead of camels for transportation. Today oil is helping people find new ways to live in the desert.

The Australian Desert

Large deserts cover nearly half of Australia. Together they are called the Australian Desert. The Australian Desert is not as dry as the Sahara. Much of it gets about 5 inches (about 13 cm) of rain a year. The edges of the desert get enough rain for grass to grow. This is rangeland used for raising cattle and sheep.

Brahman cattle, such as the one in the lower left corner of the picture, can stand the heat and the insects of northern Australia.

Many Mongols live in lightweight tents that are easily carried by pack animals.

Mongol nomads ride strong, small horses to herd their sheep and goats.

The people who live on the Australian Desert are not nomads. Australians raise sheep and cattle on large ranches that they call **stations.** More wool comes from Australia than from any other nation.

The Gobi

The Gobi (GOH•bee) is a desert north of China in central Asia. It lies mostly in the country of Mongolia (mahn•GOHL•lee•uh). Winters are very cold in this desert. Summers are very hot.

A people called the **Mongols** (MAHN•guhlz) live in the Gobi. Many Mongols are nomads. They raise herds of sheep, cattle, goats, horses, and yaks. They move from one place to another in search of water and pasture.

In recent years the Mongolian people have begun to leave the nomadic way of life. Some are going to work in new industries in Mongolia's cities. Others have settled on farms to grow grain.

Reading Check

1. What is the world's largest desert?
2. What is an oasis?
3. Why is the camel good for desert travel?
4. Who are the Mongols?

378

SOLAR ENERGY

Solar panels for heat

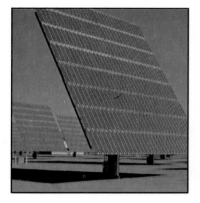

Solar cells

Space probe

Have you ever left a garden hose out in the sun? After a while, the water lying in the hose can get very hot. Sunlight made that heat. When sunlight is used for power it is called **solar** (SOH-luhr) **energy.**

Deserts get many hours of full sunlight, so they are good places for learning about solar energy. Some desert communities are now using solar energy to power machines and heat houses.

People have used the sun's heat for thousands of years. Today we have discovered new ways to use the sun's energy for heat. One way is to have sunlight heat water in pipes built into the roofs or sides of buildings. The hot water is then stored in a tank for later use.

People can also use sunlight to make electricity. **Solar cells** are batteries that turn sunlight directly into electricity. Solar cells make enough power to run radios or cook food. However, solar cells are so new that they are expensive to use. Today they are mainly used to power American **space probes.** Space probes are ships that explore our solar system. Solar cells can power a space probe for years of travel.

In the future, solar energy may also be collected in space. Today, scientists are trying to find ways to make solar energy cost less money and become more practical on Earth. Collecting and storing the sun's energy is expensive. As other fuels become more costly, however, solar energy becomes more useful. The sun's energy cannot be used up. It is free and clean. Many people hope that by the year 2000, much of our energy will come from the light of the sun.

2. THE NEGEV OF ISRAEL

To Guide Your Reading

Look for these important words:

Key Words

- Nabataeans
- Bedouins
- reclaim

Look for answers to these questions:

1. Why did the Israelis believe the Negev could be used for farming?
2. How have the Israelis changed the Negev from desert to farmland?
3. What natural resources are found in the Negev Desert?

Northwest of the Arabian Peninsula is the small country of Israel (IZ•ree•uhl). The entire southern half of this small country is desert, the Negev. No more than 4 inches (10 cm) of rain falls on the Negev each year. Yet the Israelis are slowly making the Negev a place where people can live. They have built farms, towns, and factories. They have made fertile farmland out of dry desert.

How have the Israelis done this? We must go back in history to understand. We must look at the Negev as it was 2,000 years ago.

In those days almost 300 farming towns were strung across

In the middle of a desert in Israel sprouts green, fertile farmland.

the Negev. The people who built these towns were known as the **Nabataeans** (nab•uh•TEE•uhnz). They learned to collect the little rain that fell in the desert. They built canals and tanks to save the rain. With this water they irrigated small pieces of land. They grew figs, dates, and grapes. They even raised cattle.

About 1,200 years ago, desert nomads attacked the Nabataeans. These nomads were **Bedouins** (BED•uh•wuhnz). The Bedouins were herders, not farmers. Like all nomads, they moved from place to place in search of grass and water for their animals. They had no need for farming.

Bedouins still herd their animals through unsettled areas of the Negev.

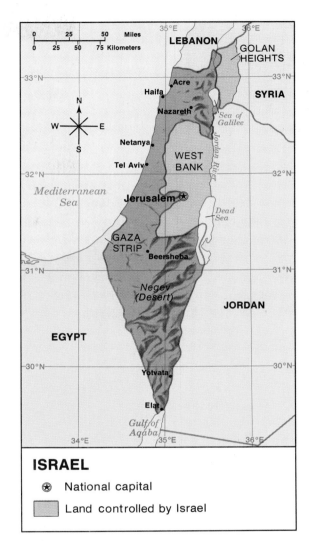

ISRAEL

⊛ National capital

☐ Land controlled by Israel

As the Nabataean towns died out, their ways of farming were forgotten. Until about 30 years ago only nomads lived on the Negev.

The nation of Israel was formed in 1948. Its new citizens, needing more land for farming, looked to the Negev. They knew that this desert was farmland long ago. They decided to try to make it farmland once again.

Though many of the Nabataeans' ways of farming are used, the Israelis also use new plastic greenhouses.

Tender strawberry plants need lots of moisture. Sheets of plastic help keep that moisture from evaporating.

Farming in the Negev Today

Today Israelis are finding that many of the old Nabataean ways of farming still work. They have built tanks under the ground to collect and store water. They have built miles of irrigation canals also. The canals carry water from the Sea of Galilee in northern Israel.

Like the Nabataeans, the Israelis make use of the moisture, or dew, that forms at night. In the desert, temperatures drop at night. During the night, dew forms on cooled surfaces. By putting stones next to plants, the Israelis collect the night dew. The small amount of water that col-

lects on the stones drips down into the soil to the roots of plants. In the Negev every drop counts!

The Israelis also have ways of farming that the Nabataeans never even dreamed of. They are using plastic to change the Negev. They have built huge plastic greenhouses that hold in moisture. Sheets of plastic also cover the soil. They keep water in the ground. Water drips right to the roots of plants through thin plastic pipes buried underground. If the plants were sprinkled from above, much of the water would evaporate in the dry desert air.

These ways of farming save water. New ways and old ways are making the Negev green again.

Low plastic tunnels cover crops in the Negev. Water from the Sea of Galilee is pumped south through canals and pipelines for irrigation.

Other Natural Resources of the Negev

The people of Israel have found other natural resources in the Negev besides farmland. They discovered some oil as well as minerals for fertilizers. The Israelis also found a 3,000-year-old copper mine and are now using it. The Israelis use clay from the Negev for pottery and some of the desert's sand for glass. The Negev is much more useful than it once seemed!

Israelis hope that many people will settle in the Negev in the next 20 years. These people will **reclaim,** or take back, more land from the desert. They will turn it into settlements. Today, there is just sand and stone in these places. In 20 years farms may bloom everywhere.

Reading Check

1. Where is the Negev?
2. What did the Israelis learn from the Nabataeans?
3. Name three ways that desert farmers use plastic.
4. Why is underground watering better than sprinkling plants from above?

SKILLS FOR SUCCESS

COMPARING AND CONTRASTING

Read these two groups of ideas:

a. Like the Sahara, the Negev is a desert.

b. The Nabataeans settled villages and farmed the land. The Bedouins moved from place to place and did not farm.

Sentence *a* tells how two things are alike. The Negev is like the Sahara because they are both deserts. When you **compare** things or people, you look for ways in which they are alike. You want to find out what these things or people have in common.

The sentences in *b* explain differences. The Nabataeans were different from the Bedouins. The Nabataeans stayed in one place and farmed the land. The Bedouins were nomads. They raised goats and camels instead of crops. When you look for ways in which people, places, or things are different, you **contrast** them.

The Sahara in northern Africa is the world's largest desert.

The Negev is a desert that covers the entire southern half of Israel.

	Ginny	Tom
Age	10	10
Height	54 inches (about 85 cm)	56 inches (about 90 cm)
Weight	67 pounds (about 30 kg)	75 pounds (about 34 kg)
Eye/Hair Color	brown eyes, brown hair	blue eyes, blond hair
School	Fox Park	Fox Park
Favorite Food	strawberry yogurt	apples

Comparing and contrasting things is nothing new for you. For example, it is easy for you to tell when two things are alike in shape. It is easy to tell when two things are different in color. Comparing or contrasting things can be more difficult, however. There may be many parts to the things you are comparing or contrasting.

Meet Ginny and Tom. You can learn some things about them from the chart above.

In some ways Ginny and Tom are alike. They are both 10 years old. They both go to the Fox Park School. In some ways they are different. For example, Ginny has brown hair, but Tom has blond hair. How many other differences can you name?

Now you know some of the ways Tom and Ginny are alike and different. What else do the facts in the chart tell you about them?

CHECKING YOUR SKILLS

Copy each sentence. Next to each sentence write *compare* if the sentence shows how deserts are alike. Write *contrast* if the sentence shows how they are different from each other.

1. All deserts get less than 10 inches (about 25 cm) of precipitation a year.

2. The Sahara has about 90 oases, but the Rub'al Khali in Saudi Arabia has none.

3. Sheep and cattle are raised on the Australian Desert and the Gobi.

4. Australians raise sheep on stations, but the Mongols move their sheep from place to place.

5. Kuwait and Saudi Arabia are both wealthy nations because of the oil found in their deserts.

3. YOTVATA, A KIBBUTZ IN THE NEGEV

To Guide Your Reading

Look for these important words:

Key Words
- kibbutz
- moshav

Look for answers to these questions:

1. What is the difference between a kibbutz and a moshav?
2. What did the early settlers of Yotvata do to change the desert?
3. What do kibbutz members raise on their desert lands?

In Israel people farm the land on two different kinds of settlements. One kind of settlement is called a **kibbutz** (kib·UHTZ). *Kibbutz* means group in Hebrew, the language of Israel. Almost everything is shared on a kibbutz. The members own the land together. They live and work together. They build houses and grow food for one another. Some kibbutz members teach school or are doctors and nurses.

The other type of settlement in Israel is the **moshav** (moh· SHAHV). Unlike a kibbutz, each family on a moshav owns part of the land. The government provides supplies and helps farmers sell their crops.

A Difficult Beginning

Yotvata (yot·VOT·uh) is a kibbutz in the Negev. When it began in 1951, Yotvata was only a few tents in one of the hottest, driest parts of the Negev. Eighty men and women started Yotvata. They put in a pump to draw water from under the ground. Then they built houses and cleared spaces in the sand and rock for fields.

The Negev was a challenge to the early settlers at Yotvata. They tried all sorts of crops. Only dates and tomatoes did well at first. Then the settlers built fences to protect their crops from wind and sand. They covered their fields with sheets of plastic. The plastic kept water from escaping into the

Yotvata is a modern kibbutz that provides schools, food, and medical care for all its members.

hot desert air. They put pipes in the ground to water the roots of their plants. Little by little the people of Yotvata brought their part of the Negev to life.

Yotvata Today

Today Yotvata is an example of what people can do to change the desert. If you were to visit the kibbutz, you would see many surprising things. Fields of flowers blooming on this dry land are the first surprise. To grow flowers the kibbutz members must remove the salt from their well water. Desert soil is very salty, so the water below it is salty, too. The kibbutz members filter the water to remove the salt. They use the water in their gardens. They also use it for their cattle.

Yotvata is very proud of its 200 dairy cows. Raising cows in the desert is not easy. Since the cows have no place to graze, they live in sheds. The kibbutz members bring food to the cows every day. During the summer they give the cows three showers a day. The showers keep the animals cool. The kibbutz also raises more than 10,000 chickens.

Kibbutz members sell the food they raise to nearby towns. The money they earn belongs to everyone at Yotvata. They use this money for food, clothing, medical care, and education. Some of the

Kibbutz members eat meals together.

Dates are one of the kibbutz's products.

Milking machines speed up milking.

Kibbutz trucks bring food to towns.

money is used for air conditioning to make life in the desert a little more pleasant.

Daily life at Yotvata begins at four o'clock in the morning. People have to start work early, before it gets too hot. By afternoon the sun beats down on the desert. The kibbutz members take naps during the early afternoon. It is too hot then to do anything else.

Life at Yotvata is not easy. Still, the people of Yotvata are happy there. They like the challenge of making the desert green. The kibbutz members are always trying out new ways of living in the desert. What they learn may help people in other dry places all over the world.

Reading Check

1. What is a kibbutz?
2. From where do the kibbutz members get much of their water?
3. How do the people of Yotvata raise dairy cows in the desert?
4. Because of the hot desert climate, when must the kibbutz members work?

CHAPTER 18 REVIEW

WORDS TO USE
Copy the words numbered 1 to 5. Next to each word write its meaning from the list below.

1. **kibbutz**
2. **nomads**
3. **oasis**
4. **reclaim**
5. **station**

a. Place in the desert with water
b. People who move from place to place
c. Australian cattle ranch
d. A kind of community in Israel
e. Take back

FACTS TO REVIEW

1. How much rainfall do deserts receive?

2. Why do desert nomads move from place to place?

3. How is life changing in the deserts of Saudi Arabia?

4. Name one way people of the Sahara are different from people of the Negev.

5. Name two ways farming in the Negev is the same today as in the past. Name a way it is different today.

6. Why have the Israelis settled in the Negev?

7. How is a moshav different from a kibbutz?

8. How did the people of Yotvata change the Negev?

9. Why do the people of Yotvata filter their water?

10. How can Yotvata help people who live in deserts?

IDEAS TO DISCUSS
How does life on American deserts differ from life on the Sahara, the Gobi, or the Negev?

◯ SKILLS PRACTICE
Comparing Things Copy each sentence. Next to each sentence, write *compare* or *contrast*.

1. Like the Gobi, the Australian Desert is very dry.

2. The people of the Gobi are nomads, but the ranchers of the Australian Desert are not.

3. On a kibbutz almost everything is shared, but on a moshav each family owns its land and provides for itself.

CHAPTER 19

Plains Around the World

About
this
chapter

More than half of all land on Earth is made up of plains. Many of the world's largest cities are on this flat or rolling land. As in the United States, people all over the world grow crops or herd cattle in plains regions.

Not all plains around the world are alike. Some plains are at sea level and some are at higher elevations. Other plains are in dry, cold places or in hot, rainy ones. In this chapter you will find out where some large plains areas are and how people living on these plains use them.

1. PLAINS REGIONS OF THE WORLD

To Guide Your Reading

Look for these important words:

Key Words
- Calgary Stampede
- Masai
- steppe

Places
- Calgary, Alberta
- Nairobi, Kenya
- European Plain
- Ukraine
- Moscow

Look for answers to these questions:

1. How are the Canadian Plains like our Great Plains?
2. What is unusual about the plains in the country of Kenya?
3. What are the land and the climate like on the plains of the Soviet Union?
4. How do people make a living on the European Plain?

The United States has two large areas of plains, the Interior Plains and the Coastal Plain. The farmlands of the Interior Plains produce much of the food our country needs. Some of our largest cities lie on the Coastal Plain and on the Interior Plains.

Plains in other parts of the world are also places for cities, farms, and ranches. Most plains produce food for many people. As you read about each large plain, find it on the world map on the next page.

The Canadian Plains

The Interior Plains of the United States stretch into Canada, our neighbor to the north. These Canadian Plains reach across most of Canada's western half.

The Canadian Plains are much like our Great Plains. They have rich soil, enough rainfall, and a growing season just right for raising wheat. Each year farms on these plains grow thousands of bushels of wheat. Like American farmers, Canadian farmers

391

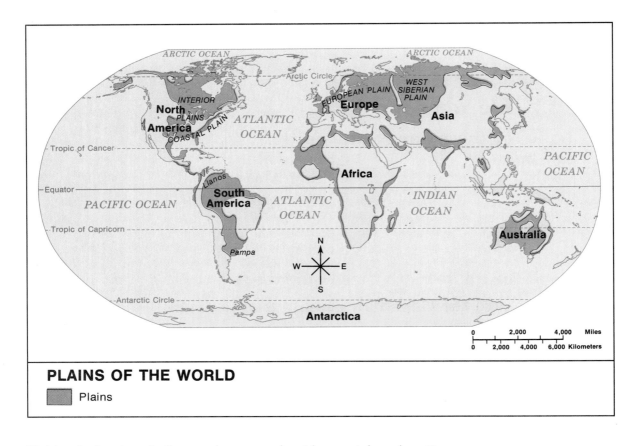

PLAINS OF THE WORLD

Plains

Fields of wheat and other grains spread out in a patchwork pattern across the fertile Canadian Plains.

The chuck wagon races are only part of the fun at the Calgary Stampede.

Herds of elephants and many other animals roam the plains of Kenya.

watch the weather carefully. Canada's interior has very cold winters. Farmers worry that early snows will ruin their wheat.

The western part of the Canadian Plains is not flat enough for growing wheat. This land, near the Canadian Rockies, is cattle country. **Calgary, Alberta,** is a city in the heart of cattle country. Every year it holds a rodeo called the **Calgary Stampede.** Many people come to Calgary's rodeo to see cattle shows and wagon races.

Beneath the rich soil of the Canadian Plains lies another valuable resource, large fields of oil. Oil from these plains has become one of Canada's most important products.

The Plains of Kenya

Plains cover three-quarters of Kenya. Kenya is a nation on the east coast of Africa. Look at the world map on page 392. First, find Africa. Then find where the equator crosses Africa's east coast. The plains of Kenya lie near this point. The climate of the plains of Kenya is different from our Interior Plains. In Kenya it is warm all year long. Why, do you think, is this so?

Kenya's plains are often dry. Except for the rainy seasons in spring and fall, little rain falls during the year. Only bushes and short grasses grow on this land.

The grasslands of Kenya are the home of elephants, lions,

zebras, and other wildlife. The government in Kenya's capital city, **Nairobi** (ny•ROH•bee), has set up huge parks to protect its wildlife. The parks are one of the few places where these animals can live in their natural home. Visitors from around the world come to Kenya to see them.

The **Masai** (mah•SY) are nomads of Kenya's plains. Herding cattle is the main way these people make a living. Yet few of the cattle are killed for meat. They are valued for their milk and used in trading. The Masai make their living mostly from their herds.

The Masai move with their herds of cattle across the land.

For thousands of years the Masai have lived on some of Kenya's driest lands.

When the cattle have eaten all the grass in one place, the Masai move to another. The Masai keep the cattle from running away by herding them into corrals. The fences are made from thorn bushes that grow on the land.

The Plains of the Soviet Union

In size the Soviet Union is the world's largest country. It is so large that it reaches across parts of two continents, Europe and Asia. The Soviet Union is divided by the Ural Mountains. The Urals are very old, low mountains like the Appalachian Mountains. East of the Ural Mountains is Soviet Asia. This covers all of the northern part of Asia. West of the Urals is the European part of the Soviet Union. It covers the eastern half of Europe.

A vast plain covers more than half of the Soviet Union. It lies mostly in Europe. This large plain, called the **European Plain,** is made up of rolling hills and flat land.

The southern part of this plain stretches into Asia and includes the **steppe** (STEP), or grassy plain. This treeless grassland of the Soviet Union has dark, rich soil and grows wheat and other grains. Where the steppe is very dry, it is used as grazing land.

Beef and dairy cattle graze on parts of the steppe too dry or too cold to farm.

The wheat crop of the Ukraine helps feed many of the Soviet Union's people.

Summers on the steppe are hot and have little rain. They can be too dry for growing wheat, which causes poor harvests. The steppe is far from the Atlantic Ocean. Winds from the Atlantic reach the steppe, but by then they have lost almost all their rain. Parts of the steppe may get as little as 8 inches (about 20 cm) of rain a year. The hot, dry winds can kill the wheat crop. Cold can be a problem, too. In some years the bitterly cold winter kills the plants before they can be harvested.

Bordering the steppe in the southwestern part of the Soviet Union is the **Ukraine.** The Ukraine region of the Soviet Union has the best farmland of the country. This part of the plain is often called the "breadbasket" of the Soviet Union.

North of the Ukraine and the steppe are more humid regions. At one time the land was covered by maples, oaks, and other broadleaf trees. Much of this land is cleared today. The Soviet Union's largest cities and largest factories are here.

More than 275 million people live in the Soviet Union. Three of every four live on the European Plain. One reason they live here is the climate. Although much of the plain is hot in summer and very cold in winter, the climate is better here than in most other parts of the Soviet Union.

Located in the heart of the European Plain, Moscow is the political, industrial, and cultural center of the Soviet Union.

Another reason so many people live here is the area's natural resources. This area has minerals and fuels for industry. Large amounts of iron, coal, oil, and natural gas mean jobs for people in factories and refineries. The area also has good soil for growing grain, potatoes, sugar beets, and sunflowers. The oil from sunflower seeds is used for cooking and making soap.

Among the cities in this region **Moscow** is the largest. Moscow is the capital of the Soviet Union. The area around Moscow is the nation's leading factory center. Cars, trucks, and buses are made in factories here. Moscow is also an important center of transportation. Highways and railroads connect Moscow to other parts of the nation. A canal and the Volga River connect Moscow to some of Europe's seas.

Reading Check

1. What plain is much like the Great Plains of the United States?
2. Where do most of the wildlife of Kenya live?
3. Why is the steppe of the Soviet Union very dry?
4. Why do most people of the Soviet Union live on the European Plain?

RETURN OF THE HORSE

Before the car and tractor were invented, the horse was one of the most useful animals. For thousands of years people used horses in sport, hunting, and war.

The **draft horse** was one kind of horse useful in both war and farming. Long ago the draft horse carried a knight wearing heavy armor. Later farmers in Europe and America used draft horses.

Draft horse in earlier times

Draft horses are the giants of the horse world. The tallest are the Shires of England. These horses measure 6 feet (about 183 cm) from shoulder to ground. Draft horses weigh more than a ton (about 0.9 metric ton), as much as a small car.

Draft horses have thick legs and strong muscles. They can pull very large loads. Though they are huge, these horses are gentle and easy to handle.

Many farmers stopped using draft horses when the tractor was invented. They thought tractors were better and cheaper. A tractor did not have to be fed when it wasn't working. Horses needed oats and hay every day. They ate whether or not they worked.

Today tractors are expensive. So is gasoline. Some farmers in Europe and the United States have decided to use horses again. On small farms a horse may be more practical than a tractor. Horses do not get stuck in the mud, as tractors sometimes do. Horses can work on steeper hills. Horses can eat food that is grown on the farm.

Draft horses today

A horse can do something else that tractors cannot do. Horses can make new horses. A tractor cannot make new tractors!

SKILLS FOR SUCCESS

CONSERVING ENERGY

More than 4 billion people live in the world today. All these people use huge amounts of natural resources. More natural resources will be needed in the future. What can we do to make our resources last longer?

One thing we can all do is to **conserve,** or save, energy. Coal, gas, and oil are used to make energy. How can you help save energy? It all begins at home!

- In cold winters, you can try using less heat. Wear warm clothes instead of turning up the heat. At night close window curtains to keep the heat inside the house.

- In summer, try not to use an air conditioner. Instead, keep window curtains closed. That way the house will stay cool during the day.

- It's easy to save electricity. Turn on only the lights you need. Turn off lights when you leave a room. Turn off the television or radio when no one is using it. After you take something from the refrigerator, close the door.

- Using the car too much is a waste of gas. Instead of going by car, see if you can walk or ride a bike. If you are going on a trip, perhaps you can use a bus or train. Share rides with friends when you are going to the same place.

Taking public transportation often saves time and energy.

Newspapers are one of the easiest, most inexpensive materials to recycle.

Recycling cans prevents waste from building up in the environment.

- **Recycling** saves both energy and natural resources. To recycle means to use materials again. Many American towns and cities now have recycling centers. People can bring cans, bottles, and newspapers to them. Recycling saves the raw materials that go into making these things. Recycling also saves energy. It takes less energy to turn used cans, bottles, and newspapers into new products than it does to start with raw materials.

- Being a careful consumer is another good way to save resources. When you buy something you don't really need, you waste resources. Buy only the things you actually need. Use what you have for as long as it lasts.

CHECKING YOUR SKILLS

Write answers to these questions.

1. What are two ways you can save energy in winter?

2. What are two ways you can use less electricity in your house?

3. How can you save energy when you go on a trip?

4. What are some other ways you can save energy?

2. THE PAMPA OF ARGENTINA

To Guide Your Reading

Look for these important words:

Key Words
- pampa
- alfalfa
- estancias

Places
- Buenos Aires
- Salado River

Look for answers to these questions:

1. What kind of rainfall and climate does the pampa have?
2. What important products come from the pampa?
3. Why is meat packing an important industry in Argentina?
4. What are estancias?

Argentina is the second largest country in South America, after Brazil. Along the western edge of the country are the Andes Mountains. As you have read, these mountains are steep and cold.

To the east of the Andes is a large, dry plateau called Patagonia. Though mostly desert, Patagonia does support a few people as well as some unusual wildlife.

One unusual animal that lives along the coast is a type of penguin. These penguins actually only live on land for a short time, when they are raising their

Though awkward looking on land, penguins are graceful swimmers.

Buenos Aires, Argentina's capital, is the center of its government and trade.

LANDFORM MAP OF ARGENTINA

- Mountains
- Hills
- Plateaus
- Plains

chicks. The rest of the year they spend swimming in the Atlantic Ocean.

Northeast of Patagonia, in the middle of Argentina, is a large grassland called the **pampa.** *Pampa* is the Spanish word for plain. Argentina's pampa is one of the world's largest plains.

Most of Argentina's products come from the pampa. More than half of Argentina's people live there, too. Most of them live in Argentina's capital city, **Buenos Aires** (BWAY·nuh SAR·eez).

Buenos Aires is a large, modern city with skyscrapers and wide highways. It lies on the eastern edge of the pampa, near the Atlantic Ocean. Buenos Aires is also a busy port. Ships from around the world dock in its harbor.

The Pampa

Spreading out from Buenos Aires for hundreds of miles is the pampa. Endless fields of wheat and grass stretch out in all directions.

401

Each rainy season produces a thick growth of grass that makes the pampa Argentina's most valuable grazing land.

The pampa has a mild climate and good rainfall. The western part of the pampa receives about 20 inches (about 51 cm) of rain each year. The eastern half receives close to 40 inches (about 102 cm) of rain a year. Yet you can travel for miles across the pampa and not see a stream. The **Salado River** is the only large river that flows across the pampa. You will, however, see windmills rising above the flat land. They pump water from under the ground.

Argentina is in the Southern Hemisphere. Therefore the seasons are just the opposite of those in our Northern Hemisphere. January is the hottest month on the pampa. June through August are the winter months. However, the winters are mild. They are much like winters in our southern states.

Farmlands and Cattle Ranches

The rich soil of the pampa makes it one of the world's best farmlands. Wheat, corn, and **alfalfa** are three of the important crops of the pampa. Alfalfa is a leafy plant grown as cattle feed. Much of the wheat and corn crops is exported to other countries.

By far the most valuable product of the pampa is beef cattle. The grasslands and alfalfa crop feed many large herds of cattle.

Spanish settlers of the *estancias* built beautiful houses like those of Europe. Today, this *estancia* mansion houses a university.

After about two years the cattle are ready for market. They are shipped to meat-packing plants in Buenos Aires. Meat packing is Argentina's most important industry. Much of Argentina's beef is exported to other countries.

Cattle were first brought to Argentina by Spanish settlers. Like most South American countries, Argentina was settled by the Spanish. Many Italian, German, and English people settled there later. However, Argentina is still a Spanish-speaking country.

Some of the settlers from Europe started **estancias** (es•TAHN•see•uhs), or large ranches, on the pampa. The *estancias* covered thousands of acres. The owner of each *estancia* built a large, beautiful house filled with costly furniture from Europe. Near the house the owner planted trees and gardens.

Estancia owners divided the land among family members over the years. Today most of the old *estancias* are much smaller. Yet some *estancias* still stretch for thousands of acres.

Reading Check

1. What is the most important city of Argentina's pampa?
2. What is the most important product of the pampa?
3. Why is alfalfa important in Argentina?
4. Why have *estancias* grown smaller over the years?

403

3. LIFE ON AN ESTANCIA

To Guide Your Reading

Look for these important words:

Key Words
- gauchos
- facón

- lasso
- round up
- asado

Look for answers to these questions:

1. What was the life of a gaucho like 150 years ago?
2. What tools does a gaucho need?
3. In what ways has gaucho life changed?

Most of the people who own *estancias* live a comfortable life. During the year they might invite guests to their ranches to enjoy their swimming pools, tennis courts, and gardens. Some *estancia* owners live on their ranches all year. Others live in Buenos Aires most of the year. Some even live in other countries.

The first *estancias* were built when the pampa was a wild, unsettled land. Modern conveniences are part of life today.

Gauchos of the pampa have rich traditions in music and poetry.

A gaucho sips *maté* from a gourd through a metal straw.

The *estancia* owners hire **gauchos** (GOW•chohs) to take care of their cattle. Today's gauchos are ranch hands. About 150 years ago, however, they were the cowboys of Argentina.

Many people in Argentina remember the gauchos of the past and consider them heroes. Poems and songs praise their brave deeds. They tell of the free life on the pampa in days gone by.

Gauchos Long Ago

Before the *estancias* were built, gauchos lived on the pampa in small groups. They chased the wild cattle there. These animals had been born to cattle that had escaped from Spanish settlers. The gauchos hunted the cattle for food and for hides.

Gauchos later herded cattle for the owners of large *estancias*. The gauchos followed the herds for hundreds of miles across the pampa. There were no fences or roads, just miles and miles of flat grassy lands. The gauchos led a hard life. They spent many days in the saddle. They slept on the ground and lived mostly on beef and a bitter tea called *maté* (mah•TAY).

Few things were more important to the gaucho than his horse. Without his horse he could not chase the cattle. Without his horse he was not free to go anywhere he wished. Gauchos took good care of their horses. They were known for their skills on horseback.

In the early days the gauchos drove cattle herds to Buenos Aires. There the cattle were sold for meat. Then refrigerated railroad cars came to the pampa. The long drives were no longer needed. Meat could now be shipped long distances without spoiling.

Other countries began to buy more beef from Argentina. Cattle ranching soon became very important on the pampa. More people moved to the pampa to start cattle ranches. They brought new kinds of cattle to improve their herds. The herds of cattle grew larger. The ranchers planted fields of alfalfa to feed the cattle.

Immigrants from Europe came to work in the fields. The ranchers built fences. Now the gauchos were no longer free to wander anywhere they chose.

Gauchos Today

Today fences, highways, and railroads cross the pampa. Life for the gaucho has changed. Gauchos no longer live out in the open. They live with their families in small houses on *estancias*. Their children go to schools in small towns near the ranches. Not many schools are open for older children, however. They may have to travel a long way to go to school.

Although the gaucho's life is different today, his clothes remain the same. A gaucho still wears baggy pants and sometimes high

Gauchos once lived on the open range. Now they live and work as ranch hands on the fenced lands of the *estancias*.

Gauchos show off their famous roping and riding skills at rodeos much like the ones held in the western part of our country.

leather boots. He ties a bright scarf around his neck and wears a hat with a broad brim.

Gauchos still carry a long knife, a **facón** (fah•KOHN). It is tucked into a cloth or leather belt. Gauchos use the *facón* for many things, from cutting rope to slicing beef. No gaucho goes anywhere without his *facón*.

On the saddle of the gaucho's horse is another important tool. It is the **lasso.** The lasso is a rope with a loop tied at the end. When the rope is pulled, the loop gets smaller. Gauchos use the lasso to rope horses or cattle. Like the cowboys of our country, they make roping animals look easy.

A workday starts early for the gauchos. They have saddled their horses by the time the sun comes up. On some days the gauchos **round up** calves for branding. *Rounding up* means herding the animals together. On horseback the gauchos separate a few cattle from the herd. Then the gauchos chase the calves. They throw out their lassos as they ride. When a calf is caught, it is thrown to the ground. Then the calf is branded.

On other days the gauchos round up the cattle to move them to another pasture. Gauchos also check for broken fences and watch for sick cows.

407

A gaucho chef prepares steaks, ribs, and sausages as part of the menu for a big outdoor feast called an *asado*.

When gauchos are not working, they may get together to sing songs or tell stories. Sometimes they have an **asado** (ah•SAH•doh), or barbecue. At an asado guests often dine on a whole cow! The beef is roasted over an open pit. Asados have been a custom since the early days of the huge estancias.

If you were invited to an asado, you might hear the guests talk about how the pampa has changed. There are more estancias now, but they are smaller. Roads, railroads, and highways crisscross the pampa. Gaucho families are changing, too. In the past a son would become a gaucho like his father. Fewer choose this life now. Many children from gaucho families leave the estancia. They go to Buenos Aires to find jobs. They are still proud of their past, though.

Yet some things have not changed on the pampa. The grand houses of the old estancias remain. So do many customs of the early Spanish settlers. The gauchos remain, too. They still ride proudly across the wide pampa.

Reading Check

1. What is a gaucho's job?
2. What animal was most important to the gaucho?
3. How did refrigerated railroad cars change the way gauchos worked?
4. Why are there fewer gauchos today than in the past?

CHAPTER 19 REVIEW

WORDS TO USE

Copy these sentences. Fill in the blanks with the right words from the list.

alfalfa   **round up**
estancia   **steppe**
gauchos

1. The drier southern part of the Soviet Union's vast plain is called the _____.

2. An _____ is a large ranch in Argentina.

3. A leafy plant used as animal feed is _____.

4. The cowboys of Argentina are called _____.

5. Gauchos _____ calves for branding.

FACTS TO REVIEW

1. Name two ways the Canadian Plains are like our Great Plains.

2. Name two ways the plains of Kenya are different from our Interior Plains.

3. Why do most Soviet people live on the European Plain?

4. Why is the pampa good for raising cattle?

5. How do gauchos take care of cattle?

IDEAS TO DISCUSS

1. Gauchos have held on to many of their old ways. Would it be difficult for gauchos to change their lives? Why or why not?

2. To help protect wildlife, the government of Kenya has started parks. Some people want to use this land, though. If you were a leader in Kenya, how would you solve this problem and how would you protect Kenya's wildlife?

◯ SKILLS PRACTICE

Conserving Energy Copy the sentences below. Write *save* after the statements that are ways to conserve energy. Then explain why doing each would conserve energy.

1. Wear warm clothes instead of turning up the heat.

2. In winter, keep the window curtains open at all times.

3. Turn off lights when you leave a room.

4. Throw away cans, bottles, and newspapers.

CLOSE-UP

PROTECTING THE ENVIRONMENT

Today many people all over the world talk about "protecting the environment (in•VY•ruhn•muhnt)." What do they mean? What is the "environment"?

We call nature and all its resources our environment. Air, land, water, plants, and animals are parts of our environment. Pollution, however, is a threat to our environment. We must protect our environment from pollution.

Factory smoke pollution

Automobile pollution

Air Pollution

For thousands of years, people made fires to cook food and keep warm. The fires sent smoke and dust into the air. There were few people then, however, and the air could carry the smoke and dust away.

Several hundred years ago people started building factories. Air pollution became much worse. Factories burn large amounts of coal and oil. Burning coal or oil sends huge amounts of waste into the air. Inventions like the automobile have added much more pollution to the air. In fact, much of the world's air pollution comes from gases that cars give off.

Air pollution can be dangerous to our health. It can burn our eyes and skin and make us feel

410

People are trying to find ways to solve the serious air pollution problems that, in many cases, they themselves cause.

dizzy or sleepy. It can make us cough. It can make breathing difficult.

Water Pollution

Our rivers, lakes, and oceans are not as clean as they once were. Chemicals dumped into our waters have caused most water pollution.

Many factories use water from nearby lakes and rivers to clean and cool machines. Often the used water is dumped back into the lake or the river. Chemicals in the waste water can poison fish and plant life. The used water may also be too hot for many fish. Such hot water kills more than 200 million fish a year.

Oil spills cause some water pollution in the oceans. Huge oil tankers carry oil around the world. An accident at sea may spill millions of gallons of oil. An offshore oil well may leak oil into the water. The water becomes coated with a layer of oil called an **oil slick.**

411

Laws can help protect our water supply from the dangers of pollution.

An oil spill made this beach unsafe for people or wildlife.

Cleaning up the oil can be very difficult. Oil slicks kill fish, birds, seals, and other sea life. They also kill the tiny plants that live on the water's surface. Whales and many other animals depend on these plants for food.

Pittsburgh, Pennsylvania

Years ago pollution was a serious problem in Pittsburgh, Pennsylvania. The giant smokestacks of Pittsburgh's steel mills sent great clouds of black smoke into the air. Burning coal to heat homes added to the pollution. The city's three rivers ran dark and dirty.

Groups of Pittsburgh's citizens decided that something had to be done. The city passed some laws. Factories cleaned up smoke before it went out the chimneys. People stopped burning coal in their homes.

412

It took many years to make a difference, but little by little the air got better. Today the citizens of Pittsburgh are still working together to clean their city's air.

Lake Erie

Twenty years ago Lake Erie, one of the Great Lakes, was dying. How can a lake die? For many years factories and cities had been dumping their wastes into the lake. The lake became polluted. Many kinds of fish were dying. Swimming in the lake was dangerous to people's health.

People along Lake Erie began to take action. They asked their state governments to pass strong laws against pollution. They prevented some of the wastes from entering the lake.

Because of pollution controls, fishing, boating, and swimming are once again safe activities on Lake Erie.

413

Save energy.

Don't be a litterbug!

Recycle what you can.

Today Lake Erie is cleaner. More fish live in the lake. People can even swim in Lake Erie now. The lake is not yet as clean as it once was. Still, people working together have made it much better.

What Can You Do?

Cleaning up air and water pollution is expensive. It may take several years to see a difference also. Sometimes it takes many people working together to get the job done.

Can one person do anything to help protect the environment? Yes! Everyone can do his or her part. Each person can help stop pollution in the following ways:

- Conserve, or save, energy. If you use less energy, less smoke goes into the air.

- Recycle bottles, newspapers, and aluminum and tin cans. Huge amounts of land are used to bury garbage. Recycling helps cut down on a community's garbage. You can make and display posters telling people about your community's recycling center. If your community does not have one, your class may want to find out how to start one.

- Throw litter in trash cans. Being careful with your own litter will make a difference.

- Whatever you take into a wilderness area, take out again. Do not bury garbage.

- With a group of people, try to clean up just one river or playground in your community. Doing your part helps make your community more pleasant for everyone.

414

UNIT 5 REVIEW

WORDS TO REMEMBER

Copy the paragraph below. Use the words in the list to complete the sentences.

communes	pampa
export	rain forest
flood plain	reclaimed
gauchos	steppe
nomads	terraces

How people make a living often depends on the place where they live. Few people live in the hot, wet (_____)(1) of the Amazon basin. The groups who do live there grow crops in small fields and hunt. The floods of the Yangtze River have built up a rich (_____)(2). Here farming villages, or (_____)(3), grow rice and other crops. The Swiss mainly raise herds of dairy cattle in the Alps. They (_____)(4) much of the cheese they make to other countries. The people of the Andes Mountains grow potatoes on (_____)(5) built on the mountain slopes. The (_____)(6) of deserts travel with their herds in search of food and water. On the Israeli kibbutz of Yotvata people have found ways to grow crops with little water. By doing this they have (_____)(7) land from the desert. On the dry (_____)(8) of the Soviet Union, people grow wheat. Herds of beef cattle are raised on the (_____)(9) of Argentina. (_____)(10) take care of the cattle on the estancias.

FOCUS ON MAIN IDEAS

1. Why do so many people live near the world's large rivers?

2. Why is the Yangtze River important to the Chinese?

3. Give two reasons why mountain regions are difficult to live in.

4. What ways of life help people live in the Andes Mountains?

5. What is an ancient way of making a living in the desert? What is a modern way?

6. How have the people of Israel made the Negev into fertile farmland?

7. In what ways do people make a living in plains regions? What natural resources allow them to do their work?

8. How did the gauchos live about 150 years ago? What tools do gauchos still use today as they did long ago?

415

9. How has the pampa of Argentina changed?

10. Name three ways Cuzco, Nanking, and Buenos Aires are alike. Name three ways they are different.

ACTIVITIES

1. **Research/Writing** Choose one place discussed in this unit. Use the library to find out how people of your age live in that place. What do their houses look like? What foods do they eat? Do they go to school? What do they study? Write a report about what you find out.

2. **Research/Mapmaking** You may want to work in a group for this activity. Choose one of the following: rivers, mountains, deserts, or plains. In an almanac or an encyclopedia find the ten largest of the feature you choose. Using different colors for each feature, mark and label each on an outline map of the world. Label the continents and the oceans also.

3. **Remembering the Close-Up** Choose a plant or an animal in which you are interested. Find out where it lives and what it needs in order to live. If possible, learn how the plant or animal helps people. Is air or water pollution a danger

to it today? Make a fact sheet showing what you find out. You may wish to draw the plant or animal in its environment on your fact sheet.

⬤ SKILLS REVIEW

1. **Reading Graphs**

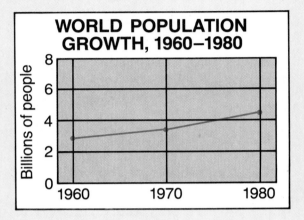

WORLD POPULATION GROWTH, 1960–1980

a. Look at the graph on this page. What does it show?

b. In what year was the population the highest? In what year was the population closest to 3 billion?

2. **Making Comparisons** Copy each sentence. Next to each sentence, write *compare* or *contrast*.

a. Buenos Aires is on a plain, but Cuzco is in the mountains.

b. Like Nanking, Lima is a port city.

c. The Soviet Union, the United States, and Canada raise wheat on their plains.

YOUR STATE

In this unit you have seen how people live in different parts of the world. You have seen that they use their land and natural resources in many different ways. By learning how other people live, we can sometimes learn more about ourselves.

Below are some things you can do to find out more about the people and places of your state.

LEARNING ABOUT HISTORY

1. Many city governments have made old buildings into landmarks. They keep reminders of the past in museums. Pick a large city in your state. Use a library to find out some of the landmarks in this city. Why are they important? Make a catalog of these landmarks. If possible, draw pictures of each one.

2. People have come to our country from all parts of the world. Use the library to find out what countries people in your state have come from. What holidays or customs are celebrated in these countries? Share what you find out with your class.

LEARNING ABOUT PEOPLE

3. Use a library to find out what famous people come from your state. Collect facts about one person. Share what you learn about this person with your class.

LEARNING ABOUT GEOGRAPHY

4. Suppose that someone from another country will be visiting your home. What would you especially like to show this person in your state? How would you make him or her comfortable? Plan a tour of the state for your guest.

5. Choose a mountain range, desert, or plain you have read about in this unit. Compare it with a part of your state that is like it. For example, perhaps your state has a large river. You might compare it with the Yangtze River. Do you live on a plain? You could compare ways of farming or ranching in your state with those on the pampa of Argentina or the European Plain of the Soviet Union.

UNITED STATES OF AMERICA: REGIONS, STATES, AND CITIES

CANADA

WASHINGTON (WA)
• Seattle
⊛ Olympia
Spokane •

Portland •
⊛ Salem
Columbia River

Eugene •

OREGON (OR)

PACIFIC STATES

⊛ Boise

IDAHO (ID)

Idaho Falls •
Pocatello •
Snake River

Helena ⊛
Butte •

Great Falls •

MONTANA (MT)

Billings •

Missouri River

NORTH DAKOTA (ND)
Grar Fork

⊛ Bismarck

Missouri

• Rapid City

SOUTH DAKOTA (SD)

• Pierre ⊛

PLAINS STATES

WYOMING (WY)

Casper •

Laramie •
Cheyenne ⊛

NEBRASKA (NE)

Grand Island •

Platte River

• Reno
⊛ Carson City

Sacramento ⊛

San Francisco

NEVADA (NV)

Great Salt Lake
• Ogden

Salt Lake City ⊛
Provo •

MOUNTAIN STATES

UTAH (UT)

Green River

Colorado River

• Boulder
⊛ Denver

COLORADO (CO)
• Colorado Springs

Pueblo •

KANSAS (KS)
Sali

• Wichita

CALIFORNIA (CA)

Las Vegas •

Los Angeles •

San Diego •

ARIZONA (AZ)

Phoenix ⊛ • Mesa

Gila River

Tucson •

• Santa Fe
• Albuquerque

NEW MEXICO (NM)

SOUTHWEST

Roswell •

Las Cruces •

OKLAHOMA (OK)

Oklahoma City ⊛

Lawton •

Brazos River

TEXAS (TX)

Pecos River

PACIFIC OCEAN

MEXICO

Rio Grande

Austin ⊛

San Antonio •

ARCTIC OCEAN

SOVIET UNION

ALASKA (AK)
Fairbanks •

Yukon River

PACIFIC STATES

CANADA

Arctic Circle

Anchorage •

Juneau ⊛

| 250 | 500 Miles |
250 500 750 Kilometers

PACIFIC OCEAN

418

Tropic of Cancer

PACIFIC OCEAN

Kauai

Oahu **HAWAII (HI)**
Honolulu •

Maui •

PACIFIC STATES

| 100 | 200 Miles |
100 200 300 Kilometers

Hilo
Hawaii

CANADA

Lake Superior

MINNESOTA (MN)

Fargo
Duluth
Minneapolis • ⊛ St. Paul

WISCONSIN (WI)

Green Bay
Milwaukee •
Madison ⊛

MICHIGAN (MI)

Lake Michigan
Lake Huron

Grand Rapids
Lansing ⊛
Detroit •

IOWA (IA)

Sioux Falls
Cedar Rapids •
Davenport •
Des Moines ⊛

Rockford •
Chicago •
Gary •
Fort Wayne •

GREAT LAKES STATES

ILLINOIS (IL)

INDIANA (IN)

Indianapolis ⊛
Springfield ⊛

Omaha •
Lincoln •

Topeka ⊛
Kansas City •
St. Louis •

MISSOURI (MO)

Jefferson City ⊛

Missouri River
Mississippi River

Cincinnati •

OHIO (OH)

Columbus ⊛
Wheeling •

Cleveland •

PENNSYLVANIA (PA)

Buffalo •
Harrisburg ⊛
Pittsburgh •
Philadelphia •

Lake Ontario
Lake Erie

St. Lawrence River

NORTHEAST

NEW YORK (NY)

Albany ⊛
Springfield •
Hartford ⊛
Bridgeport •
Newark •
New York City •
Trenton ⊛

MAINE (ME)

Augusta ⊛
Lewiston •
Portland •

Burlington •
Montpelier ⊛

VERMONT (VT)

Rutland •

NEW HAMPSHIRE (NH)

Concord ⊛
Manchester •
Boston ⊛

MASSACHUSETTS (MA)

Providence ⊛

RHODE ISLAND (RI)

CONNECTICUT (CT)

NEW JERSEY (NJ)

Dover ⊛

DELAWARE (DE)

MARYLAND (MD)

Baltimore •
Washington, D.C. ⊛
Annapolis ⊛

Ohio River
Wabash River

Louisville •
Frankfort ⊛
Lexington •

Huntington •
Charleston ⊛

WEST VIRGINIA (WV)

VIRGINIA (VA)

Richmond ⊛

Norfolk •
Virginia Beach •

KENTUCKY (KY)

Nashville ⊛
Knoxville •

Greensboro •
Raleigh ⊛

NORTH CAROLINA (NC)

Charlotte •

Tulsa •

Arkansas River

TENNESSEE (TN)

Memphis •

Greenville •
Columbia ⊛

SOUTH CAROLINA (SC)

Charleston •

ARKANSAS (AR)

Fort Smith •
Little Rock ⊛
Pine Bluff •

SOUTHEAST

Atlanta ⊛

Dallas •

Red River

Shreveport •
Vicksburg •
Jackson ⊛

Birmingham •

ALABAMA (AL)

Montgomery ⊛

Columbus •

GEORGIA (GA)

Savannah •

Tennessee River

MISSISSIPPI (MS)

LOUISIANA (LA)

Hattiesburg •
Mobile •
Tallahassee ⊛
Jacksonville •

Sabine River

Houston •

Baton Rouge ⊛
Biloxi •
New Orleans •

ATLANTIC OCEAN

FLORIDA (FL)

Tampa •

Gulf of Mexico

Miami •

BAHAMAS

Tropic of Cancer

CUBA

— National boundary
— State boundary
( ) Postal abbreviation
⊛ National capital
⊛ State capital
• Large city

N
W E
S

0   100   200   300 Miles
0 100 200 300 400 Kilometers

419

UNITED STATES OF AMERICA: THE LAND

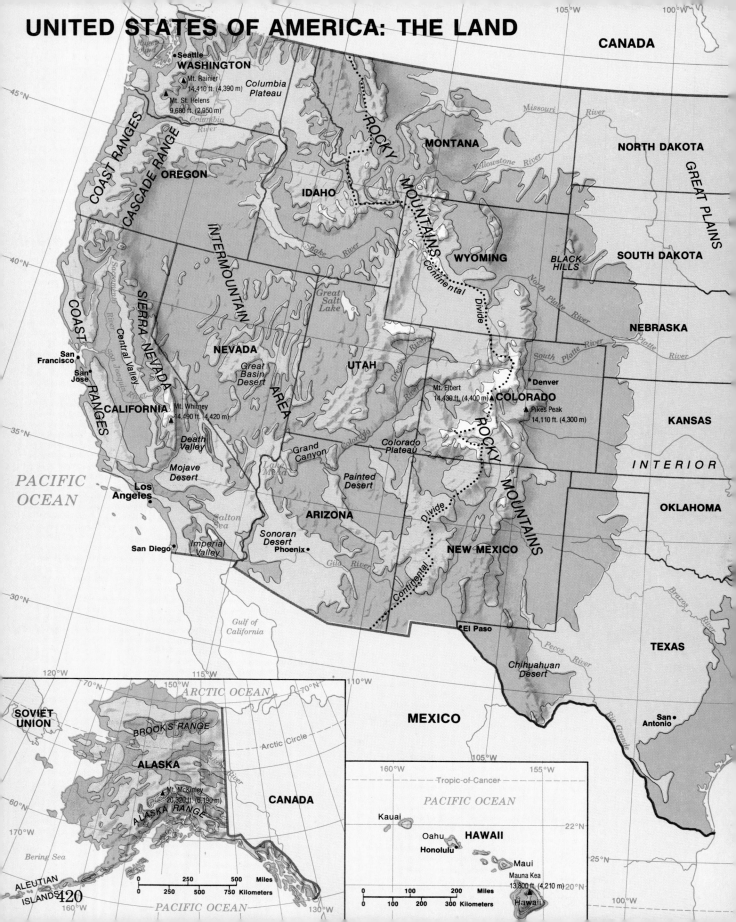

CANADA

WASHINGTON • Seattle
▲ Mt. Rainier
14,410 ft. (4,390 m)
▲ Mt. St. Helens
9,680 ft. (2,950 m)

Columbia Plateau

Columbia River

COAST RANGES

CASCADE RANGE

OREGON

ROCKY MOUNTAINS

MONTANA

NORTH DAKOTA

GREAT PLAINS

Missouri River

Yellowstone River

IDAHO

Shake River

INTERMOUNTAIN

Great Salt Lake

Continental Divide

WYOMING

BLACK HILLS

SOUTH DAKOTA

SIERRA NEVADA

San Francisco •

San Jose •

CALIFORNIA

▲ Mt. Whitney
14,490 ft. (4,420 m)

Central Valley

San Joaquin River

Sacramento River

COAST RANGES

NEVADA

AREA

Great Basin Desert

UTAH

Green River

Mt. Elbert
14,430 ft. (4,400 m) ▲ **COLORADO**

• Denver

▲ Pikes Peak
14,110 ft. (4,300 m)

South Platte River

North Platte River

Platte River

NEBRASKA

KANSAS

Death Valley

Mojave Desert

Los Angeles •

San Diego •

Salton Sea

Imperial Valley

Lake Mead

Grand Canyon

Colorado River

Painted Desert

Colorado Plateau

ROCKY MOUNTAINS

INTERIOR

OKLAHOMA

ARIZONA

Sonoran Desert

Phoenix •

Gila River

Divide

NEW MEXICO

Continental

Divide

PACIFIC OCEAN

Gulf of California

• El Paso

Chihuahuan Desert

Pecos River

TEXAS

San Antonio •

Brazos River

Rio Grande

MEXICO

SOVIET UNION

ARCTIC OCEAN

BROOKS RANGE

ALASKA

Arctic Circle

▲ Mt. McKinley
20,320 ft. (6,190 m)

ALASKA RANGE

CANADA

Bering Sea

ALEUTIAN ISLANDS

420

PACIFIC OCEAN

| 0 | 250 | 500 | Miles |
| 0 | 250 | 500 | 750 | Kilometers |

Tropic of Cancer

PACIFIC OCEAN

Kauai

Oahu **HAWAII**

Honolulu

Maui

Mauna Kea
13,800 ft. (4,210 m)

Hawaii

| 0 | 100 | 200 | Miles |
| 0 | 100 | 200 | 300 | Kilometers |

CANADA

MINNESOTA

Lake of the Woods

MESABI RANGE

Lake Superior

WISCONSIN

MICHIGAN

Lake Michigan

Lake Huron

Minnesota River

Mississippi River

Milwaukee

IOWA

Chicago

Des Moines River

Detroit

Lake Erie

Cleveland

Lake Ontario

St. Lawrence River

MAINE

VERMONT

NEW HAMPSHIRE

Boston

Cape Cod

MASSACHUSETTS

RHODE ISLAND

CONNECTICUT

NEW YORK

PENNSYLVANIA

ILLINOIS

INDIANA

OHIO

Indianapolis

Columbus

Hudson River

Connecticut River

New York City

Philadelphia

NEW JERSEY

MARYLAND

Baltimore

DELAWARE

WEST VIRGINIA

Washington, D.C.

CENTRAL PLAINS

Missouri River

Kansas City

St. Louis

MISSOURI

GREAT PLAINS

PLAINS

Wabash River

KENTUCKY

VIRGINIA

Fall Line

Chesapeake Bay

ATLANTIC OCEAN

APPALACHIAN MOUNTAINS

Mt. Mitchell 6,680 ft. (2,040 m)

NORTH CAROLINA

Cape Hatteras

COASTAL PLAIN

Ozark Plateau

Nashville

TENNESSEE

ARKANSAS

Memphis

Piedmont

SOUTH CAROLINA

Tennessee River

Atlanta

GEORGIA

MISSISSIPPI

ALABAMA

Pearl River

Savannah River

COASTAL PLAIN

Dallas

LOUISIANA

Sabine River

Red River

COASTAL PLAIN

Houston

New Orleans

Mississippi Delta

Jacksonville

FLORIDA

Cape Canaveral

Lake Okeechobee

Everglades

Gulf of Mexico

Florida Keys

BAHAMAS

Tropic of Cancer

CUBA

Elevations

Feet	Meters
Above 10,000	Above 3,000
7,000	2,000
3,000	1,000
700	200
0	0
Below sea level	Below sea level

—— National boundary

—— State boundary

☐ Glaciers (Alaska)

▲ Mountain peak

• Large city

N
W   E
S

| 0 | 100 | 200 | 300 Miles |
| 0 | 100 | 200 | 300 | 400 Kilometers |

THE WORLD

—— National boundary

ARCTIC OCEAN

180° 160°W 140°W 120°W 100°W 80°W 60

Arctic Circle
ALASKA

60°N

CANADA

North
America

40°N

UNITED STATES

PACIFIC
OCEAN

ATLANTIC
OCEAN

MIDWAY IS. (U.S.)

MEXICO

BAHAMAS

Tropic of Cancer

HAWAII

CUBA

20°N

DOMINICAN
REPUBLIC

JAMAICA HAITI

VIRGIN IS. (U.S.)

GUATEMALA BELIZE
HONDURAS

PUERTO RICO (U.S.)

EL SALVADOR NICARAGUA

COSTA RICA

TRINIDAD AND TOBAGO

PANAMA

VENEZUELA GUYANA
SURINAME
FRENCH GUIANA (Fr.

COLOMBIA

0° Equator

ECUADOR

South
America

PERU

BRAZIL

WESTERN
SAMOA

AMERICAN
SAMOA
(U.S.)

FRENCH

POLYNESIA

BOLIVIA

TONGA

20°S

TAHITI

(Fr.)

PARAGUAY

Tropic of Capricorn

URUGUAY

PACIFIC
OCEAN

CHILE

ARGENTINA

40°S

FALKLAND IS.
(U.K.)

60°S

Antarctic Circle

Antarctica

80°S

180° 160°W 140°W 120°W 100°W 80°W 60

ALB. Albania
AUST. Austria
BEL. Belgium
C. AF. REP. Central African Republic
CZECH. Czechoslovakia
E. GER. East Germany
HUNG. Hungary
NETH. Netherlands
SWITZ. Switzerland
U. ARAB EMIR. United Arab Emirates
W. GER. West Germany
YEMEN (P.D.R.) People's Democratic
   Republic of Yemen
YUGO. Yugoslavia

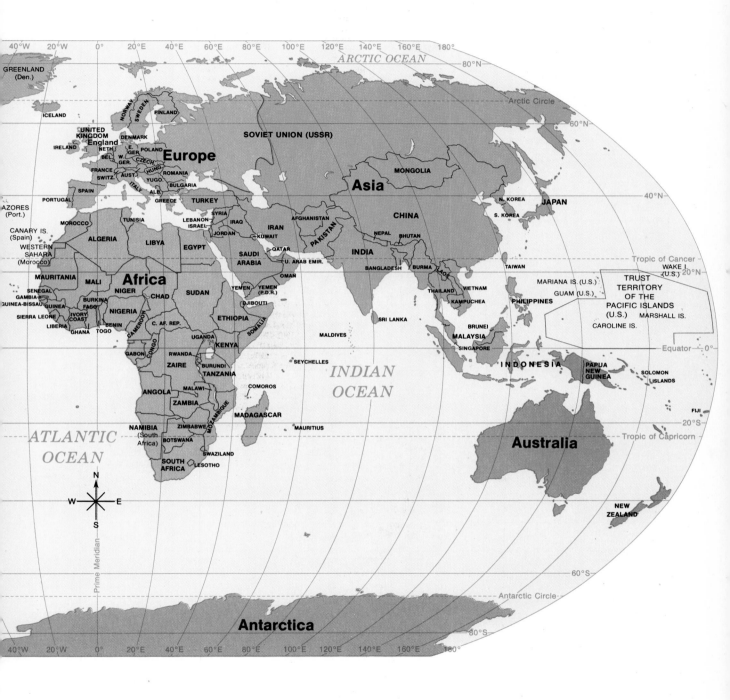

GREENLAND
(Den.)

ICELAND

ARCTIC OCEAN

Arctic Circle

80°N

SOVIET UNION (USSR)

60°N

NORWAY SWEDEN FINLAND

UNITED KINGDOM
England
IRELAND

DENMARK
NETH.
BEL. E. POLAND
W. GER.
GER. CZECH
FRANCE
SWITZ. AUST. HUNG.
ITALY YUGO. ROMANIA
ALB. BULGARIA
GREECE

Europe

MONGOLIA

Asia

40°N

SPAIN

PORTUGAL

TURKEY

N. KOREA JAPAN

S. KOREA

AZORES
(Port.)

CANARY IS.
(Spain)

MOROCCO

TUNISIA

LEBANON SYRIA
ISRAEL IRAQ
JORDAN

IRAN

AFGHANISTAN

CHINA

WESTERN
SAHARA
(Morocco)

ALGERIA

LIBYA

EGYPT

KUWAIT
QATAR
SAUDI
ARABIA
U. ARAB EMIR.

PAKISTAN

NEPAL

INDIA

BHUTAN

BURMA
LAOS

TAIWAN

Tropic of Cancer

WAKE I.
(U.S.)

20°N

MAURITANIA

MALI

Africa

NIGER

CHAD

SUDAN

OMAN

YEMEN YEMEN
(P.D.R.)

DJIBOUTI

BANGLADESH

THAILAND
VIETNAM

KAMPUCHEA

MARIANA IS. (U.S.)

GUAM (U.S.)

PHILIPPINES

TRUST
TERRITORY
OF THE
PACIFIC ISLANDS
(U.S.)

MARSHALL IS.

SENEGAL
GAMBIA
GUINEA-BISSAU GUINEA
SIERRA LEONE
LIBERIA

BURKINA
FASO
IVORY
COAST
GHANA TOGO

BENIN

NIGERIA

CAMEROON

C. AF. REP.

ETHIOPIA

SOMALIA

SRI LANKA

MALDIVES

BRUNEI

MALAYSIA

SINGAPORE

CAROLINE IS.

Equator

0°

GABON

CONGO

UGANDA

RWANDA
BURUNDI

ZAIRE

KENYA

TANZANIA

SEYCHELLES

INDIAN
OCEAN

INDONESIA

PAPUA
NEW
GUINEA

SOLOMON
ISLANDS

ANGOLA

MALAWI

ZAMBIA

MOZAMBIQUE

COMOROS

MADAGASCAR

MAURITIUS

FIJI

ATLANTIC
OCEAN

NAMIBIA
(South
Africa)

ZIMBABWE

BOTSWANA

SWAZILAND

SOUTH
AFRICA

LESOTHO

Tropic of Capricorn

20°S

Australia

N
W E
S

NEW
ZEALAND

60°S

Prime Meridian

Antarctic Circle

Antarctica

80°S

40°W 20°W 0° 20°E 40°E 60°E 80°E 100°E 120°E 140°E 160°E 180°

0 500 1,000 1,500 2,000 Miles

0 1,000 2,000 Kilometers

423

FACTS ABOUT THE STATES

STATE (Abbreviations)	STATE CAPITAL	STATE POPULATION*	STATE NICKNAME	STATE BIRD	STATE FLOWER
Alabama (Ala., AL)	Montgomery	3,959,000	Yellowhammer State; Heart of Dixie; Cotton State	common flicker	camellia
Alaska (Alaska, AK)	Juneau	479,000	Last Frontier; Land of the Midnight Sun	willow ptarmigan	forget-me-not
Arizona (Ariz., AZ)	Phoenix	2,963,000	Grand Canyon State; Sunset State; Apache State	cactus wren	saguaro (giant cactus)
Arkansas (Ark., AR)	Little Rock	2,328,000	Land of Opportunity	mockingbird	apple blossom
California (Calif., CA)	Sacramento	25,174,000	Golden State	California valley quail	golden poppy
Colorado (Colo., CO)	Denver	3,139,000	Centennial State	lark bunting	Rocky Mountain columbine
Connecticut (Conn., CT)	Hartford	3,138,000	Constitution State; Nutmeg State	robin	mountain laurel
Delaware (Del., DE)	Dover	606,000	First State; Diamond State	blue hen chicken	peach blossom
Florida (Fla., FL)	Tallahassee	10,680,000	Sunshine State	mockingbird	orange blossom
Georgia (Ga., GA)	Atlanta	5,732,000	Empire State of the South; Peach State	brown thrasher	Cherokee rose
Hawaii (Hawaii, HI)	Honolulu	1,023,000	Aloha State	nene (Hawaiian goose)	hibiscus
Idaho (Idaho, ID)	Boise	989,000	Gem State; Spud State	mountain bluebird	syringa (mock orange)
Illinois (Ill., IL)	Springfield	11,486,000	Land of Lincoln; The Inland Empire	cardinal	native violet
Indiana (Ind., IN)	Indianapolis	5,479,000	Hoosier State	cardinal	peony
Iowa (Iowa, IA)	Des Moines	2,905,000	Hawkeye State	eastern goldfinch	wild rose
Kansas (Kans., KS)	Topeka	2,425,000	Sunflower State; Jayhawker State	western meadowlark	sunflower
Kentucky (Ky., KY)	Frankfort	3,714,000	Bluegrass State	Kentucky cardinal	goldenrod
Louisiana (La., LA)	Baton Rouge	4,438,000	Pelican State; Bayou State	brown pelican	magnolia
Maine (Maine, ME)	Augusta	1,146,000	Pine Tree State	chickadee	white pine cone & tassel
Maryland (Md., MD)	Annapolis	4,304,000	Old Line State; Free State	Baltimore oriole	black-eyed Susan
Massachusetts (Mass., MA)	Boston	5,767,000	Bay State; Old Colony	chickadee	mayflower
Michigan (Mich., MI)	Lansing	9,069,000	Wolverine State; Water Wonderland	robin	apple blossom
Minnesota (Minn., MN)	St. Paul	4,144,000	Land of 10,000 Lakes; Gopher State	common loon	pink & white lady's slipper
Mississippi (Miss., MS)	Jackson	2,587,000	Magnolia State	mockingbird	magnolia

*These population figures reflect the most recent available estimates.

STATE (Abbreviations)	STATE CAPITAL	STATE POPULATION*	STATE NICKNAME	STATE BIRD	STATE FLOWER
Missouri (Mo., MO)	Jefferson City	4,970,000	Show Me State; Gateway to the West	bluebird	hawthorn
Montana (Mont., MT)	Helena	817,000	Treasure State	western meadowlark	bitterroot
Nebraska (Nebr., NE)	Lincoln	1,597,000	Cornhusker State	western meadowlark	goldenrod
Nevada (Nev., NV)	Carson City	891,000	Silver State; Battle Born State	mountain bluebird	sagebrush
New Hampshire (N.H., NH)	Concord	959,000	Granite State	purple finch	purple lilac
New Jersey (N.J., NJ)	Trenton	7,468,000	Garden State	eastern goldfinch	purple violet
New Mexico (N. Mex., NM)	Sante Fe	1,399,000	Land of Enchantment; Sunshine State	roadrunner	yucca
New York (N.Y., NY)	Albany	17,667,000	Empire State	bluebird	rose
North Carolina (N.C., NC)	Raleigh	6,082,000	Tar Heel State; Old North State	cardinal	dogwood
North Dakota (N.Dak., ND)	Bismarck	680,000	Sioux State; Flickertail State	western meadowlark	wild prairie rose
Ohio (Ohio, OH)	Columbus	10,746,000	Buckeye State	cardinal	scarlet carnation
Oklahoma (Okla., OK)	Oklahoma City	3,298,000	Sooner State	scissortailed flycatcher	mistletoe
Oregon (Oreg., OR)	Salem	2,662,000	Beaver State	western meadowlark	Oregon grape
Pennsylvania (Pa., PA)	Harrisburg	11,895,000	Keystone State	ruffed grouse	mountain laurel
Rhode Island (R.I., RI)	Providence	955,000	Little Rhody; Ocean State	Rhode Island red	violet
South Carolina (S.C., SC)	Columbia	3,264,000	Palmetto State	Carolina wren	Carolina yellow jessamine
South Dakota (S.Dak., SD)	Pierre	700,000	Coyote State; Sunshine State	ring-necked pheasant	American pasqueflower
Tennessee (Tenn., TN)	Nashville	4,685,000	Volunteer State; Big Bend State	mockingbird	iris
Texas (Tex., TX)	Austin	15,724,000	Lone Star State	mockingbird	bluebonnet
Utah (Utah, UT)	Salt Lake City	1,619,000	Beehive State	seagull	sego lily
Vermont (Vt., VT)	Montpelier	525,000	Green Mountain State	hermit thrush	red clover
Virginia (Va., VA)	Richmond	5,550,000	Old Dominion; Mother of Presidents	cardinal	dogwood
Washington (Wash., WA)	Olympia	4,300,000	Evergreen State; Chinook State	willow goldfinch	coast rhododendron
West Virginia (W. Va., WV)	Charleston	1,965,000	Mountain State	cardinal	rhododendron
Wisconsin (Wis., WI)	Madison	4,751,000	Badger State; America's Dairyland	robin	wood violet
Wyoming (Wyo., WY)	Cheyenne	514,000	Equality State; Cowboy State	meadowlark	Indian paintbrush

*These population figures reflect the most recent available estimates.

Glossary

This glossary contains important social studies words and their definitions. Each word is pronounced as it would be in a dictionary. When you see this mark ' after a syllable, pronounce that syllable with more force than the other syllables. The page number at the end of the definition tells where to find the word in your book.

add, āce, câre, pälm;   end, ēqual;   it, īce;   odd, ōpen, ôrder;   tŏok, pōol;   up, bûrn; yōo as u in *fuse*;   oil;   pout;   ə as a in *above*, e in *sicken*, i in *possible*, o in *melon*, u in *circus*; check;   ring;   thin;   this;   zh as in vision.

adobe (ə•dō′bē) Sun-dried clay bricks used to build homes in the Indian pueblos. (p. 234)

alfalfa (al•fal′fə) A leafy plant grown as cattle feed. (p. 402)

almanac (ôl′mə•nak) A book of facts and figures, brought up to date every year. (p. 119)

altitude (al′tə•tōod) The elevation or height of the land. (p. 77)

aluminum (ə•lōo′mə•nəm) A lightweight metal. (p. 273)

arctic (ärk′tik) Very cold. Climate zones farthest from the sun are Arctic zones. (p. 340)

area (âr′ē•ə) Amount of land. (p. 104)

assembly line (ə•sem′blē līn) A moving belt where each worker adds a part until the car is finished. (p. 190)

assembly plant (ə•sem′blē plant) A place where the parts of the cars are put together, or assembled. (p. 190)

atlas (at′ləs) A book of maps. (p. 118)

axis (ak′səs) The imaginary line around which the Earth turns. The line runs from the North Pole to the South Pole. (p. 338)

bamboo (bam•bōo′) A giant grass. (p. 344)

barge (bärj) A large, flat-bottomed boat used to carry goods from place to place. (p. 64)

barter (bär′tər) To trade for goods. (p. 182)

basin (bā′sən) Low, bowl-shaped land. (p. 33)

bay (bā) A body of water partly surrounded by land. (p. 135)

bison (bī′sən) Buffalo. (p. 205)

border (bôr′dər) The outside edge of a place, shown as a line on a map. (p. 3)

boundary (boun′də•rē) The border, or outside edge of a place. (p. 27)

branch (branch) 1. A smaller river or stream that joins a river; a tributary. (p. 56) 2. One of the three main parts of the government. (p. 313)

brand (brand) To mark calves or sheep to show who owns them. (p. 86)

canal (kə•nal′) A stream or river built by people. (p. 102)

canyon (kan′yən) A narrow valley with steep sides. (p. 33)

capital (kap′ə•təl) A city where laws are made. (p. 29)

cardinal directions (kär′də•nəl di•rek′shənz) The four main directions; north, south, east, and west. (p. 138)

century (sen′chə•rē) A period of 100 years. (p. 145)

chaff (chaf) The outside cover of the grain. (p. 210)

citizen (sit′ə•zən) A person who is a member of a nation. (p. 173)

climate (klī′mət) The weather a place has year after year. (p. 36)

climate zone (klī′mət zōn) A wide band that circles the Earth. Places in a climate zone all have about the same climate. (p. 340)

coast (kōst) The land next to the ocean. (p. 29)

colony (kol′ə•nē) A place that is ruled by another country. (p. 141)

combine (kom′bīn) A huge machine that cuts and threshes the wheat. (p. 210)

commonwealth (kom′ən•welth) A kind of territory that governs itself. (p. 172)

communication (kə•myōo•nə•kā′shən) The way we send and receive messages. (p. 299)

compass rose (kum′pəs rōz) A symbol on a map that shows directions. (p. 3)

competition (kom•pə•tish′ən) A contest between producers to get customers. (p. 304)

conservation (kon•sər•vā′shən) Saving something by using it wisely and carefully. (p. 87)

conserve (kən•sûrv′) To save, or keep from being used up. (p. 398)

consumer (kən·soo′mər) A person who spends money to buy things. (p. 292)

council (koun′səl) The lawmakers of a community. (p. 319)

county (koun′tē) Part of a state that has its own government. (p. 214)

county seat (koun′tē sēt) A town or city that is the center of government for a county. (p. 213)

courts (kôrts) The branch of government where judges make sure that people are obeying the laws. (p. 315)

cross section (kros sek′shən) A slice or piece of something to show its insides. (p. 89)

crude oil (krūd ôil) The name for oil when it is pumped from the earth. (p. 167)

dam (dam) A wall built to hold back the water flow of a river. Also used to store water for drinking and irrigation. (p. 61)

delta (del′tə) A triangular piece of land at the mouth of a river. (p. 60)

democracy (də·mo′krə·sē) A government where people are free to choose their government leaders. (p. 20)

desert (dez′ərt) A region where the land is mostly dry and few or no plants grow. (p. 33)

dictionary (dik′shə·ner·ē) A book that tells what words mean and how to spell and say them. (p. 118)

distance scale (dis′təns skāl) A guide on a map where a small distance on the map stands for the actual distance on the Earth. (p. 5)

downstream (doun′strēm) Towards the river's mouth. (p. 71)

drought (drout) A time of little or no rainfall. (p. 115)

economy (i·kon′ə·mē) The way a country provides and uses goods and services. (p. 304)

elect (i·lekt′) To choose by vote to a position in government. (p. 185)

elevation (el·ə·vā′shən) The height of the land. (p. 70)

encyclopedia (en·sī·klə·pē′dē·ə) A book with articles on many subjects, arranged in alphabetical order. (p. 117)

equator (ē·kwā′tər) A make-believe line around the Earth halfway between the North Pole and the South Pole. (p. 5)

erode (i·rōd′) To wear away the Earth's surface. (p. 60)

erosion (i·rō′zhən) The slow wearing away of large areas of land. (p. 60)

executive (ig·zek′yə·tiv) The branch of government that makes sure the laws are carried out. (p. 315)

export (ex′pôrt) To send something to another country to be sold. (p. 357)

fact (fakt) A statement that can be checked and proved. (p. 235)

farming commune (fär′ming kom′yoon) A kind of village where people live and work together. (p. 348)

federal government (fed′ər·əl guv′ərn·mənt) Government of a country. (p. 310)

feedlot (fēd′lot) A large pen where cattle are fed grain to fatten them for market. (p. 114)

fertile (fûr′təl) Full of minerals that make plants grow. (p. 108)

finished product (fin′isht pro′dəkt) Something such as clothing or furniture that is made from raw materials. (p. 110)

flood (flud) The overflowing of a river, caused by heavy rains or melting snow. (p. 61)

flood plain (flud plān) An area of fertile land formed by river floods. (p. 343)

free enterprise (frē en′tər·prīz) An economy where people are free to own and run businesses and industries. (p. 304)

frontier (frun·tir′) The place where the settled areas ended and wilderness began. (p. 162)

fuel (fyool) Something such as coal, oil, or natural gas that is used to make heat and to run machines. (p. 38)

gaucho (gou′chō) A ranch hand in Argentina. Long ago, gauchos were cowboys. (p. 405)

geography (jē·og′rə·fē) The study of the Earth's surface. (p. 1)

geyser (gī′zər) A spring of water that shoots steam and hot water into the air. (p. 251)

globe (glōb) A model of the Earth in the shape of a sphere, or ball. (p. 5)

goods (goodz) Things people buy and sell. (p. 17)

government (guv′ərn·mənt) A group of people who lead a city, a state, or a country. (p. 20)

governor (guv′ər·nər) The head of the state government's executive branch. (p. 318)

grain elevator (grān el′ə·vā·tər) A tall tower that stores harvested grain. (p. 209)

graph (graf) A drawing that show numbers. (p. 98)

graze (grāz) To feed on grass. (p. 86)

grid (grid) A pattern of crossing lines in a chart or drawing. (p. 58)

hailstorm (hāl′stôrm) A storm that drops pieces of ice. (p. 203)

harbor (här′bər) A place on a coast where ships can dock safely. (p. 31)

harvest (här′vəst) To gather crops in late summer or autumn. (p. 187)

hemisphere (hem′ə•sfir) Half of a ball or globe. (p. 81)

heritage (her′ə•tij) A way of life and beliefs. (p. 21)

history (his′t•rē) Past events. (p. 140)

immigrant (im′ə•grənt) A person who moves to a new country. (p. 11)

import (im′pôrt) To bring something into a country for sale. (p. 356)

industrialize (in•dus′trē•əl•iz) To make a place have a huge number of industries. (p. 300)

industry (in′dəs•trē) A business that manufactures things. (p. 65)

ingot (ing′ət) A block formed from molten, or melted, steel. (p. 190)

inset (in•set′) A boxed area set inside a map. (p. 44)

interdependence (in•tər•də•pen′dəns) The need or dependence of people or regions on others for products or services. (p. 293)

intermediate directions (in•tər•mē′dē•ət di•rek′shəns) Directions in between the cardinal directions. (p. 138)

interview (in′tər•vyoo) To talk with someone to find out information. (p. 244)

irrigation (ir•ə•gā′shən) Bringing water to dry land to grow crops or other plants. (p. 38)

junk (junk) A light boat with tall square sails. (p. 345)

kibbutz (kib•ŏots′) A kind of settlement in Israel where the members own the land together. (p. 386)

labor (lā′bər) Work. (p. 292)

landforms (land′fôrmz) Shapes of the land on the Earth's surface. (p. 1)

latitude, line of (la′tə•tood) A line going across a map from east to west. (p. 80)

law (lô) A rule for all to follow. (p. 20)

legislature (lej′ə•slā•chər) The lawmaking branch of a government. (p. 318)

llama (la′ma) An animal in the Andes that looks somewhat like a camel without a hump. Its wooly coat is used for clothing and blankets. (p. 363)

local government (lō′kəl guv′ərn•mənt) The government for a city or community. (p. 310)

longitude, line of (lon′jə•tood) A line going across a map from north to south. (p. 80)

majority rule (mə•jôr′ə•tē rool) A way of deciding something where whoever or whatever gets the most votes wins. (p. 309)

manufacturing (man•yoo•fak′chər•ing) Making goods. (p. 17)

map key (map kē) A guide that shows what symbols on a map stand for. (p. 3)

mayor (mā′ər) The head of the local government's executive branch. (p. 319)

meridian (mə•rid′ē•ən) A line of longitude, or a line on a map going from north to south. (p. 80)

mesa (mā′sə) A flat-topped hill. *Mesa* is the Spanish word for "table." (p. 220)

metropolitan area (met•rə•pol′ə•tən âr′ē•ə) A large city with other cities near it. (p. 191)

mission (mish′ən) A church and a school started by priests. (p. 225)

monument (mon′yoo•mənt) Something that is built to remind people of the past. (p. 199)

moshav (mō•shav′) A type of settlement in Israel where each family owns a part of the land. (p. 386)

mulberry tree (mul′ber•ē trē) A plant of the Yangtze River in China. Silkworms feed on the leaves. (p. 344)

municipal court (myoo •nis′ə•pəl kort) A court that judges people accused of breaking laws in the city. (p. 319)

nation (nā′shən) A country. (p.11)

natural features (nach′ər•əl fē′chərz) Things on the Earth, such as landforms and bodies of water, that have not been made by humans. (p.2)

natural region (nach′ər•əl rē′jən) A large area that has something natural in common. Mountain and plains regions are two examples. (p. 53)

natural resources (nach′ər•əl rē′sôr•səz) Things in nature that people can use. (p. 38)

nomads (nō′madz) People who move from place to place. (p. 375)

northeast (nôrth•ēst′) The direction between north and east. (p.138)

northwest (nôrth•west′) The direction between north and west. (p. 138)

oasis (ō•ā′səs) A desert place with water. (p.375)

offshore well (ôf′shôr′ wel) A well off the coast that drills and pumps for oil under the ocean floor. (p. 230)

open-pit mine (ō′pən pit mīn) A mine where giant machines dig the ore from deep, open holes in the ground. (p. 188)

opinion (ə•pin′yən) A statement that tells what a person thinks or believes. (p. 235)

ore (ôr) Rock that has a mineral in it. (p. 137)

paddies (pad′ēz) Rice fields. (p. 343)

pampa (pam′pə) The Spanish word for plain. Argentina's pampa is one of the world's largest plains. (p. 401)

parallel (par′ə•lel) A line of latitude, or a line on a map going from east to west. (p. 80)

peninsula (pə•nin′•sə•lə) Land with water on three sides of it. (p. 153)

pioneers (pī•ə•nirz′) The first people to settle in a new place. (p. 184)

plain (plān) A large area of flat, low land. (p. 29)

plantation (plan•tā′shən) A huge farm on the Coastal Plain in early America. (p. 159)

plateau (pla•tō′) An area of high, flat land, like a table. (p. 33)

pollute (pə•lōōt′) To make dirty; to make unclean by dumping wastes from cities and factories. (p. 62)

population (pop•yōō•lā′shən) The number of people who live in a place. (p. 104)

port (pôrt) A city with a large, busy harbor. (p. 65)

poultry (pōl′trē) Chickens and turkeys, raised for their meat and eggs. (p. 148)

prairie (prâr′ē) Another name for the Central Plains; an area of level, grassy land. (p. 111)

precipitation (pri•sip•ə•tā′•shən) Rain or snow. (p. 36)

producer (prə•dōō′sər) A person who makes goods or provides services. (p. 292)

product (prod′ət) Something people make or get from nature. (p. 38)

profit (prof′ət) The money that is left over after you sell your product and pay your costs. (p. 293)

pueblo (pweb′lō) An Indian village built on the sides of cliffs in the Southwest. *Pueblo* is the Spanish word for "village." (p. 234)

pulp (pulp) Ground-up wood mixed with water used to make paper. (p. 168)

quality (kwal′ə•tē) How good a product is. (p. 294)

rain forest (rān′ fôr′əst) A place where trees, vines, and other plants grow close together. (p. 336)

range (rānj) Miles of grassland where animals graze, or eat. (p. 86)

raw materials (rô mə•tir′ē•əlz) Materials used to make something else. (p. 110)

reclaim (ri•klām′) To take back. (p. 383)

recycle (rē•sī′kəl) To use materials again. (p. 399)

reference book (ref′ər•əns book) A book that is full of facts. (p. 117)

refinery (ri•fīn′ər•ē) A factory where crude oil is changed into gasoline and heating oil. (p. 167)

represent (rep•ri•zent′) To act or speak for the people in government. (p. 310)

republic (ri•pub′lik) A government where the people elect their leaders. (p. 20)

reservoir (rez′ər•vwär) A lake that stores water held back by a dam. (p. 229)

revolution (rev•ə•lōō′shən) One trip by the Earth around the sun. Each revolution takes 365 days, or one year. (p. 339)

revolve (ri•volv′) To move in a circle. (p. 339)

right (rīt) A freedom that belongs to a person. (p. 21)

river basin (ri′vər bā′sən) The area of land drained by a river and its branches. (p. 56)

road map (rōd map) A map that shows drivers how to get from one place to another. (p. 204)

rotate (rō′tāt) To spin, like a top. The Earth rotates on its axis every 24 hours. (p. 338)

ruins (rōō′ənz) The remains of buildings, towns, and cities. (p. 365)

salmon (sa′mən) A fish that lives in coastal waters. (p. 261)

sampan (sam′pan) A type of fishing or cargo boat in China. (p. 345)

sand dunes (sand dōōnz′) Large, rounded piles of sand, found in some deserts. (p. 94)

sea level (sē lev′əl) The level of the surface of the ocean. (p. 36)

self-government (self guv′ərn•mənt) The ruling of a country by its own people. (p. 313)

self-sufficient (self sə•fish′ənt) Able to do everything for oneself. (p. 291)

service (sur′vəs) An activity that people do for others. (p. 17)

silkworm (silk′wûrm) A kind of caterpillar that spins silk to make its cocoon. (p. 344)

silt (silt) The soil washed into the river. (p. 56)

skyscraper (skī′skrā•pər) A tall building. (p. 29)

slave (slāv) A person owned by another. (p. 13)

slavery (slā′və•rē) The owning of slaves. (p. 13)

sod (sod) A layer of grass-covered earth. (p. 208)

solar (sō′lər) Having to do with the sun, as in solar energy, which is used to heat homes. (p. 379)

source (sôrs) The place where a river begins. (p. 55)

southeast (south•ēst′) The direction between south and east. (p. 138)

southwest (south•west′) The direction between south and west. (p. 138)

soybean (soi′bēn) A small bean used in many foods. (p. 166)

spawn (spôn) To lay eggs in pools of water. (p. 272)

specialization (spesh•əl•ə•zā′shən) When a person does only one special kind of job. (p. 292)

spring wheat (spring wēt) Wheat that grows in the northern Great Plains. It is planted in spring and harvested in summer. (p. 210)

standard of living (stan′dərd uv liv′ing) A measure of how well people live in a country. (p. 305)

state government (stāt guv′ərn•mənt) The government that handles a state's problems, such as building highways and paying for schools. (p. 310)

station (stā′shən) A large ranch where Australians raise sheep and cattle. (p. 378)

steel mill (stēl′mil′) A place where steel is made. (p. 65)

steppe (step) The grassy plain in Asia. (p. 394)

sugar beet (shŏŏ′gər bēt) A white beet from which sugar is made. (p. 252)

sugar cane (shŏŏ′gər kān) A tall grass from which sugar is made. (p. 165)

symbol (sim′bəl) Something that stands for something else. (p. 322)

tax (taks) The money that government collects from people who work or own property. (p. 320)

technology (tek•nol′ə•jē) Building, using, repairing, and improving modern machines. (p. 300)

temperate (tem′pər•ət) Mild climate. (p. 340)

temperature (tem′pər•ə•chər) How warm or cold a place is. (p. 36)

terrace (ter′əs) A flat shelf built on a mountainside and planted with crops. (p. 362)

territory (ter′ə•tôr•ē) A place that is governed by another nation. (p. 172)

textiles (teks′tīlz) Cloth. (p. 166)

thresh (thresh) To separate the wheat from its chaff, or outside cover. (p. 210)

timeline (tīm′līn) A line showing a period of time and important events of a certain period. The events are marked in order on the timeline. (p. 144)

time zone (tīm zōn) An area where people use the same clock time. (p. 302)

tornado (tôr•nā′dō) A tall, dry funnel of whirling wind. Also called a "twister." (p. 202)

trade (trād) The buying and selling of goods. (p. 149)

transportation (tranz′pər•tā•shən) Moving people and things from place to place. (p. 69)

treaties (trē′tēz) Written agreements between the United States government and the Indians. (p. 207)

tributary (trib′yə•ter•ē) A smaller river or stream that joins a river. Also called a branch. (p. 56)

tropics (tro′piks) Climate zones between the equator and tropic lines. Places there have warm climates. (p. 340)

tundra (tun′drə) Flat, treeless land that stays frozen most of the year. (p. 262)

united (yōō•nī′təd) Joined together. (p. 289)

upstream (up′strēm) Against the flow of the river. (p. 71)

volcano (vol•kā′nō) A crack in the Earth's surface through which hot, melted rock, called lava, comes. Lava builds up around the crack over many years and forms a cone-shaped mountain. (p. 75)

vote (vōt) To choose a leader. (p. 20)

wage (wāj) Money paid for work. (p. 292)

waterway (wô′tər•wā) A body of water that ships can use. (p. 64)

wharves (wôrvz) Platforms where ships load and unload cargo. (p. 350)

windmill (wind′mil) A machine used to drive pumps. Windmills have wide blades set in the shape of a wheel. When wind strikes the blades, the wheel turns, making the pump work. (p. 202)

winter wheat (win′tər wēt) Wheat that grows in the southern Great Plains. It is planted in the fall. (p. 210)

yak (yak) A large animal of the Himalayas. It is cousin to the American bison. (p. 358)

Index

1982: 193. After-Image, © Christopher Springman: 194L. After-Image, © Michael Philip Manheim: 194R. Taurus Photos, © Frank Siteman: 199. West Light, © Larry Lee: 209. West Light, © Chuck O'Rear: 210. Photo Researchers, Inc., © Len Rue, Jr.: 221B. International Stock Photo, © Chad Ehlers: 223. Woodfin Camp and Associates, © George Hall: 229. Bruce Coleman Inc., © Michael Freeman, 233TR. Archive, © Ethan Hoffman: 234. Bruce Coleman Inc., © Steve Solum: 241. Magnum Photos, Inc., © Dennis Stock: 242R. After-Image, © John L. Marshall: 243TR. Peter Arnold, Inc., © Stephen J. Kraseman: 243TL. © John Elk III: 251. Peter Arnold, Inc., © James H. Karales: 252. © Peter Menzel: 253. Taurus Photos, © Scott Ransom: 254. Woodfin Camp and Associates, © George Herbert: 263L. © Peter Menzel: 263R. After-Image, © John L. Marshall: 264TL. Peter Arnold, Inc., © Stephen J. Kraseman: 264R. © Steve McCutcheon: 264B. After-Image, © Jack Fields: 266. After-Image, © Holly Reckford: 269. Woodfin Camp and Associates, © Robert Frerck: 271L. © Tom Tracy: 273, 276. Bruce Coleman Inc., © Bob and Clara Calhoun: 277. Woodfin Camp and Associates, © Craig Aurness: 279R. © Alec Duncan: 279L. © Kit Hedman: 280. West Light, © Chuck O'Rear: 288. Stock, Boston, © Stacy Pick 1982: 301C. Stock, Boston, © Tom Bross: 303L. The Image Works, © Mark Antman: 305L. © Peter Arnold, Inc.: 305R. Contact, © Gianfranco Gorgoni 1982: 306. Click, Chicago, © Jim Pickerell: 314. West Light, © Glenn Cruickshank: 318. Woodfin Camp and Associates, © William Hubbell 1982: 319. Taurus Photos, © Vance Henry: 325. Contact, © Chuck Fishman: 326. Magnum Photos, Inc., © Eve Arnold: 330. Magnum Photos, Inc., © Inge Morath: 334BL. After-Image, © Albert J. Gordon: 334BR. Woodfin Camp and Associates, © Loren McIntyre: 337. International Stock Photo, © Kit Luce: 344B. Click, Chicago, © D. E. Cox 1983: 345L. Peter Arnold, Inc., © Susan Pierres: 345R. Woodfin Camp and Associates, © Bob Davis 1980: 346. Click, Chicago, © Art Brown: 348, 349. Magnum Photos, Inc., © Bruno Barbey: 350, 351. Peter Arnold, Inc., © Stephanie Fitzgerald: 352T. Magnum Photos, Inc., © Bruno Barbey: 352B. © John Elk III: 356B. Magnum Photos, Inc., © Martine Franck: 357L. Magnum Photos, Inc., © Bruno Barbey: 357R. Woodfin Camp and Associates, © Craig Aurness 1981: 358. Woodfin Camp and Associates, Roger Werthers, © 1980 Longview Daily News: 359T. Photo Researchers, Inc., © Rick Golt 1977: 359B. Bruce Coleman Inc., © Giorgio Gualco: 361T. © Moss Henry: 362. Peter Arnold, Inc., © Jacques Jangoux 1975: 364. © Elliott Varner Smith: 366B. © Moss Henry 1981: 367. Bruce Coleman Inc., © Giorgio Gualco: 375. Woodfin Camp and Associates, © Robert Azz 1980: 376L. The Image Bank, © Harvey Lloyd: 376R. Click, Chicago, © Robert Frerck 1979: 376R. Photo Researchers, Inc., © George Holton 1972: 378L. Woodfin Camp and Associates, © Howard Sochurek 1980: 378R. Woodfin Camp and Associates, © Fred Mayer: 380. Contact, © Alan Reininger: 381L. © Bill Apton: 382L, 382R, 383. Woodfin Camp and Associates, © Fred Mayer: 384L, 384R. West Light, © Craig Aurness: 392T, 392B. Contact, © Douglas Kirkland: 393R. Woodfin Camp and Associates, © Marvin E. Newmann 1980: 394. Magnum Photos, Inc., © Rene Burri: 406. Click, Chicago, © Jim Pickerell: 410B. Taurus Photos, © Eric Kroll 1978: 412L. Click, Chicago, © Hamilton and Hamilton: 413.

PHOTOGRAPH ACKNOWLEDGMENTS

KEY: T, Top; B, Bottom; L, Left; C, Center; R, Right.

HBJ PHOTOS: 303, 320, 399L.

HBJ PHOTOS by Rick Der: 15T, 89, 282L, 282R, 293.

HBJ PHOTOS by Alec Duncan: 7, 213, 214L, 214R, 215, 233, 255L, 255R, 256T, 256B, 414C.

HBJ PHOTOS by John Green: 281L, 281R.

HBJ PHOTOS by Elliott Varner Smith: 15C, 23, 72T, 72C, 117, 118, 244L, 244R, 245, 292L, 292R, 294, 296, 301T, 301B, 310, 312, 317, 323, 414T, 414B.

HBJ PHOTO by Tom Tracy: 399R.

RESEARCH CREDITS: NASA: blind folio x. Taurus Photos: 8. Grant Heilman Photography, John Colwell: 17. Grant Heilman: 32. Bruce Coleman Inc., M. W. Grosnick: 34R. Milt and Joan Mann: 37. Grant Heilman: 56, 57. Bruce Coleman Inc., Keith Gunnar: 61. Photri, A. Novak: 63. Milt and Joan Mann: 65. Nancy Creedman: 69. Grant Heilman: 77L, 77R. New York State Department of Environmental Conservation, J. Goerg: 88T, 88C, 88B. Grant Heilman: 95. Taurus Photos, Katherine S. Thomas: 96. U. S. Department of Interior Indian Arts and Crafts Board: 97T, 97C. Courtesy Museum of New Mexico, Arthur Taylor: 97B. Click, Chicago, Bob Brudd, 108R. Milt and Joan Mann: 110. International Stock Photo, John Zoiner: 112TR. Bruce Coleman Inc., Lynn M. Stone: 112B. Grant Heilman: 115L. Living History Farms, Des Moines, Iowa: 115R. Grant Heilman: 116. Office of Tourism Development, Frankfort, Kentucky: 120T. Thomas Gilcrease Institute of American History and Art, Tulsa, Oklahoma: 120B. The Bettman Archive Inc.: 142. Peabody Museum of Salem: 143T. International Stock Photo, Smallman: 146. Stock, Boston, Cary Wolinsky: 148. Peter Arnold, Inc., James H. Karales: 150. Art Collection of the Union League of Philadelphia: 161L. Independence National Historical Park Collection: 161R. Kentucky Office of Tourism Development: 162T. Taurus Photos, C. B. Jones: 167. Stock, Boston, Edith G. Haun: 168. Bruce Coleman Inc., James H. Carmichael: 169L. Commonwealth of Puerto Rico Tourism Company: 175. Stock, Boston, John Running: 177. Grant Heilman: 178. Milt and Joan Mann: 180. Courtesy Architect of the Capitol, Washington, D. C.: 183T. Grant Heilman Photography, Lou Jacobs, Jr.: 184. Library of Congress: 185. U. S. Postal Service: 186T. Grant Heilman: 186, 188. Milt and Joan Mann: 190BL. Grant Heilman: 191. Grant Heilman: 201. Photri: 202. Bruce Coleman Inc., E. R. Degginger: 203. National Museum of American Art, Smithsonian Institution, gift of Mrs. Joseph Harrison, Jr., *Black Rock, A Two-Kettle Chief*, George Catlin: 205. Smithsonian Institution, *Held Up*, N. H. Trotter: 206. Solomon D. Butcher Collection, Nebraska State Historical Society: 208. Click, Chicago, Fred Leavitt: 212. Stock, Boston, John Running: 221T. Photo Researchers, Inc., Joe Munro: 222. International Museum of Photography at George Eastman House: 227. The Bettman Archive Inc., 228T. Contact, David Burnett: 228B. Stock, Boston, Owen Franken: 230. Woodfin Camp and Associates, Adam Woolfitt: 232. Grant Heilman: 242. Thomas Gilcrease Institute of American History and Art, Tulsa, Oklahoma: 250T. Steve McCutcheon: 265. Milt and Joan Mann: 268T, 268BL. Tom Tracy: 268BR. Stock, Boston, Cary Wolinsky: 271BR. Freelance Photographers' Guild International, Windsor Publications: 272. National Cowboy Hall of Fame, Oklahoma City: 278. Photri: 297. Illinois Bell: 300. Taurus Photos, L. L. T. Rhodes: 322. Photo Researchers, Inc., Farrell Grehan: 336. Herman Wong: 342B. Stock, Boston, Richard Balzer: 343L. Betty Crowell: 343R. Stock, Boston, Bill Gillette, 344T. China Pictorial Magazine: 347. Stock, Boston, Richard Balzer: 352C. Stock, Boston, Ira Kirschenbaum: 363L. Taurus Photos, L. L. T. Rhodes: 363R. Betty Crowell: 366TL. Virginia Ferrero: 368. John Elk III: 374B. Grant Heilman Photography, Schoenberger: 379T. Betty Crowell: 379C. NASA, research courtesy Grant Heilman: 379B. John Elk III: 384L. Motke Avivi, Kibbutz Yotvata: 387, 388. Milt and Joan Mann: 393L. Tass from SovFoto: 395L, 395R, 396. Scala/Art Resource, Inc.: 397T. Peter Arnold, Inc., Clyde Smith: 397B. Alec Duncan: 398. Bruce Coleman Inc., Jen and Des Bartlett: 400. Woodfin Camp and Associates: 401L. Leo Hertzel: 402, 403, 404, 405L, 405R, 407, 408. Grant Heilman: 410T. Tom Tracy: 411. Betty Crowell: 412R.

ART ACKNOWLEDGMENTS

David Broad: 195. John Garcia: 138, 250. Jane Heaphy: 3, 172. Intergraphics: 4, 34B, 36, 46, 47, 48, 58, 62, 66, 79, 81, 82, 89, 90, 98, 99, 103, 104, 105, 108, 128, 144, 145, 181, 193, 196, 211, 224, 231, 295, 311, 315, 316, 328, 338, 339, 340, 359C, 369L, 369R, 370, 416. Cheol-sa Kim: 324. Aline Ordman: 162, 174, 249. Jim Pearson: 216, 226, 235, 274. Julie Peterson: 22, 24. Sue Rother: 10, 26, 54, 74, 92, 106, 132, 152, 176, 198, 218, 238, 260, 290, 308, 332, 354, 372, 390. Charles Scogins: 12, 141, 183, 247.

MAP CREDITS

R. R. Donnelly Cartographic Services: 13, 28, 30–31, 40, 41, 42, 43, 44, 50, 59, 64, 70, 76, 80, 85, 94, 109, 113, 114, 134, 139, 155, 173, 200, 220, 240, 248, 262, 267, 270, 276, 283, 298, 299, 302, 334–335, 342T, 356T, 365, 381R, 392T, 401R, 418–419, 420–421, 422–423.

COVER CREDIT

Stock, Boston, © Terry E. Eiler.

438